Blogging from Egypt

Edinburgh Studies in Modern Arabic Literature
Series Editor: Rasheed El-Enany

Writing Beirut: Mappings of the City in the Modern Arabic Novel
Samira Aghacy

Autobiographical Identities in Contemporary Arab Literature
Valerie Anishchenkova

The Iraqi Novel: Key Writers, Key Texts
Fabio Caiani and Catherine Cobham

Sufism in the Contemporary Arabic Novel
Ziad Elmarsafy

Gender, Nation and the Arabic Novel: Egypt 1892–2008
Hoda Elsadda

The Unmaking of the Arab Intellectual: Prophecy, Exile and the Nation
Zeina G. Halabi

Post-War Anglophone Lebanese Fiction: Home Matters in the Diaspora
Syrine Hout

Prophetic Translation: The Making of Modern Egyptian Literature
Maya I. Kesrouany

Nasser in the Egyptian Imaginary
Omar Khalifah

Conspiracy in Modern Egyptian Literature
Benjamin Koerber

War and Occupation in Iraqi Fiction
Ikram Masmoudi

Literary Autobiography and Arab National Struggles
Tahia Abdel Nasser

The Arab Nahdah*: The Making of the Intellectual and Humanist Movement*
Abdulrazzak Patel

Blogging from Egypt: Digital Literature, 2005–2016
Teresa Pepe

Sonallah Ibrahim: Rebel with a Pen
Paul Starkey

Minorities in the Contemporary Egyptian Novel
Mary Youssef

edinburghuniversitypress.com/series/smal

Blogging from Egypt

Digital Literature, 2005–2016

Teresa Pepe

EDINBURGH
University Press

Edinburgh University Press is one of the leading university presses in the UK. We publish academic books and journals in our selected subject areas across the humanities and social sciences, combining cutting-edge scholarship with high editorial and production values to produce academic works of lasting importance. For more information visit our website: edinburghuniversitypress.com

Edinburgh University Press Ltd
The Tun – Holyrood Road
12 (2f) Jackson's Entry
Edinburgh EH8 8PJ

First published in hardback by Edinburgh University Press 2019

Typeset in Adobe Garamond by
Servis Filmsetting Ltd, Stockport, Cheshire, and

A CIP record for this book is available from the British Library

ISBN 978 1 4744 3399 0 (hardback)
ISBN 978 1 4744 3400 3 (paperback)
ISBN 978 1 4744 3401 0 (webready PDF)
ISBN 978 1 4744 3402 7 (epub)

Contents

Figures

Series Editor's Foreword

Edinburgh Studies in Modern Arabic Literature is a new and unique series that will, it is hoped, fill in a glaring gap in scholarship in the field of modern Arabic literature. Its dedication to Arabic literature in the modern period, that is, from the nineteenth century onwards, is what makes it unique among series undertaken by academic publishers in the English-speaking world. Individual books on modern Arabic literature in general or aspects of it have been and continue to be published sporadically. Series on Islamic studies and Arab/Islamic thought and civilisation are not in short supply either in the academic world, but these are far removed from the study of Arabic literature qua literature, that is, imaginative, creative literature as we understand the term when, for instance, we speak of English literature or French literature. Even series labelled 'Arabic/Middle Eastern Literature' make no period distinction, extending their purview from the sixth century to the present and often including non-Arabic literatures of the region. This series aims to redress the situation by focusing on the Arabic literature and criticism of today, stretching its interest to the earliest beginnings of Arab modernity in the nineteenth century.

The need for such a dedicated series, and generally for the redoubling of scholarly endeavour in researching and introducing modern Arabic literature to the Western reader, has never been stronger. Among activities and events heightening public, let alone academic, interest in all things Arab, and not least Arabic literature, is the significant growth in the last decades of the translation of contemporary Arab authors from all genres, especially fiction, into English; the higher profile of Arabic literature internationally since the award of the Nobel Prize in Literature to Naguib Mahfouz in 1988; the growing number of Arab authors living in the Western diaspora and writing both in English and Arabic; the adoption of such authors and others by mainstream, high-circulation publishers, as opposed to the academic publishers of the past; the establishment of prestigious prizes, such as the International Prize for Arabic Fiction (IPAF) (the Arabic Booker), run by the Man Booker Foundation, which brings huge publicity to the shortlist and winner every year, as well as translation contracts into English and other languages; and, very recently, the events of the Arab Spring. It is therefore part of the ambition of this series that it will increasingly address a wider reading public beyond its natural territory of students and researchers in Arabic and world literature. Nor indeed is the academic readership of the series expected to be confined to specialists in literature in the light of the growing trend for interdisciplinarity, which increasingly sees scholars crossing field boundaries in their research tools and coming up with findings that equally cross discipline borders in their appeal.

When we think Arabic literature, we think books, publication, distribution, reader reception, critical reception, to the end of stages and processes associated with print. This book looks for Arabic literature elsewhere, and extends research in the subject into territories as yet little trodden: those of digital literature, where the author is also the publisher; where publication is simultaneous with the act of creation; where distribution is worldwide and cost-free; where censorship, if an issue, is bypassed; where a first-time author stands as much of chance of being published as those renowned and established; where readers are interactive and can instantaneously make their views known to the author who also can if he/she wishes enter into conversation with them; where all the author needs to publish and all the reader needs to receive is a computer and connection to the Internet: we are in the realm of digital literature and particularly blogging, the subject of this monograph, which traces the emergence of the phenomenon internationally, harking back to its print premonitions such as autofiction and theoretical germination, before turning its focus on the evolution and development of literary blogging in Egypt from the beginnings of the twenty-first century and up to the Egyptian uprising of 25 January 2011 which toppled the autocratic regime of Hosni Mubarak. Examined in the book is the role of blogging in the years leading up to the uprising, with its pronounced political and social criticism and calls for reform, tolerance and pluralism both in the political establishment and in social attitudes. In this book we are afforded a rare direct glimpse into a powerful, if short-lived, literary phenomenon that broke away from literary conventions as we have known them for centuries.

Professor Rasheed El-Enany, Series Editor,
Emeritus Professor, University of Exeter

Acknowledgements

I would like to express my gratitude to the people who have accompanied me on this journey, and without whose help I would not have been able to reach the final destination. My first word of thanks goes to the series editor Rasheed El-Enany, who has supported this project with enthusiasm and has provided constructive comments and suggestions throughout this process. Many thanks also to his editorial team, in particular to Kirsty Woods, Nicola Ramsey and Rebecca Mackenzie.

I would also like to thank Stephan Guth and Yves Gonzalez-Quijano for supervising this research project at the University of Oslo. Stephan has welcomed this project with great academic curiosity and has contributed to it with inspiring suggestions, as well as immense attention to details and, not least, his great sense of humour. Yves has engaged with me in long Skype conversations that have always been inspiring and thought-provoking.

I also wish to express my gratitude to Tarek el-Ariss, Tetz Rooke, Ferial Ghazoul, Francesca Corrao, Gunvor Mejdell, Rana Issa, Wael Philip Gallab, Moumita Sen, Gennaro Gervasio, Mona Abdel-Fadil, Bjørn Olav Utvik, Albrecht Hofheinz, Saphinaz Amal Naguib, Helge Jordheim and Abeer Salama, for contributing to this project with invaluable feedback.

This book would not have been written without the help of the bloggers, who dedicated their time to this research even in periods of stress and anxiety due to the unstable political situation in Egypt. Special thanks go to Ahmed Naji, Nael Eltoukhy, Amr Ezzat, Bilal Husni, Mona Seif, Youssef Rakha, Abeer Soliman, Mohammad Rabie, and Al-Baraa Ashraf – who sadly could not see this book published. I would also like to thank Mohammad Farag, Ashraf Youssef, Tamer Fathy and Omar Said for the long conversations and debates we had about Arabic literature and culture.

A word of thanks goes also to those who have invited me to present this material in draft stage and offered valuable feedback, such as Jill Walker and the Electronic Literature research group affiliated to the University of Bergen, Lucia Carminati at the Center for Middle Eastern Studies at the University of Arizona, Anna Forne at the Department of Language and Literature, University of Gothenburg, and Ilka Eichkof and Rudolf de Jong at the Netherlands-Flemish Institute in Cairo. I would also like to thank Philippe Gasparini for his e-lectures on French autofiction and for sharing many thoughts about the possibility of Arabic autofiction.

An enormous thank you to the artist Qarm Qart (Carmine Cartolano) for designing the cover of this book and for providing me with a new lens through which to imagine Egypt, through his art and literary writing.

This book would not have been possible without the moral support of my dear friends Lucia, Gianni, Erminia, Adriana, Athos, Cettina, Shady and Reda, who have sent me good vibes and immense support from Italy and Egypt.

My immense gratitude goes to my family: Mamma, Papà and Mario, who have always encouraged me to travel, learn new languages, discover new cultures, and to appreciate and give back hospitality. They have dealt with new technologies and planes to follow me everywhere and make me feel their presence. *Vi voglio un bene immenso.*

Last, but not least, very special thanks go to my husband Giosuè Sapienza, for sharing with me every single moment of this journey, for bearing endless conversations and monologues about autofiction and blogging, for constantly pushing me to think out of academic boxes, and calming me down, always, with his smile, his know-how and cute dog pictures.

This book is dedicated to the memory of my intimate friend Mahmud Farag. Our ways tragically parted in the middle of this journey. It is through his stories, movies and drawings that I discovered the Egypt I know.

Portions of the book have appeared previously in the following publications: 'From the Blogosphere to the Bookshop: Publishing Literary Blogs in Egypt', *Oriente Moderno*, Nuova Serie, Anno XCI, vol. 1 (Between Everyday Life and Political Revolution: The Social Web in the Middle East), 2011, pp. 75–89; 'Improper Narratives: Egyptian personal blogs and the Arabic notion of *adab*', *LEA Lingue e Letterature d'Oriente e d'Occidente*, vol. 1,

2012, pp. 547–62; 'Autofiction on screen', in *Women and New Media in the Mediterranean Region*, ed. Fatima Sadiqi, Imprimerie des Universités (Fez), 2012, pp. 243–56; 'Cultivating the Self and Building Communities in Egyptian Autofictional Blogs', in *La littérature à l'heure du Printemps arabe: analyse et perspectives*, *Proceedings of EURAMAL 10*, eds Sobhi Boustani and Rasheed al-Enany, 2016, pp. 333–48; 'When Writers Activate Readers: How the autofictional blog transforms Arabic literature', *Journal of Arabic and Islamic Studies*, vol. 15, 2015, pp. 73–91; 'Mixed Arabic as a Subversive Literary Style (2005–2011)', in *Philologists in the World: A Festschrift in Honour of Gunvor Mejdell*, eds Nora Eggen and Rana Issa, Novus Forlag, 2017, pp. 363–94. I am grateful to all the editors and reviewers.

Note on Transliteration and Translation

I have followed the IJMES system for transliterating Arabic names and titles. While *ayn* (ᶜ) and *hamza* (ᵓ) are shown throughout the book, diacritical marks are not used. The full transliteration is used for Arabic technical terms.

Popular and widespread names, however, are spelt in accordance with their most common English rendition, such as Gamal Abdel Nasser and Hosni Mubarak. Also, names of authors whose works are available in English translation appear as they do in the extant English spelling, such as Ahmed Naji, Youssef Rakha and Nael Eltoukhy. As for the bloggers' names, I have used the transliteration they give on their blogs, such as Emraamethlya or Abeer Soliman, if existent. In all such cases, the standard Arabic transliteration is indicated upon first mention in the text.

Transliteration of texts in Egyptian colloquial Arabic follows the IJMES system, with the addition of the dialect vowels /e/, /ē/, /o/ and /ō/.

All translations from Arabic are mine unless otherwise noted.

Introduction: Egyptian Blogs between Fiction and Autobiography

The adoption of the Internet has favoured the proliferation of new forms of autobiographical writing and literary creativity all over the world. Blogs, in particular, are used by Internet users worldwide as a means of recording and sharing their writing.

The popularity attained by the blogging phenomenon and the original features of blog texts have attracted the interest of international scholars. More specifically, a specific kind of blog defined as the 'personal blog', which consists of 'a blog written by an individual and focusing on his or her personal life' (Walker 2005), has spurred significant debate. Most academics agree that personal blogs should be considered as forms of diaries (Lejeune 2000; McNeill 2003), thus inserting them into the category of biographical writing (in effect, history). It is true that the personal blog shares a number of features with the diaristic genre, as its content is mainly autobiographical and it consists of dated entries, arranged chronologically in reverse order. However, besides recording one's life, personal blogs allow users to play with their identity, to reveal aspects of their personality while inventing new ones.

Take for example, the blog *Gay Girl in Damascus*, which in June 2012 spurred on so much controversy worldwide. This personal blog was purportedly written by 'Amina Abdalla Arraf Omar', who claimed to be a lesbian Syrian-American living in Damascus, in the midst of the political uprising instigated a few months before. Her story left readers worldwide in suspense when a post appeared on her blog, claiming to be from her cousin, announcing that Amina had been kidnapped by three armed men. International human rights organisations, journalists and even the American embassy took active steps for her release. The Facebook page rallying to the cause to 'Free Amina' gathered 15,000 people from all around the world. When it turned out that 'Amina' was actually Tom MacMaster, a forty-year-old American living in Edinburgh, and that the blog was fictional, everybody accused him of 'lying'.[1]

The above incident points to the fact that blogs are usually read as factual accounts, but at the same time the form gives their authors the opportunity to play with identities, to reveal aspects of one's personality, while at the same time inventing new ones. It shows that blogs are symptomatic of how the Internet questions many of the assumptions we make about texts, and therefore their generic conventions need to be studied in greater depth (Himmer 2004).

In his article 'The Labyrinth Unbound: The Weblog as Literature', Steve Himmer points out that besides the record of the blogger's daily life, personal blogs include short stories, film reviews, comments about music, book reviews, song videos, and calls for meetings, social events and political demonstrations; therefore 'the fictional is blended with the outside reality and the extra-literary world, the personal is strongly intermingled with the public, and the personal and the political are not discernible' (2004). Building on these remarks, in her article 'The Pleasure of the Blog', Kathleen Fitzpatrick argues that 'reducing the personal blog to no more than online diaries or domestic ranting, we are effectively casting aside un-theorized an entire mode of blogging that has a significant literary potential' (2007: 173), therefore personal blogs might fruitfully be approached as an 'emergent literary form' (2007: 168). So far, the question of how blogging may be studied as a literary form remains to be investigated. This book takes up this challenge by focusing on the Egyptian blogosphere as a case for analysis.

Indeed, since 2005, blogging has emerged as a noteworthy phenomenon in Egypt. In January 2002, the Egyptian government invested largely in IT infrastructure while keeping the Internet relatively uncensored. As a result, the number of users – that was estimated at 220,000 in 1999 – increased to 5.2 million by September 2006 (Abdulla 2007: 48). In particular, the introduction of Web 2.0 technology and blogging tools to write in Arabic in 2005 encouraged many young Egyptians to use blogs as a space for self-expression and literary experimentation, rendering the subgenre of personal blogs particularly prominent. Indeed, in a period of political and social turmoil, and of state and self-censorship in both traditional media and society, blogs appeared to many Egyptian young people as the best tool for self-expression and self-discovery. The availability of personal spaces, unedited and relatively uncensored, encouraged amateur and more skilled writers to pursue their literary ambitions and to try their hand at writing in the form of a new, uncategorised genre. The anonymity of the medium allowed young people, and particularly women, to talk about themselves in a way they were not allowed to, both in traditional media (for religious and political reasons, but also because of the difficulty of entering the cultural field) and in public (because of social pressures), to express criticism and frustration about daily life without losing social credibility. The interactive nature of blogs made it possible to connect people with similar interests and values, and to receive immediate feedback and advice on their writing. In addition, the possibility of combining writing with hyperlinks to other texts, audio and video elements favoured the proliferation of new styles and new aesthetics. The absence of gatekeepers on the Internet allowed bloggers to experiment with a writing style that mixes elements from the vernacular, standard Arabic, youth slang and English, in a way that finds no precedent in modern Arabic literature.

Since 2008, blogs have also left an important mark in the Arabic/Egyptian literary field. This came after more and more publishers started to search the Arabic blogosphere to find new literary voices, attracted by the original style and content of these blogs, and by the high number of followers that they had managed to gather. In particular, in 2008, three Egyptian blogs written by three women bloggers were published by Dar al-Shuruq, the biggest private Egyptian publishing house, and entered the best-seller lists of Cairo bookshops.[2] Arab literary critics and academic scholars were divided into those who devalued the digital space as a space for amateurs and non-professional writers, and those who highlighted the original literary features of these texts.[3] Thus, since then, terms such as '*mudawwanāt adabiyya*' (literary blogs) and '*adab al-mudawwana*' (blog literature) have appeared frequently in several newspapers, literary journals, academic papers and conference panels. The use of these terms evidences that blogs are looked at as a unique genre in Arabic literature. However, their specific literary features, including the reading pact on which they are based (whether they should be read as fictional/non-fictional), remain unexplored.

More than ten years after its emergence, blogging has prompted a boom of literary publications written by young emergent writers that span memoirs, novels and satirical literature and that mix formal and more informal varieties of Arabic. Many of these authors have come to print publication after testing their writing in the form of blog posts, Facebook notes and tweets. Among them, names like Ahmed Naji (Aḥmad Nājī), Mohammad Rabie (Muḥammad Rabīᶜ), Nael Eltoukhy (Nāᵓil al-Ṭūkhī), Muhammad Aladdin (Muḥammad ᶜAlāᵓ ad-Dīn) and Youssef Rakha (Yūsuf Rakhā) appear now at the forefront of the Arabic and global literary scene, as their novels have appeared in multiple prints in Arabic and have been translated into several European languages. This new Egyptian writing deserves further exploration; it needs to be studied at the intersection of print and digital, as the novel is in continuous dialogue with the author's blog and social networks profile.

Arabic Blogging: Beyond the 'New' and 'Political'

So far, Egyptian bloggers have attracted academic interest mainly for their political activity, leaving a knowledge gap on the influence of the Internet in the social and cultural domains (Hofheinz 2011: 1422). This came as a result of their active role in the numerous demonstrations and political campaigns that have taken place in Egypt from 2005, leading eventually to the downfall of the Mubarak regime in February 2011. Most of the existing studies on the impact of blogging and social media in the Arab world are based on interviews with the bloggers and have oscillated between the hope that blogs could bring democracy and alternative voices to the public sphere, and the admission that media alone could not unsettle the regime's stability in the region.[4] Sahar Khamis and Katherine Vaughn (2011) argued that blogs and social networks in Egypt enabled an effective form of citizen journalism, through the provision of forums for ordinary citizens to document the protests; to spread the word about ongoing activities; to provide evidence of governmental brutality; and to disseminate their own words and images to each other, and, most importantly, to the outside world through both regional and transnational media.

However, it must be noted that after 2006, political activists constituted only a small number of bloggers, while the blogosphere enlarged to include different topics and social groups, among which were blogs written by religious and sexual minorities, cultural and art enthusiasts, that were mainly 'personal' or 'autobiographical' (Radsch 2008). This leaves open the question: who are the authors of these blogs? Why did they resort to blogging as a means of writing the self? What made these blogs so compelling to read?

This preoccupation with the political in regard to Arabic blogging is coupled with an obsession with the 'new'. Walter Armbrust has pointed out that the study of digital technologies in the Arab region is marked by 'a relentless presentism' (2012), where Internet technology is treated as if it were the first new media to be implemented in the Arab world. Actually, the introduction of the Internet has provoked a number of questions and debates that had already taken place with the introduction of print technology. For example, the debate concerning the ontological status of blogs and their literary status may be compared to the same preoccupations revolving around the novelistic genre in both the European and Arabic literary scene in the eighteenth to nineteenth centuries, after the spread of the periodical press. Therefore, one of the questions that this study will address is which continuities and ruptures may be identified between blogs and previous forms of Arabic literature published in print?

An important contribution to this area is given by the studies carried out by the scholars Hoda el-Sadda (2010), Marié-Thérèse Abdel-Messih (2009) and Valerie Anishchenkova (2014) on the book-blogs published by Shuruq publishing house. Anishchenkova regards the book-blog *ᶜAyzah Atgawwiz* (*I Want to Get Married*) by Ghada Abdel Aal (Ghāda ᶜAbd al-ᶜĀl) as an 'autoblography' (2014: 170), evidencing that blogs should be studied as the last form of autobiographical writing in contemporary culture. In her article entitled 'Arab Women Bloggers: The Emergence of Literary Counterpublics', Hoda el-Sadda compares blogs to early twentieth-century literary salons and magazines, and argues that 'blogging has resulted in the creation of literary counterpublics, forums for alternative literary genres, languages and style that are adjacent or parallel to mainstream literary centers' (2010: 315). By studying the same book-blogs studied by el-Sadda and comparing them to three Egyptian print novels, Abdel-Messih argues that a new generation of writers has emerged from the world of blogging and techno-writing that has initiated a break with former narrative modes (2009: 515). Similarly, in his article 'Hacking the Modern', Tarek el-Ariss looks at the intersection between print and digital in the avant-garde novel *An Takun ᶜAbbas al-ᶜAbd* (*Being Abbas el Abd*, 2003) by the Egyptian author Ahmed Alaidy (Aḥmad al-ᶜAydī), and points out that the new technologies are used to foster politically and aesthetically subversive transformations in Arabic literature (2010: 545).

These studies emphasise the importance of exploring the continuities and ruptures introduced by Internet technologies in Arabic literature. But, since they are still bound to the analysis of print literary works, they highlight the urgency of studying these transformations by exploring the intricate web of the blogosphere. An initial attempt in this sense is constituted by Gail Ramsay's book *Blogs & Literature & Activism: Popular Egyptian Blogs and Literature in Touch* (2017). Here, Ramsay analyses blog narratives against the background of a long tradition of criticising society through literary expression in the Egyptian national framework. However, her study is based on a sample of five Egyptian, top-ranked blogs. *Blogging from Egypt* instead stems from the awareness that only by looking at a large sample of online texts will we be able to understand the unique features that Arabic literature (*adab*) is developing on the Web.

Trials of Imagination

The question concerning the fictionality of the Internet and the relation between blogs and print literature may sometimes have serious consequences, as shown by the case of imprisonment of the blogger and novelist Ahmed Naji, who figures among the authors analysed in this study.

On 1 February 2016, Naji was sentenced to two years in jail for defaming public morals (*khadsh hayāʾ al-mujtamaᶜ*).[5] The charge came after Naji published a chapter of his last novel, *Istikhdam al-Haya* (*Using Life*, 2014), in the section 'Ibdāᶜ' ('Creativity') of the state-owned literary magazine *Akhbar al-Adab*, for which he works as an editor. In October 2015, one year and three months following publication, an Egyptian citizen named Hani Salah Tawfiq (Hānī Ṣalāḥ Tawfīq) went to court and filed a case against Naji, and against the magazine's Editor in Chief, Tariq al-Tahir (Ṭāriq al-Ṭāhir), accusing them of having published a 'sexual article' (*maqāla jinsīya*) that harms not only his moral health, but also that of all of Egypt! Between 2016 and 2017 Naji spent one year in prison, while the editor Tahir was fined 10,000 EGP for failing to live up to his responsibilities as Editor-in-Chief, as he claimed that he had not read the chapter in question before allowing its publication. In the history of modern Arabic literature, Naji is the first writer to be imprisoned for having written a work of fiction.

The chapter of the novel under discussion is narrated in the first person. It recounts a normal day in the life of the twenty-three-year-old Bassam Bahjat (Bassām Bahjat), spent in the alienating city of Cairo. It contains explicit sexual content, as many works of Arabic literature do.[6] In a Facebook statement, Naji explained that the accusation assumes that the text published is an article (*maqāla*) and not part of a novel (*riwāya*), and therefore a work of literature (*adab*). The prosecutors have failed to understand the difference between a piece of journalism (supposedly based on true events) and a work of fiction (based on imagination). Therefore, they have attributed the harmful thoughts and actions of the novel's protagonist, Bassam Bahgat, to the author himself. Moreover, during the trial, the prosecution used a number of posts retrieved from Naji's blog, *Wassi*ᶜ *Khayalak*, as evidence of Naji's immoral lifestyle, which imply drug use and sex outside marriage.

What is the ontological status of these texts? Why are they read as factual accounts, despite the fact that they are presented as works of imagination? How does Naji's blog relate to the condemned novel? These are some of the questions that will be addressed in the present book.

Autofiction: An Explanation of the Term

My research into the Egyptian blogosphere highlights that the experimentation with blogging, and in particular with the subgenre of personal blogs, has led to the emergence of a new writing genre in Arabic literature that may be defined as the 'autofictional blog'. The genre consists of an online literary autobiographical account that is characterised by an indiscernible mix of fiction and non-fiction. It is a hybrid genre that mixes autofictional narrative strategies with the aesthetic features provided by the Internet structure, which is the possibility of combining writing with links, audio and video elements.

The term 'autofiction' was coined in 1977 by the French scholar and author Serge Doubrovsky to define a form of autobiographical writing in which the line between fiction and non-fiction is blurred. With this term, Doubrovsky wanted to fill a gap in the theory of autobiographical writing illustrated by Philippe Lejeune in his book *Le pacte autobiographique* (*The*

Autobiographical Pact, 1975).[7] Lejeune had defined autobiography as a first-person narrative prose genre that, unlike the novel, is based on an implicit contract between the narrator and the reader that implies that the narrated facts are real. In this theory, a work of fiction in which the name of the protagonist is the same as the name of the author would be an impossible combination; it would result in rejection by the reader.[8] In his novel *Fils* (*Threads/Son*),[9] Doubrovsky created a character who bears his own name, a character who narrates his story in first person. The novel includes numerous autobiographical elements, but its subtitle, 'novel', makes it clear that the narrated events do not correspond with Doubrovsky's real life. On the back cover of his novel, Doubrovsky explains the term 'autofiction' thus:

> Autobiography? No, that is a privilege reserved for the important people of this world, at the end of their lives, in a refined style. Fiction of events and facts strictly real; autofiction, if you will, to have entrusted the language of an adventure to the adventure of a language, outside of the wisdom and the syntax of the novel, traditional or new.[10]

As we can see from his words, an element of Doubrovsky's motivation to use this style of writing lies in his need to overcome the exclusive social norms that used to characterise traditional autobiography. In fact, while autobiography in the past was a privilege of the important and famous, Doubrovsky advocates autofiction as a means to give the common man a voice.[11] Moreover, while autobiography tends to look at lives that are over, autofiction moves away from the mythical figure of an omniscient writer looking back and taking stock of his life; it rather 'tries to grasp the meaning of a life that is still in progress, in a fragmented state, whilst avoiding the temptation to fall into any totalizing representation, since any attempt to recapitulate is in vain' (Laouyen 2002: 6; my translation).

While Doubrovsky's novel *Fils* remained untranslated, the term 'autofiction' inspired a significant international debate that continues to the present day. Since the publication of his novel, many have asked, and still ask, whether autofiction is in fact a new genre, and in which way it differs from autobiography. There seems to be a lack of consensus, especially with regards to which part of the term – auto- or -fiction – is considered dominant.

In a doctoral thesis completed under the guidance of Gérard Genette in 1989, Vincent Colonna asserted the importance of the term; however, at the same time he questioned its novelty. According to Colonna, autofiction may be seen as synonymous with the 'autobiographical novel', since the phenomenon of fictionalising the self is universal. 'We would do well to restrict the neologism autofiction to authors who invent a personality and a literary existence for themselves', he argues, providing as examples Dante's *Divine Comedy* (1555) and Borges's *Aleph* (1949). However, Doubrovsky refuted Colonna's argument by pointing out that 'even classic autobiographers knew that they were writing fiction'. He was aware of the fact that he was not the first to have produced a text in which there is a nominal link in identity between the author, narrator and protagonist, but in his writing, his playing with non-referential elements is overtly signalled to the reader. Genette himself also contributed to the debate by arguing that in autofiction, the fictional is the element that allows the self to enter into the realm of literature; therefore autofiction uses the self to produce fiction. For Doubrovsky, instead, autofiction represents the fictionalisation of a framework, through which one can represent a 'deeper' truth of selfhood (Jones 2009: 178).[12] As for the question of genre, Doubrovsky clarified that autofiction does not mark the end of the traditional autobiography, but rather it should be seen as a 'different type of autobiography', a late twentieth-century form of autobiographical writing that is symptomatic of a gradual evolution of the literary form, rather than a sharp break with tradition. Indeed, he claimed: 'At the end of the 20th century you don't do things the way you could at the end of the 18th' (Doubrovsky, quoted in Jones 2009: 178).

The French scholar Philippe Gasparini provided a further contribution to the debate. In his *Autofiction: une aventure du langage* (*Autofiction: An Adventure of Language*, 2008), based on the analysis of a number of autofictional works published in France in recent years, Gasparini came to a definition of autofiction as an 'autobiographical and literary text that features numerous oral qualities, formal innovation, narrative complexity, fragmentation, separation from the self, disparateness and auto-commentary, which tends to problematize the relationship between writing and experience' (2008: 311).[13] Besides, for Gasparini and other autofictional theorists, a recurring element in autofictional texts is the indication in the paratext of the book that the text is a novel, and the linked identity of the narrator-author-protagonist (2004).[14] The combination of these two features creates what Laouyen has defined 'an oxymoronic pact' that confuses the reader's expectations and constitutes the real novelty of this genre (1999). Readers of autofiction have to approach the text by keeping in mind that it includes both fictional and non-fictional elements. It is this uncertainty and confusion that provides the pleasure of the autofictional text.

Despite the controversies regarding its definition and periodisation, the term 'autofiction' has undergone a slow but sure process of recognition. The scholar Ferreira-Meyers reports that the concept was included in the *Encyclopedia Universalis* in 1984, defined along the same lines as Doubrovsky's theory (2012: 104). The website autofiction.org has been established, featuring articles that discuss specific works of autofiction and contemporary French authors, while opting for a vague definition of the term as 'writing that shakes notions of reality, truth, sincerity, fiction, plowing through the unattended galleries in the field of memory'.[15] The term has also travelled outside of France and has inspired the coinage of similar terms, such as 'surfiction', 'faction' (used especially in England) or 'Double Contract', as defined by the Danish critic Poul Behrendt.[16]

In Arabic, 'autofiction' was translated by the Moroccan author and critic Mohamed Berrada (Muḥammad Barrāda) as '*al-takhyīl al-dhātī*' (literally: self-imagination) during a literary discussion held in Rabat in 1996, to describe his novel *Mithla sayf lan yatakarrar* (*Like A Summer That Will Not Come Back*, 1999). In 2004, the Moroccan author Abdelkader Chaoui (ᶜAbd al-Qādir al-Shāwī) used the term '*al-takhyīl al-dhātī*' on the cover of his book *Dalil al-ᶜunfwan* (*Signs of Vigor*, 2004) (Dahi, quoted in Genon 2009). The use of this term especially in the Maghreb leads us to think that these authors are influenced by the French debate over the definition of the term 'autofiction'. In fact, in a conference held in Lyon in 2008, entitled 'Autofiction(s) and Culture(s)', aimed at discussing how the term and genre developed in several countries around the world, including the Arabic nations, the Moroccan scholar Muhammad Dahi (Muḥammad al-Dāhī, quoted in Genon 2009) acknowledged that the term remains unclear in the Arab world, just as it is unclear in the West, because Arab critics rely heavily on Western literary debate and have not tried to instigate their own critical debate on Arabic autofiction.[17]

Overall, we can see that in recent years several authors, writing in a variety of languages, have inserted fictional characters into their work who carry their own name, rendering autofiction as a global literary phenomenon and showing that autofiction is read and appreciated by readers, despite literary critics not being able to come to a consensus on its meaning, its definition and its precise field of application.[18]

According to Gasparini, the boom in autofictional writing is linked to socio-cultural context and is highly influenced by (1) the rise of psychoanalysis, (2) a postmodern cultural sensibility, (3) the rise of individualisation and (4) globalisation (2008: 322). Chiming with the post-structuralist theories, primarily of Lacan but also Foucault, Derrida and Barthes, autofiction, then, is seen as a form of autobiographical writing attuned to an age in which the subject is no longer accepted as a unified, simple whole. Also, autofiction is linked to a major shift towards individualism in society, which asserts the moral importance of the individual in opposition to traditional social groups and authorities. As evidence of that, Gasparini points out that the genre first emerged in the aftermath of the May '68 movement in France, which saw the rise of feminist and anarchist movements and homosexual rights organizations, and was primarily adopted by authors belonging to sexual and ethnic minorities.[19] Finally, he sees autofiction as a form of a resistance against the economic and political forces of globalisation that tend to impose common patterns of behaviour and lifestyle. By linking autofiction to individualism, Gasparini predicts that autofictional writing is likely to spread in societies that are hampered by dictatorial regimes, integralism and communitarianism, which tend to suppress individual expression. In this sense, writing the self takes the form of a 'refuge'; it becomes a way of asserting one's voice and existence in society. It is not surprising, then, that autofiction is a literary form that has taken ground in Arabic societies and especially on the Internet.

Autofiction in Arabic Literature

The mixing of fiction and factual elements in life-writing has been a constant feature of Arabic autobiographical writing since the early twentieth century.

Dwight Reynolds' study *Interpreting the Self: Autobiography in the Arabic Literary Tradition* (2001) has shown that autobiography has ancient roots in Egyptian culture and that autobiographical materials were disseminated through classical Arabic literature. However, autobiographical elements entered Arabic literature more prominently during the Nahda (*nahḍa*), a period of political and cultural reforms marked by an intense contact with Europe and the introduction of new technologies (such as the printing press) that took place between the end of the nineteenth century and the beginning of the twentieth.[20] In this period of transformation, Arab authors borrowed and adapted modern literary forms among which were the novelistic genre and the autobiographical genre from European literary tradition, as they were particularly apt for dealing with the question of individuality and society, a question that had become particularly prominent at this time.[21] Since their first emergence, the novel and autobiography interlinked and borrowed traits from each other. However, authors would opt for a factual or fictional reading pact, depending on the content of the story and the historical circumstances in which it was narrated.

Several scholars, among them Enderwitz (1998a) and Philipp (1993), have shown how the first half of the twentieth century witnessed a boom in conventional autobiographies. They were written by members of the new intellectual class that emerged with the Nahda. In line with conventional autobiography, these life stories were based on a factual reading pact and provided a coherent, retrospective account of the authors' life, and were written upon the author's reaching an age and level of maturity (Philipp 1993: 591).[22] The writing of these autobiographies was driven by the intellectual will to set an example for fellow citizens, as they were equated with a new and original national history (Enderwitz 1998a: 78). Autobiographists felt that their personal history and the history of their generation were worth recording because they bridged two radically different historical periods. They thought their life could serve as a source of inspiration and guidance for others.

More private issues, such as love or personal failures, were more likely to be narrated through fiction. The cover provided by fiction allowed authors to sneak in private aspects of their life, feelings, emotions, that they would not dare to attribute to their own public figure. An example of this is Taha

Hussein's (Ṭāhā Ḥusayn) novelised autobiography *Al-Ayyam* (*The Days*, 1929, 1939, 1973), which tells the story of a young boy from the countryside who strives against poverty and blindness, and manages to affirm himself in society as an intellectual. According to Malti-Douglas (1988), the novelistic format was a means for the author to distance himself from his poor background and his physical handicap, something that an intellectual at this time would not be proud of. The author only recognised it as an autobiography in 1973: the reason, according to Guth, was that it was still a successful story (1998: 142). Tetz Rooke has demonstrated that the novel inspired the proliferation of 'autobiographies of childhood' (which he claims is a genre of its own in Arabic literature) throughout the entire Arab world, a genre distinguished by the length of their narratives, which is characteristically short; by its narrative mode, which is predominantly novelistic; and by its narrative structure, which is epic. In these texts, the boundary between novel and autobiography is blurred (Rooke 1997: 111). Still, the typical plot of these autobiographies can be encapsulated in the expression: 'I can become what I want, thanks to my own individual effort.' They focus on the fortunes of an unimportant child, often of humble origin, who, thanks to education and personal ambition, surmounts a series of difficulties before the breakthrough that is adulthood.

Anishchenkova's study *Autobiography in Contemporary Arabic Culture* (2014) in this series shows that Arabic autobiographical writing underwent major transformation in the 1960s. Philipp also notes that the defeat of 1967, and the crises that shook the Middle East thereafter, no longer allowed for the writing of autobiography, 'at least not the kind that demonstrates the mastery of different worlds by successfully forming one's own life between and from them' (1993: 602). In addition, authors seemed not to be concerned anymore with the maintenance of social respectability and in telling a successful life story, as they were living in a society of anti-heroes. This condition did not only concern intellectuals, but society as a whole (Hafez 2007: 323).

An example of this transition could be seen in Edwar al-Kharrat's (Idwār al-Kharrāṭ) 'text' *Turabuha zaᶜfaran* (*City of Saffron*, 1985), which, according to Pflitsch, marks the shift between modernism and postmodernism in Arabic literature (2010: 80). If early modern writers had shown the importance of the self-conscious subject, the individual, al-Kharrat shows that the end of grand narratives proclaimed by postmodernism also pertains to the narration of one's life. After the clash of external reality (identified with the Arab defeat of 1967, the fall of Nasser's regime and the politics of economic liberalisation started by his successor, Sadat), it was no longer possible to write about one's existence, if not in the form of fragmentation and a breach of the chronological order (Pflitsch 2010: 83). According to Guth, al-Kharrat's *City of Saffron* also inaugurates a new phase with regard to the factual-fictional pact established with readers, as in this text the author makes clear that the distinction between fiction and reality no longer exists (1998: 147). The story revolves around episodes in the life of a sensitive young Christian boy growing up in Egypt in the 1930s. Although the author inserts a fictional character, Mikhail, we can still identify many autobiographical elements; however, the author himself defines it as 'Alexandrian texts' (*nuṣūṣ iskandarāniyya*) rather than an autobiography. The framework of fiction is not predicated on a protection of the writer's respectability (as in the Nahda) but is in order to show that truth and imagination are both conceptual constructions. Writing an autobiography means also writing a fictional account.[23]

This ontological and stylistic innovation in autobiographical writing is carried on by the Egyptian generation of writers in the 1990s. A major feature of these authors is a preoccupation with the self. Indeed, an author belonging to this generation, Mustafa Dhikri (Muṣṭafā Dhikrī), has stated that they all write autobiographies but with various different approaches. However, Hafez writes that they establish a complex referentiality with the extrinsic world. They ask the reader to treat them as novels while at the same time they confuse the aesthetic and generic expectation to which the form gives rise (Hafez 2011: 132). Christian Junge (2011) has analysed two novels published in the 1990s, Nura Amin's (Nūrā Amīn) *Qamis wardi farigh* (*An Empty Pink Shirt*, 1997) and Mustafa Dhikri's *Huraʾ Mataha Qutiyya* (*Much Ado about a Gothic Labyrinth*, 1997), defining them as 'autobiographic metafiction', a genre that does not necessarily deal with the historical author outside the text; instead, it deals mainly with the fictional author within the text. He affirms that a similar tendency can be found in the novels *Awraq al-Narjis* (*Leaves of Narcissus*, 2001) written by Sumayya Ramadan (Sumayya Ramaḍān) and *Dunyazad* (*Dunyāzād*, 1997) by May Telmissany (Mayy al-Tilmisānī). Similarily, al-Kharrat suggests reading these novels as trans-generic writing (*kitāba ᶜabra nawᶜiyya*), to indicate that they eschew traditional genre classifications. Like al-Kharrat's text, they are characterised by a fragmented narrative and a self-reflexive narration; the plot is often circular and involves the presence of multiple narrators.

Overall, we could say that the literary works written by the 1990s generation of authors in Egypt anticipate some of the tendencies that we find in Egyptian autofictional blogs. This does not only concern the aesthetics of their work, but also how they choose to publish that work. The writers of the 1990s distanced themselves from state-controlled publishing houses and opted for private publishing, where they had to pay for the publication out of their own pockets.[24] Self-publication may be seen as an antecedent of online self-publication. In fact, its relative independence from state-controlled publishing allows the introduction of demographic patterns, themes and styles that will be absorbed and pushed further by autofictional blogs.

The link between the novels written by the 1990s generation of Egyptian authors and autofictional blogs will be further elaborated in the book. However, for now suffice to say that the fact that the author Ahmad Alaidy, who belongs to this generation of writers, inserts in the opening and the last pages of his novel *An Takun ᶜAbbas al-ᶜAbd* (*Being Abbas el Abd*) his real phone number and writes 'CALL ME', can clearly be interpreted as a bridging point between the fictionalised autobiographies produced in the 1990s and the interactive digital autofiction analysed in this study. Alaidy steps into his own fictional world and makes an open invitation to the reader to join him in recollecting the fragments of a lost individuality and reshaping the surrounding reality. This paves the way for the emergence of a new generation of urban, tech-savvy and streetwise young authors who open up their lives to a larger public and invite readers to take active participation in the construction of a multimedia self-narration.[25]

Autofiction and Internet Writing

The global spread of autofiction has coincided with the growing use of the Internet as a platform for self-expression and communication. According to several autofictional scholars, this is not a mere coincidence.

In 1997, the Canadian scholar and writer Regine Robin was the first to argue in her book *Le Golem de l'écriture: de l'autofiction au cybersoi* (1997) that the Internet seems to be an ideal environment for autofictional representation of the self in the form of a mosaic or collage. In 1997, she launched her own personal website entitled *Papiers perdus*, in which she displayed her 'fragmented self' in the form of short texts, pictures and links. Inspired by Donna Haraway's 'Cyborg Manifesto' (1991), Robin writes in her article 'Le texte cyborg' that cyberspace creates a 'fictionalized version of the daily life'. By referring to multi-user domains (MUD), online forums, email conversations and personal websites, she writes, 'imaginary characters, pseudonyms, autofictional experiments on personal webpages, role-games, and dramatized dialogues … everything in this simulated universe tends towards a blurring of true and false' (2000: 18).[26]

More recently, Thomas C. Spear, in his article 'Identité virtuelle', included in the proceedings of the conference *Autofiction(s) and Cultures*, affirms that the Internet is a space that privileges autofiction (2010: 459) as it allows the creation of multiple identities and gives the authors the opportunity to express 'who they want to be' (2010: 452). Spear mentions Internet forums, chat rooms, social networks like MySpace, as well as blogs written by well-known authors.

While these works anticipate that autofiction could be a useful term to understand self-presentation on the Internet, so far the original features that autofiction acquires on the Internet are yet to be explored. This book will explore this isssue by focusing on a sample of blogs written from Egypt. However, a few similarities between personal blogs and the autofictional novel will be introduced here.

We can already see that personal blogging shares with autofiction the aim of democratising the act of writing life. As we will see in Chapter 2, blogs and social networks allow anyone to share their own life stories, and especially writers coming from minority groups. Chapter 3 will demonstrate how the blog and autofictional novel share a fragmented structure. Blogs are always in progress, always evolving and transforming. The blogger's life is constituted of disparate fragments, posted online in the form of short texts mixed with audiovisual elements, and left to the readers to recollect and make sense of. However, unlike the novel that is based on a fictional reading pact, blogs are based on an unclear reading pact, but are usually read as factual accounts (Walker 2008: 92). As the book shows, the fact that readers do not expect much in the way of fiction shapes the way they approach a blog, and it also shapes the way the bloggers write about themselves.

Therefore, what distinguishes autofictional blogs from other personal blogs is the oxymoronic reading pact that confuses the readers' expectations regarding the truthful/fictional nature of the account. As already argued by scholar Kathleen Fitzpatrick, some personal blogs may be considered emergent literary forms because of the self-conscious work they do in documenting the self, and at the same time developing it as fictional (2007: 178). In this sense, the 'autofictional blogs' are the ones in which the blogger breaks the autobiographical reading contract, on which blogs are apparently based, and opens a grey area between the fictional and the documentary. The presence of this oxymoronic reading pact, which results in the readers' uncertainty and confusion, will be considered the main essence of autofiction in this study.

Methodology

The study is based on a sample of forty Egyptian blogs, written between 2005 and 2011, and two novels published in the aftermath of the Arab uprising. The blogs were picked (1) through search engines; (2) through recommendations from other bloggers; (3) from among the ones characterised as '*mudawwanāt adabiyya*' (literary blogs) or '*mudawwanāt shakhṣiyya*' (personal blogs) by the editors of *Wasla* magazine (a print journal derived entirely from blogs); and (4) from printed collections of blog texts.

My selection for the sources is based on the following criteria: I have chosen 'personal' blogs (*mudawwanāt shakhṣiyya*) whose primary subject is the author's life. I have excluded blogs focusing exclusively on politics, current events or social commentary. The blogs encountered in this study do include some commentary on politics: news, first-hand accounts of political events, but these issues are mostly presented from a personal point of view. They are all written by Egyptian citizens and mainly written in Arabic (see Chapter 3 for more on mixed language varieties). They are publicly accessible on the Web (in others the access may be restricted by a password and you may need an invitation from the author in order to access it), because I want to respect the privacy of my informants. They are written by an almost equal number of male and female authors (25/15). Among this large sample, I have selected six blogs as case studies, on which I have decided to put more emphasis in this book. These six blogs are 'representative' of Egyptian blog autofiction as they embody many of the literary traits that characterise this genre. At the same time, they embody the variety of the Egyptian blogosphere, as their authors come from different professional or social backgrounds and therefore present different life stories. The selection of these case studies is also based on frequency (the blogger has been writing regularly for at least two years) and popularity (the blog is followed by more than 4,000 visitors, as attested to by the visitor counter displayed on the blog page, and as confirmed by the bloggers interviewed;[27] blogging has helped the authors achieve certain notoriety in the cultural field).

In view of such a large amount of texts, the question of value also had to be addressed. The notion of 'literariness' has been a concern for several scholars dealing with cyber/digital literature (Aarseth 1997; Hayles, quoted in Rettberg 2007). In my selection of sources, I have not considered literariness as a criterion for selection, for two main reasons: the first is that, as Aarseth argues in reference to the literariness of 'digital literature', we live in an age where the 'inherent' quality of literature (or any other previously dominant mode of discourse) is no longer self-evident. Secondly, even if traditional literary studies have attempted to set notions of canon, I was interested in observing how these texts challenge these same canonical ideas. The same method is followed by Serfaty, who argues in her study of American online diaries (2004) that evaluating these forms with regard to their literary value sheds light on new forms of writing that might change the same notion of what literature is and how the Internet changes traditional notions of literariness.

In this corpus, I investigate the relationship between the authors and the online characters they create in their blogs, using theories and methods that mainly belong to the field of literary studies (plot analysis, investigation of linguistic and stylistic choices, study of titles, choices of authorship, etc.). According to Hayles (quoted in Rettberg 2007), literary interpretations bring out some of the richness of digital texts that would be lost in approaches from other perspectives. She argues, in fact, that this is a vital part of twenty-first-century literature, and if we leave it aside it will impoverish our understanding of all literature, including print literature.

The literary analysis is carried out against the backdrop of the testimonies offered by the people behind the screen, the blog authors themselves.

Out of forty bloggers, I have interviewed thirty, of whom twenty-one are men and nine women. The interviews were conducted mainly in Arabic (see Chapter 2). In the interviews, I inquired about their reasons for blogging, the effect of fictional self-construction on their daily life, and how blogging helped them to depict their internal world (their emotions and bodies) and to deal with the constraints of the outside reality, including their families and social groups, traditional religious authorities and the spheres of politics and professional life.

Besides, using theories and methods from sociolinguistics, I have studied the unique style to be found in these blogs. The text-based linguistic analysis is coupled with the meta-linguistic statements provided by the blog authors.

Researching online literature presents several challenges. The first derives from the extensive amount of texts present on the Internet. Navigating through the blogosphere and choosing blogs that might be classed as 'representative' was a huge challenge. The sample I eventually came up with cannot claim to be fully representative. Yet, I have tried to give it at least a certain degree of representativity by applying some precise criteria for the selection of the sources.

The second challenge has to do with the ephemeral, volatile nature of material stored on the Internet. Blogs are inherently unstable objects, constantly changing, sometimes disappearing altogether. It is difficult to determine the object of analysis when it is constantly changing. In order to solve this problem, I have taken screen shots with the software Zotero, which has helped me to save web pages and date of access. I have also used the 'Wayback Machine' at the Internet Archive – a non-profit group site that has archived Web pages from 1996 to the present.

Another challenge lies in the language in which Egyptian blogs are written. First of all, they require a good understanding not only of Modern Standard Arabic, Egyptian dialect and idiomatic expressions, but also an intimate familiarity with the so-called '*lughat al-shabāb*' ('youth language', Rizk 2007) and Cairene and Alexandrian slang. They also contain many references to Egyptian popular culture. In addition, since the texts are not edited and are written by non-professional authors, they include typographical errors and unclear sentence structures. Indeed, authors prefer to keep the spontaneity of blog-writing rather than bothering about the accuracy of their style because they consider 'naturalness' an inherent feature of the blog style. The translation of all the texts is my own (unless otherwise stated) and very few of these texts have appeared in English before (existing translations are signalled in endnotes). I have opted for a literal translation, while trying at the same time to convey the sense of the text and finding equivalent idiomatic expressions in English (literal translation of idioms is indicated in brackets). I have indicated typographical errors and mistakes only if they rendered the meaning of the text obscure (otherwise there would have been too many 'corrections' and this would have 'blown up' the endnote sections). In order to give readers of the study who are familiar with the Arabic language the opportunity to go back to the original wording I have inserted the original Arabic text after each translation. The Arabic text is copied and pasted from the blog as it is, with all of the 'mistakes' intact.

The final challenge has to do with the fact that this study analyses a very recent cultural phenomenon. In terms of media history, the current age could be described as an era of 'media transition', where the digital is slowly replacing print tools in many sectors (Thorburn and Jenkins 2003). This is mirrored in the fact that digital technologies are still looked at with a mix of anxiety and enthusiasm. Blogs appeared in Egypt for the first time in 2003 (Radsch 2008) and since then the use of the Internet has spread and evolved very quickly. While I think it is urgent to study the cultural implications of Internet media on Arabic society, it is also difficult to make claims about a phenomenon that is changing rapidly. Referring to electronic literature, Hayles points out, 'we're in the process of disciplinary transformation right now. In twenty years, we will look back at talks like this one and laugh and think, how silly' (quoted in Rettberg 2007). Likewise, Tarek el-Ariss, in his article 'Fiction of Scandals' on new writing in Egypt, argues

> it would require at least a couple of decades before we could begin to understand these texts' aesthetic and political significance in a larger historical context. All one can do is expose the way new writing is being defined and practiced by its practitioners (authors, poets, bloggers, translators) as they struggle with, dismiss, and reassert the question of literature. (el-Ariss 2012: 530–1)

On top of this, the political situation in Egypt has changed drastically since I started this research. I started in October 2010 when 'something was in the air', but nobody was expecting a 'revolution' to take place. The uprising of January 2011 led to the ousting of President Mubarak and the start of an unstable political situation that continues to the present day (September 2017). I carried out fieldwork in Egypt immediately after the 25 January revolution (February–May 2011), in the following year (December 2011–May 2012), and between August 2015 and May 2016. Immediately after the uprising, everyday life in Cairo was somehow safe, as protests and demonstrations would usually take place in a limited number of specific areas. However, many of my informants were often busy with political activities, interviews, or were simply stuck to their mobiles or laptops to check what was going on and to share news and updates. In addition, the themes of discussion would easily shift to politics, which seemed a more urgent topic at that moment. When I returned to Cairo in 2015, for one year, I found my informants struggling with depression and political despair. The revolution seemed like a far-off dream that had been replaced by a much more cruel nightmarish reality.

Outline of the Book

The book is organised as a journey that takes the readers through an exploration of the blogging literary movement in Egypt. The first chapter provides the historical context in which these blogs appeared. Drawing on ethnographic research on the Internet and in the Egyptian literary sphere, it shows that the introduction of Internet tools in the Arab world was soon accompanied by the emergence of numerous platforms for distributing and discussing Arabic literature, literary websites, online publishing houses, the Internet Arab Writers Union, and so on. This atmosphere was conducive to the adoption of blogs as a platform for literary experimentation in Egypt. The chapter then focuses on blogging in Egypt, providing a short history of its development and how it impacted the literary sphere. In the second chapter, the book shifts to an analysis of the blogs as autofiction. This section deals with the paratext, which includes titles, choices of authorship and private conversations with the blog authors. The paratext is a strong indication of the autofictional nature of the blog; it also reveals the social backgrounds of the bloggers and their reasons to blog. In the third chapter, I link the political and collective nature of blogging evidenced in the previous chapter to the bloggers' linguistic choices. I analyse the linguistic style of blogs as a 'deterritorialized language', using Deleuze and Guattari's theory of minor literature (1983). Furthermore, I show some examples of editorial choices made concerning this style when blogs are turned into books. Chapter 4 looks at the ways in which the blog transforms the practice of writing the self in Arabic literature. It focuses on three major aspects: interactivity, multimedia and visual elements. The chapter shows that the blog implies a transformation of Arabic literary self-writing into a game of 'strip-tease' to be played among authors and readers, away from the gatekeepers of the literary field, such as editors, publishers and censors. Literary hoaxes, self-conscious narrators, links and visual elements and the use of Mixed Arabic are used as a means of activating the readers and inviting them to discover the author's identity, as well as to contribute and change the literary texts and the reality surrounding them. While the previous chapters take into consideration the paratext and narrative and stylistic strategies, Chapter 5 focuses on the main contents and themes developed in the blog. Here, the body is identified as the recurring theme in blogger's identity construction. Indeed, the blog is conceived as an attempt at recollecting the scattered pieces of the body, as it allows the description of feelings and emotions, which are considered the true attributes of one's individuality. At the same time, the body is re-imagined in the forms of animals, objects, Egyptian goddesses and small children, as a means of taking refuge from the constraints of daily reality. While autofictional authors worldwide are often accused of exhibitionism and narcissism, I argue that for these Egyptian bloggers, writing the body is political because it displays in public how power is imposed on their bodies. The chapter also elaborates on the fact that writing the body on the blog was conducive to the exposure of the body in the 25 January uprising, as evidenced by the mobilisation for Khaled Said's (Khālid Saᶜīd) murder at the hands of the police, the public discussions on sexual harassment, and Aliaa al-Mahdi's (ᶜAlyāᶜal-Mahdī) nude pictures on her blog *Mudhakkirat Thaᵓira* (*A Rebel's Diary*, 2011–). Chapter 6 discusses how blogs have evolved in the years after 2011 and what is left of the blog in Arabic literary production. Here I show that blogging continues to be an important phenomenon in the Arab world, even though blogging practices have changed following the spread of social networks such as Facebook and Twitter. In addition, the blog continues to impact Arabic print literature, in terms of young authors' access to the literary field, their experimentation with language and genre, and the importance of the visual. The novel *Istikhdam al-Haya* (*Using Life*, 2014) by Ahmed Naji, mentioned before, and Youssef Rakha's novel *Bawlu* (*Paulo*, 2016) will be recalled here to discuss the link between the blog, the dystopic novel and new literary styles in Egypt.

Notes

1. See Daniel Bennet (2011), 'A "Gay Girl in Damascus", the Mirage of the "Authentic Voice" – and the Future of Journalism'. Newspapers worldwide reported the news. See for example: 'A Gay Girl in Damascus Comes Clean', *The Washington Post*, 12 June 2011, http://articles.washingtonpost.com/2011-06-12/lifestyle/35234652_1_gay-girl-foreign-media-blog (last accessed 22 August 2017). See also Yves Gonzalez-Quijano's commentary posted on his personal blog: 'Les spin doctors du Net: la vraie vie de la Gay Girl in Damascus', 28 June 2011, http://cpa.hypotheses.org/2817 (last accessed 22 August 2017).
2. The titles of these books are: *ᶜAyza Atgawwiz* (*I Want to Get Married*) by Ghada Abdel Aal, *Aruzz bil-Laban li-Shakhsayn* (*Rice Pudding for Two*) by Rihab Bassam and *Amma Hadhihi fa-Raqsati Ana* (*This is My Own Dance*) by Ghada Muhammad Mahmud.
3. For a study of these book-blogs, see T. Pepe (2011), 'From the Blogosphere to the Bookshop'; H. el-Sadda (2010), 'Arab Women Bloggers: Literary Counterpublics'; M. T. Abdel-Messih (2009), 'Hyper Texts: Avant-gardism in Contemporary Egyptian Narratives'; M. ᶜIbada (Ibadah 2008), 'Mudawwanat: Kitaba Jadida aw Ihtijaj Ijtimaᶜi?'; G. al-Ghitani (2009), 'Adab al-Kliniks'; I. Farghali (2008), 'Kitaba Iftiradiyya Hassasa Tantaqil lil-Waraq'. Exclusively on Ghada Abdel Aal's *ᶜAyza Atgawwiz*, see V. Anishchenkova (2014), *Autobiographical Identities in Arabic Culture*; on Rihab Bassam's *Aruzz bil-Laban li-Shakhsayn*, see S. Al-Muji (2008), 'Riḥab Bassam'; I. Abd al-Munᶜim (2011), 'al-Rihan ᶜala Basatat al-Mutakhayyil'.
4. Albrecht Hofheinz indicates as examples the contributions to the *Journal of Arab Media and Society*, whose aim, since its establishment in 2007, was to document a 'revolution' (2011: 1417). More recent examples of studies dealing with Egyptian political blogs include: D. Faris (2015), *Dissent and Revolution in the Digital Age*; C. Radsch (2016), *Cyberactivism and Citizen Journalism in*

Egypt: Digital Dissidence and Political Change; S. Khamis and M. el-Nawawy (2013), *Egyptian Revolution 2.0; Political Blogging, Civic Engagement, and Citizen Journalism*. For a comparative study on online activism in both Egypt and Kuwait, see J. Nordenson (2017), *Online Activism in the Middle East: Political Power and Authoritarian Governments from Egypt to Kuwait*. On blogging in Tunisia, M. Zayani (2015), *Networked Publics and Digital Contention: The Politics of Everyday Life in Tunisia*.

5. On the issue of the trial see: Pepe (2015), 'Literature is on Trial in Egypt', and Jacquemond (2016), 'Ahmed Naji, the Use of Life and the Zombies'.
6. For a more detailed account of the topic, see R. Allen and H. Kilpatrick (eds) (1994), *Love and Sexuality in Modern Arabic Literature*.
7. The publication of the novel was also accompanied by a letter addressed to Lejeune in which Doubrovsky explains his endeavour: 'I wanted very seriously to fill the space that your analysis left empty, and it is a true desire that suddenly linked your critical text to the one I was writing, if not blindly, at least in half darkness' (translated and quoted in Pitcher McDonough 2011: 19).
8. 'Le héros d'un roman déclaré comme tel, peut-il avoir le même nom que l'auteur ? Rien n'empêcherait la chose d'exister, et c'est peut-être une contradiction interne dont on pourrait tirer quelques effets intéressants. Mais, dans la pratique, aucun exemple ne se présente à l'esprit d'une telle recherche' (Lejeune, quoted in Laouyen 1999). In her presentation 'Autofiction and Technology: Broadcasting the Self in Contemporary French Literature' given at the conference 'Technologies of the Self' held in Cork in September 2011, Elise Hugueny-Leger showed that Lejeune's oft-cited definition of autobiography represents only one aspect of his work, which has evolved increasingly towards the study of writing of the self as a practice, and toward a conception of the self, and of autobiography, as fragmented and unstable.
9. In French, *fils* means 'son' if the speaker pronounces the 's' but 'threads' (plural of *fil*) if the 's' is silent; the title invites an interpretation from the reader.
10. Serge Doubrovsky (1977), *Fils*, Paris: Gallimard (Collection Folio edn) translated by Pitcher McDonough (2011: 7).
11. 'I'm not allowed into the pantheon of funeral parlors that is autobiography. OK. But I can smuggle myself in. I can sneak in, with the help of fiction, under the cover of the novel' (Doubrovsky, quoted in E. H. Jones 2009: 177).
12. Genette considers autofiction as a '*fictionalisation de soi*' (fictionalisation of the self), while Doubrosvky views it as a '*fiction référentielle*' (referential fiction): (Schmitt 2010: 122–37).

13. 'Texte autobiographique et littéraire présentant de nombreux traits d'oralité, d'innovation formelle, de complexité narrative, de fragmentation, d'alterité, de disparate et d'autocommentaire qui tendent à problématiser le rapport entre l'écriture et l'expérience' [my translation].
14. De Montremy also quotes several French autofictional works published between 1977 and 2001 that either carry the denomination 'novel' or do not specify the genre at all (Montremy 2002: 62).
15. 'Elle vient en effet poser des questions troublantes à la littérature, faisant vaciller les notions mêmes de réalité, de vérité, de sincérité, de fiction, creusant de galeries inattendues le champ de la mémoire' [my translation], available at www.autofiction.org (last accessed 20 August 2017).
16. Poul Behrendt (2006), *Dobbeltkontrakten. En æstetisk nydannelse* (*The Double Contract: a newly created aesthetic concept*).
17. The conference proceedings were published in the volume *Autofiction(s)* (C. Burgelin, I. Grell and R. Yves-Roche 2010).
18. An example of that is the best-selling Neapolitan tetralogy by the author writing under the pseudonym Elena Ferrante known as the *Neapolitan Quartet* (2012–15) or the series of six novels written by the Norwegian Karl Ove Knausgaard under the title *Min kamp* (*My Struggle*), published between 2009 and 2011. Other examples include Jonathan Coe in *The Terrible Privacy of Maxwell Sim* (2010), Damon Galgut, *In a Strange Room* (2010), Geoff Dyer, *Jeff in Venice, Death in Varanasi* (2009) Will Self, *Walking to Hollywood* (2010), Michel Houellebecq, *The Map and the Territory* (2010), Alberto Manguel, *All Men Are Liars* (2008) and Walter Siti, *Troppi Paradisi* (2006). For more examples, see 'Is auto-fiction strictly a boys "game"?', *The Guardian*, 24 September 2010, http://www.guardian.co.uk/books/booksblog/2010/sep/24/auto-fiction (last accessed 20 August 2017).
19. Frank Zipfel points out that Doubrovsky himself is Jewish (2005: 37).
20. For an exploration of new literary genres that emerged during the Nahda, see Sabry Hafez (1993), *The Genesis of Arabic Narrative Discourse*.
21. The question of whether autobiography is a genre developed under European influence or indigenous to Arabic culture has been tackled by several scholars. The issue is also inflamed by the fact that autobiography was seen as a cultural expression peculiar to Western mankind (Gusdorf, quoted in Rooke 1997: 5). Rooke (1997), Enderwitz (1998a) and Philipp (1993) agree on the fact that Arabic autobiography has been inspired and profoundly influenced by its corresponding Western genre. However, Rooke highlights that it is not the informing

mentality that has been imported from the West, but the narrative form as such. It is not an outcome of intellectual colonisation, but of social development. Philipp adds that autobiography is tied to modernity and not exclusively to Western culture, which is only a catalyst (1993: 576).

22. Examples of these early modern autobiographies are the ones written by Jurji Zaydan (Jurjī Zaydān [1908] (1968), *Mudhakkirat Jurji Zaydan* (*Juryji Zaydan's Memories*)), Ahmad Amin (Aḥmad Amīn [1950] (1952), *Hayati* (*My Life*)) and Salama Musa (Salāma Mūsā (1947), *Tarbiyat Salama Musa* (*Salama Musa's Education*)). Philipp also points out that the authors of these autobiographies were born within a few years of each other (Zaydan, 1860; Ahmad Amin, 1886; Salama Musa, 1887; Taha Hussein, 1889).
23. From the same period, Daroueche Hilali Bachar, in his doctoral thesis 'L'Autofiction en Question' (2014), analyses selected works by Mohamed Choukri (Muḥammad Shukrī), Sonallah Ibrahim (Ṣunʿallah Ibrāhīm) and Rashid al-Daif (Rashīd al-Ḍaʿīf) as autofictions, inserting them into the long tradition of fictionalisation of the self that dates back to the Nahda.
24. These novels were published by small independent publishing houses, which emerged at the same time, such as the Sharqiyyat publishing house owned by Husni Sulayman (Ḥusnī Sulaymān), and later by Dar Mirit, established by Muhammad Hashim (Muḥammad Hāshim) in 1998, whose publishing plan is based on 'freedom of expression' and 'encouraging young writers'. Self-publication was not a new phenomenon in Egypt. Yves Gonzalez-Quijano has shown in his book (1998) that several poetry collections and Islamic books were published at the author's expense. Also a significant antecedent of this practice is the experiment of *Galiri 68*, a literary journal founded and sponsored by several authors of the 1960s generation (see above), as an act of defiance against the dominant intellectual class that would not support their experimental modes of writing and critical representation of reality. This initiative did not last for long (only eight issues were published), but it helped these avant-garde authors to become well-known writers in the 1980s and 1990s. See E. Kendall (2006), *Journalism, Literature and the Avant-Garde: Intersection in Egypt*. See also Ulricke Stehli (2011), 'The Egyptian Magazine Galīrī 68: Truth, Innovation and Diversity'.
25. In the narration, the number is supposed to belong to one of the main characters, Hind. But readers actually dialled the phone number printed in the text and found out that it was the author's number.
26. 'L'environnement informatique crée un univers de fictionnalisation du

quotidien: personnages imaginaires, pseudonymie généralisée, expérimentations autofictionnelles même élémentaires sur les pages personnelles, jeux de rôle, dialogues théâtralisés … tout dans cet univers de la simulation tend vers une indifférenciation du vrai et du faux' [my translation].

27. The blog counter shows that Emraamethlya has reached 73,537 profile visitors, Amr Ezzat 412,267, Bilal Husni 4,319, Abeer Soliman 11,100 and Mona Seif 15,311(last updated April 2018). Ahmed Naji has removed the visitors' counter tool, but he affirms that the blog reached the apex of popularity between 2007 and 2008, with circa 15,000 visitors per day, among which 4,000 visitors per day were visiting the blog for the first time (Interview, April 2018).

1

Arabic Literature Goes Digital

The implementation of Internet technologies in the Arab world has undeniably revolutionised the conditions of literary and cultural production, distribution and reception, involving changes in the form and function of texts. Indeed, if in 2003 the Arab Human Report[1] spoke of books as a threatened species in the Arab world, things were going to improve after that date, as some observers hailed a 'literary revolution' enhanced by the digital medium.[2]

In the 1990s, before Internet tools were implemented in the Arab region, Arabic literary production was hindered by several challenges. The first was the problem of distribution. Arab authors and artists worked with little support from the institutions and had serious difficulties in getting their books distributed. This was due to a lack of major specialised book distributors with wide distribution networks, where books were only available in a limited number of bookshops in major cities, reflecting a weak demand. Related to that was the problem of censorship and lack of freedom of expression, where traditionally taboo subjects in Arab public discourse have been politics, religion and sex (Stagh 1993). In general, the Arabic book market is controlled by dozens of censorship authorities, whose standards may vary across the twenty-two countries of the Arab world. Authors and publishers had to accommodate the whims and instructions of twenty-two censors, with the result that books could not move easily through their market. Also, as a result of the growing Islamisation of society, civil society had started to support the State in repressing creative voices.[3] The other major problem was the low number of readers. The main reason behind that was the purchasing power for books: economic stagnation, declining purchasing power and the increasing cost of living had left the average Arab citizen preoccupied with basic issues of livelihood; therefore, books had turned into luxury items for educated elites and for students. Furthermore, the high illiteracy rate in the Arab world, coupled with the state institutions' failure to encourage people towards reading and writing, undeniably influenced the size of readership.

These factors together had created an atmosphere of stagnation and hopelessness. These feelings were felt especially among the young generation of authors, coming of age in the 1990s. The Arab world population had increased by 31 per cent (51 million) between the 1980s and 1990s and by 30 per cent between 1990 and 2010 (63 million), which means that it nearly doubled in twenty years (rising from 166 million in 1980 to 406 million in 2016 according to the World Bank Group),[4] causing a 'youth bulge' where the young people represented the major part of the population (Rivlin 2009: 12). However, in the literary field, as in larger sections of society, the youth had to deal with prolonged unemployment, corruption that had permeated every aspect of national life, state censorship and the spread of conservative religious ideologies (Hafez 2010).

Nevertheless, this data did not correspond to a decline in book production. The last decade of the twentieth century witnessed a quantitative explosion in production as, for creative literature alone, Egyptian production had at least tripled from the 1960s to the 1990s, going from 100 to 150 titles published per year to at least 500 titles per year (Jacquemond 2008: 224). Following the implementation of a new liberal economy in most Arab countries, many young writers of the 1990s had distanced themselves from state-controlled publishing houses and had opted for private publishing, where they had to pay for publication out of their own pockets. These publishing houses also functioned as gathering places for these young writers where they exchanged readings and new ideas. Unfortunately, this did not entail an increase in reading in the population. While these independent publishing houses offered more freedom in terms of styles and contents, authors lamented that books were printed in limited copy numbers, and circulated among small intellectual circles.[5]

Therefore, the advent of Internet technologies was immediately welcomed with enthusiasm and optimism by a number of Arab literati, based in the Arab region or elsewhere. The Internet offered the possibility of developing and enriching the field of Arabic literature, by surpassing geographical distances, censorship and the costs of book publication, as well as experimenting with new styles and literary forms. These digital literary initiatives prepared the ground for literary expression in the Egyptian blogosphere, as they validated the use of digital tools to innovate and distribute Arabic literature.

Drawing on ethnographical investigation, both in the online and offline sphere, this chapter first describes the appearance of a number of literary websites that have contributed to the emergence of an Arabic digital literary production. The textual analysis of these websites is combined with interviews with a number of Egyptian writers, critics and journalists, carried out between 2009 and 2010, regarding the online literary resources (journals, websites, publishing houses and so on) that they regularly visit. In the second part, the chapter focuses on the literary innovation brought by the implementation of Web 2.0 and blogging in particular. It describes the rise and development of blogging in Egypt from 2003 to the present and how it has impacted Arabic literary production. My account is largely based on the interviews I have conducted with a number of blog authors selected for this study, and on Ahmed Naji's account of the Egyptian blogosphere as delineated in his book *al-Mudawwanat: min al-Bust ila al-Twit* (*Blogs: From Post to Tweets*, 2010).

Arabic Literature 1.0

One of the first literati to establish an online presence for Arabic literature was the Bahraini poet Qasim Haddad (Qāsim Ḥaddād). In 1996, he founded the website *Jihat Shi^c^r* (*Poetry Directions*),[6] in cooperation with the Al-Nadim foundation of Bahrain. In a speech given at the Bahraini Internet Society in 2003, Haddad defines the Internet as 'a new horizon for Arabic literature' for its capacity of fostering creativity and imagination, and *Jihat Shi^c^r* as 'an example'.[7] Until today, the website functions as an online archive of Arab and international poetry, including biographies, images and poems of leading Arab poets of the past half century. The site also dedicates attention to critical writings and the role of critical thought in modern culture. Besides Arab poetry, the site also includes poems written in English, French, Italian, German, Dutch and Persian. As Haddad explains in the 'About' page of the website, *Jihat* wants to offer readers the pleasure of reading poetry, but it also aims at being a useful resource for 'the specialist, the scholar and student of poetry', by publishing works by leading critics not easily accessible in print.[8]

Following *Jihat*, a number of websites dedicated to Arabic literature started to appear. They were modelled on print literary magazines, as they included creative works, reviews and interviews of authors. For example, in 2000, the Kuwaiti author Karim Al-Haza (Karīm Al-Hazzāᶜ) and the two brothers Muhammad and Salah al-Nabhan (Muḥammad and Ṣalāḥ al-Nabhān), born in Kuwait but based in Canada, founded *Majallat Ufuq* (Horizon),[9] an online monthly literary cultural journal (*majalla adabiyya thaqāfiyya*). On the website *Ufuq* is presented as

> a bridge between the intellectual and the people, by using the interactivity of the online medium; between the print cultural sphere and electronic writing; between the reader of *fuṣḥā* and the reader of *ᶜāmmiyya*, hoping to favor the birth a new language that includes the features, senses, imagination, and mindset and tastes of both language varieties.

Among these websites, *Kika* (*Kikah*), established in March 2003 by the Iraqi writer Samuel Shimon (Ṣamūʾīl Shimᶜūn) based in London, had a major influence.[10] In 2000, Shimon and his wife, Margaret Obank, had already established the print literary magazine *Banipal*, with the aim of promoting Arabic literature in English. However, with *Kikah* they wanted to offer a channel of literary communication for Arabic authors and readers from several parts of the Arab world. Besides, *Kikah*'s marked interest in young, emergent writers, coupled with its open conception of literariness and the literary genre, was a novel addition to the cultural scene. Several Arab authors have claimed that *Kikah* has played a key role in introducing new literary voices to the Arab world.[11] In 2013, Shimon turned the website into a print literary magazine entitled *Kikah for International Literature in Arabic*.

Around the same period, several Arabic authors started to look at the Web as a means of promoting their work and enlarging their readership. Several of them, such as the Lebanese writer Emily Nasrallah (Imīlī Naṣrallāh; www.emilynasrallah.com), the late Palestinian poet Mahmud Darwish (Maḥmūd Darwīsh; www.mahmoudarwish.com) and the Moroccan essayist and novelist Fatima Mernissi (Fāṭima Mirnīsī; www.mernissi.net), established personal websites including biographical information and reviews of their books.

Conscious of the difficulties encountered by many young writers in accessing the literary field, in 2003 a young Kuwaiti author, Hayat al-Yaqut (Ḥayāt al-Yāqūt), founded the first Arabic electronic non-profit digital publishing house, *Nashiri*.[12] It provided young amateur writers with the opportunity to publish for free on a platform that already had an established audience, and to receive free editing of their texts. Over the years, *Nashiri* has become a recognised publishing house: it is established in the Kuwaiti cultural field and has been granted several awards by the Kuwaiti government. As such, writers who wish to publish on the website have to follow a set of criteria: they have to write in Modern Standard Arabic and their works must not violate the moral code or the law.

As for the problem of distribution, in 2005 the Egyptian Rami Habib (Rāmī Ḥabīb) founded *Kotobarabia*, a commercial distributor, selling digitalised versions of printed books, including titles that have been censored in Arab countries.[13] To escape censorship, the company's servers are located in the United States. His ambition is 'to build an Alexandrian Library that can't burn down' (quoted in Kulesz 2011: 60). Around the same time, various online bookstores also emerged (among which *Nil wa-Furat*[14] and *Adab wa-Fann* were located in Lebanon).

Electronic publishing houses and virtual bookstores emerged together with free online libraries (*al-maktabāt al-ᵓīliktrūniyya*). One of the first of these libraries to appear was *Maktabat al-Warraq*, founded in 2000 in Abu Dhabi.[15] The library includes traditional Arabic works, religious books and dictionaries, which can be consulted for free on the website. More recently published books can be found on the website *4shared*, founded in 2005, which offers the possibility of uploading and downloading entire books of any sort in PDF format.[16] While *al-Warraq* is managed by an editorial group, on *4shared* anybody can share books, as well as music and videos. The presence of these libraries provides Arab readers with accessibility to a wider range of global cultural products. Interesting and controversial books are now quickly known and easily available through the Internet, as national governments have very little control over what goes on in these virtual libraries.

Computer technologies have also been used to develop new literary aesthetics. In 2005, the Jordanian writer Muhammad Sanajla (Muḥammad Sanājla) published the novel *Shat* (*Chat*), the first digital novel in Arabic, composed using JavaScript and combining written text with sound and images. In the same year, he founded the Arab Internet Writers Union (*ᵓIttiḥād Kuttāb al-Internet al-ᶜArab*),[17] aimed at gathering together Arab intellectuals interested in digital culture. Sanajla also developed a theory of the 'digital realistic novel' (*riwāya raqamiyya wāqiᶜiyya*) and 'digital realistic literature' (*adab raqamī wāqiᶜī*) and invited the other 'e-writers' to develop new critical tools to analyse digital literature. In 2006, the Arab Internet Writers Union reached an agreement with the Jordanian Minister of Culture and was recognised as an official cultural institution. This might explain why the Union has a rigid structure that allows only recognised members to publish on the websites. As time progressed, the Union spread its roots into the offline literary establishment by establishing offices in Amman, Jordan, and Alexandria, Egypt. It organised conferences and meetings concerning digital culture in Damascus, Syria, in April 2006, and in Alexandria in 2010, while additionally establishing a prize for Digital Creativity.[18]

The websites mentioned above had an important role in revitalising the Arabic literary scene by offering platforms of publication and by providing material not easily accessible in print. They functioned as aggregators, as they allowed groups of like-minded writers to publish their work and that of their friends, and invited others of similar orientation to join them. However, since they were created with the technology Web 1.0, they appear static, as they mostly transfer print material into the digital realm and they allow very little interactivity between authors and readers. In addition, the fact that these projects were subsequently institutionalised for economic and bureaucratic purposes has often limited their potential. The implementation of Web 2.0, which allows for more dynamic formats, interactivity and user-generated content, gave a major boost to the Arabic digital literary sphere.

Blogging in Egypt/the Arab World

Blogging is one of the early technologies introduced with Web 2.0 that allowed anyone to open a page for free on the Internet and publish it online, with the possibility of receiving immediate feedback from other users. Before blogging, online forums and email lists were popular among many Internet users in Egypt, and many of the early bloggers had participated in them (Hofheinz 2007: 76). Among the most famous, the forum *Al-Sakhir* (*The Joker*)[19] allowed aspirant writers to publish their literary attempts and to receive feedback from the community. However, posted messages had to be approved by a moderator before they could be visible. Several bloggers report that they were frustrated with the often-uncivilised tone in discussion forums and the occasional censorship exercised there by moderators. When Blogspot, the most popular blogging platform created by Google, enabled Arabic script in its posts, many young Internet users began to move away from forums, announcing that they would instead concentrate on blogging.

Blogs had begun to spread in the US from 2001, and soon also became an extremely important feature of Persian Internet use. Iranians at home and abroad used blogs not only to publish information critical of the regime after the crackdown on the liberal press in Iran, but also for expressing themselves on personal, social and cultural matters (Mina 2007). In the Arab region, blogging was first adopted in Iraq during the 2003 war. The bloggers SalamaPax and Riverbend blogged in English in order to describe the hardships experienced by Iraqi civilians to an international audience.[20] Shortly after that, the first blogs appeared in Egypt as well. They were authored mainly by Linux geeks and 'techies', and were written in English, like their Iraqi counterparts. At that time Egypt counted nearly 3 million Internet users (Radsch 2008: 1).

In 2004, the implementation of tools to write in Arabic on blogging platforms such as Blogspot or WordPress was a turning point. Alaa Abdel Fattah (ᶜAlāᵓ ᶜAbd al-Fattāḥ) and his wife Manal, 'MaleX', 'Taq Hanak', Ahmed Naji, 'JarelKamar', Amr Ezzat[21] (ᶜAmr ᶜIzzat) and the Gharbiyya brothers (ᶜAmr and Aḥmad Gharbiyya) were among the first Egyptian bloggers to write in Arabic, to address primarily an Arabic-speaking audience and contribute to the rise of an Arabic blogosphere. For example, Ahmad Gharbiyya, who had already started blogging in Arabic in November 2003, explained that he had decided to switch to Arabic to find words in Arabic to express new concepts, such as 'computer technology', 'climate change' or 'nuclear power'. In the very first entry of his blog, he wonders about the Arabic term he should use to define what he is writing:

> What is that, then?
> Do you know any other blogs / *blugāt* written in Arabic?
> How to call the blog in Arabic, to begin with?
> And how will our brothers from Levant or Gulf pronounce it, since they

pronounce the g as [dʒ]??? Will they write b-l-w-gh [which also could be read *bulūgh*, i.e. as *maṣdar*/verbal noun/'infinitive' of the verb *balagha* 'to reach; to grow up']?

And what did Persians and Japanese and Chinese and the other nations do in order to find names for everything that is modern in their local languages? Who knows me personally, knows that I call things by [their] Arabic names, as long as there is a name for them, even if the name sounds strange to the ears of the commoners, but truly I don't know what is the name of what I am writing now and what you are reading now.[22]

إيه دا بأه!
هل تعرف أي بلُجات blogs أخرىٰ بالعربية؟
ثم ماذا يسمىٰ البلُج بالعربية أصلا؟!
و كيف سينطقه إخواننا الشوام و الخليجيون الذين ينطقون بالجيم المعجّمة. هل سيكتبونها "بلوغ"؟
و ماذا فعل الفرس و اليابانيون و الصينيون و سائر الأمم التي توجد أسماء لكل ما هو حديث بلغتها المحلية؟
من يعرفونني شخصيا بعرفون أنني أسمي الأشياء بالعربية طالما كان لها اسم، حتىٰ لو كان هذا الاسم غريبا علىٰ آذان العامة، و لكني فعلا لا أدري ماذا يسمي هذ الذي أكتبه الآن أو الذي تقرؤه أنت الآن!!

He created the Wikipedia entry in Arabic for 'blog', describing what it is, how to set up one, and promoted the term '*mudawwana*' as the Arabic term for 'blog'.[23] Inspired by these bloggers, others who had been blogging in English switched to Arabic.[24]

By blogging in Arabic, bloggers could address an audience that extended across the entire Arab region, and include Arab speakers living abroad. Interestingly, a study conducted by the Berkman Center for Internet and Society at Harvard University (Etling *et al.* 2009) showed that the Arab blogosphere divided into several national clusters. This is evidenced by the fact that national blog aggregators were created. In Egypt, Alaa Abdel Fattah and his wife Manal founded manalaa.net, the first Egyptian blog aggregator, which linked bloggers together both online and through offline meetings. This contributed to the emergence of an Egyptian blogosphere.

The study conducted by the Berkman Center reveals that in 2009 the Egyptian blogosphere comprised the largest structural cluster in the Arabic blogosphere, including nearly one-third of the blogs on the map. It also shows that almost half of the Egyptian bloggers were women, one of the highest percentages of female bloggers in any cluster of the Arabic blogosphere. In her study of Lebanese blogging practices, Sarah Jurkiewicz claims that the Egyptian blogosphere has also been a source of inspiration for other national blogospheres (2012: 64).

This is due to the fact that, unlike other national governments, the Egyptian State did not practice severe online censorship (Abdulla 2007: 85). As for the other Arab countries, Hofheinz (2005) reports that various methods of censorship were used. Filtering and banning of certain sites deemed inappropriate for moral or political reasons was common in Saudi Arabia, Syria, Tunisia and Yemen. The United Arab Emirates, Bahrain and Jordan decreased filtering, focusing on a few political opposition sites. Qatar filtered only what it deemed pornographic. Unfiltered access was available in Morocco, Algeria, Libya, Sudan, Lebanon, Iraq and Kuwait, besides Egypt. However, in some cases (e.g. Sudan, Yemen, Morocco), the cost of accessing the net has been so high for many years that it has effectively limited Internet use to a tiny minority. In countries that do not block access to sites deemed morally or politically unacceptable, such as Sudan, Internet traffic was monitored by police and security organs (Hofheinz 2005: 79–80). This relative freedom encouraged an explosion of creativity and self-expression, as well as discussion of issues that were usually suppressed in mainstream media and society.

Not surprisingly then, upon its emergence in 2004, blogging was initially adopted as a tool for political mobilisation. It was primarily used to support the grassroots *Kifaya* (Enough) movement (whose official name was *al-Ḥaraka al-maṣriyya min ajl al-taghyīr*, Egyptian Movement for Change), which appeared in 2004 on the eve of the first-ever multi-candidate presidential elections to be held in 2005. The movement called for a rejection of a further mandate for President Mubarak, opposition to dynastic succession within the Mubarak family and a commitment to electoral democracy. Bloggers supported *Kifaya* in several ways: by criticising and revealing the abuses of Mubarak's government, in line with the principles of the movement, and by using blogs to organise and coordinate demonstrations.[25]

However, the initial hope put into blogging as a political tool was swept away by a series of disillusioning events on the political scene. These comprised firstly, the re-election of Mubarak as President of Egypt in May 2005, and secondly, the election of a majority of candidates from Mubarak's ruling NDP and also from the Muslim Brotherhood at the parliamentary elections held in November 2005, achieved through systemic abuse of the voting system.[26]

Despite the political disillusion, blogging did not lose its force. On the contrary, the year 2006 witnessed the 'flood age [*ᶜaṣr al-fayaḍān*] of Egyptian blogging', as the blogger Ahmed Naji describes it (2010: 17). This was favoured by the fact that the government, probably unaware of the subversive potential enabled by the technology, improved Internet infrastructure and lowered the price to buy a computer and Internet connection. Between 2003 and 2005, the number of Egyptians with access to the Internet increased from 3 to 5 million.[27] Accordingly, between 2005 and 2006, the number of blogs had increased threefold from 400 to 1,200, according to Alaa Abdel Fattah (quoted in Radsch 2008). At that time, the Internet was becoming a fact of life especially among the younger, urban, educated elites (Hofheinz 2005: 82–3). As Naji writes,

> after the parliamentary elections the dream of a political change seemed impossible to realize. But the growing emergence of blogs as an alternative medium, and the battle towards freedom of press and opinion were impossible to stop. Therefore, instead of aiming at big issues, such as complete political change and democracy, we focused on minor issues that could improve daily life within Egyptian society. (2010: 42)

More and more young Egyptians joined the blogosphere, writing on a variety of interests, ranging from daily life, religion, culture, human rights, to women's issues, and others. The blogosphere turned into a larger space for creativity and personal expression.

At this point, bloggers also became known outside of the blogosphere. The weekly Egyptian newspaper *al-Dustur*, known for its opposition to the government, initiated a blog page to introduce the Egyptian blogosphere to a larger public. In addition, independent newspapers such as *al-Masri al-Yawm* hired bloggers as freelancers.[28]

The Egyptian State replied by harassing and imprisoning some bloggers who were actively involved in political demonstrations. In 2006, the blogger Muhammad al-Sharqawi (Muḥammad al-Sharqāwī), founder of the independent publishing house Malamih, was the victim of brutal torture. In the same year, the blogger Karim Amer (Karīm ᶜĀmir) was sentenced to four years imprisonment for spreading his secular opinions, defaming Islam and insulting the President on his blog. In response, bloggers received protection from international organisations. Bloggers began to be regarded by international human rights organisations as 'citizen journalists' (*ṣaḥāfiyyūn shaᶜbiyyūn*) and thereby became beneficiaries of the advocacy and exposure granted to professional journalists by international organisations such as the Committee to Protect Journalists, Amnesty International, Human Rights Watch and Reporters Without Borders, among others. The Egyptian couple Alaa Abdel Fattah and Manal, considered the 'parents of blogging' in Egypt, received the 'Best Blog' award from the international NGO Reporters Without Borders, which also was publicised by the Al-Jazeera news channel. Egyptian bloggers began to link with bloggers from other Arab countries, as evidenced by the fact that the first Arab Bloggers Meeting was held in Beirut in 2008, and was followed by additional activities and campaigns.

Blogging the Self in the Egyptian Blogosphere

Within this context, the sub-genre of 'personal blogs' – that is blogs focused on one's own life and interests – became particularly prominent. The Egyptian youth adopted blogging to talk about themselves in a way they were not allowed to do both in traditional media (for religious and political reasons but also because of the difficulty of entering the cultural field) and in public (because of social pressures). They were clearly dissatisfied with the logic of the mainstream cultural field. By telling their own life stories, they hoped to find a place for themselves in society and to change people's mentality. By blogging, they aimed at developing new literary styles and breaking established taboos.

A great number of women turned to blogs to recount their ordinary lives, focusing on quotidian life details, ambitions, dreams and love problems. According to Naji and to the scholars Yasmine Rifaat (2008) and Otterman (2007), women's blogs contributed to a paradigm shift in the image and role of women in Egyptian society. By writing about their ordinary life, women began to speak out about their discrimination in society, relationships with their families, and marriage problems. Most of all, bloggers brought to light the issue of sexual harassment. On 25 October 2006, bloggers reported an episode of mass sexual harassment, where dozens of women were assaulted on the streets of Cairo by gangs of men while the police stood by and watched.[29] For several days, the event was unacknowledged by the mainstream media. Therefore, in the weeks and months after the episode, a number of female bloggers wrote about their personal experiences of sexual harassment. This was considered a taboo in society, as in cases of harassment it is usually the woman who is blamed; it is assumed that she must have provoked the man with a certain behaviour or dress code.

It was not just women who found an outlet for their voices online, but also other identifiable groups that had been silenced or marginalised in society. Members of the Muslim Brotherhood (MB) organisation, which had been declared illegal by the Mubarak government, joined the blogging community. The first person to explicitly identify himself as an MB member was the young journalist ᶜAbd al-Munᶜim Mahmud (ᶜAbd al-Munᶜim Maḥmūd), on his blog *Ana Ikhwan* (*I am a Muslim Brother*), which he started in October 2006.[30] Inspired by him, a considerable number of young MBs started individual online journals in which they discussed their lives, their cultural inclinations and their family problems. Both male and female members of the Brotherhood were blogging (Lynch 2007b). Through blogs, they formed relationships with non-Brotherhood youth, each discovering the humanity of the other.[31] Bahaᵓis, whose faith is not recognised in Egypt, also took to blogging as a means to assert their rights to citizenship and to disclose their identity.[32] The first of these was *Bahaᵓi Misri* (*Egyptian Bahaᵓi*), a blog started by a young Bahaᵓi in September 2006.[33] The blog served its contributors as a public space to write and publish their diaries, and to respond to allegations and myths about the Bahaᵓi religion. At this time, several bloggers also openly described themselves as atheist or secularists, often under the shelter of a pseudonym. Furthermore, many gay people started to write about themselves, either about their love problems, social discrimination or daily life; homosexual discourse is quite absent in ordinary media for social and religious reasons (Naji 2010).

Arabic Literature Between the Online and the Offline

In 2007, the implementation of social networks like Facebook and Twitter gave even more visibility to blogging, rather than diminishing or overshadowing its importance. Some amateur writers started using Facebook to publish literary texts in the form of Facebook notes and to share them within their network. However, they often switched to blogging as they found that blogs were more apt for writing longer entries, but still linking to their blog entries on their FB page.[34]

The blogging boom also prompted the emergence of more literary websites, aimed at ruling the chaos of blogging. For example, in 2007, the leading Egyptian scholar Sabry Hafez founded a new literary journal entitled *al-Kalima*.[35] In his words, the journal aspired to bring the best practices and conventions of Arab cultural journalism – quality control, professional language, ethical critical conduct and the regular appointment with the reader – back to cultural journalism (Hafez 2017: 47). In 2009, the Egyptian poet Muhammad Abu Zayd (Muḥammad Abū Zayd) founded *al-Kitaba* (*Writing*) to give major visibility to new literary voices that had emerged online in recent years.[36] *Al-Kitaba* was founded with the aim of becoming a voice for 'marginalized writing, new writing, and serious writing, to throw light on the voices that nobody hears but that regenerate the blood of literature'.[37]

The growing use of blogging and social networks as platforms of publication did not weaken the book market, as many had feared. On the contrary, social media had a great impact in promoting print literature and introducing new themes and aesthetics. The spread of this technology coincided with the implementation of new marketing strategies aimed at revitalising the literary field. For example, new bookshops/coffee-bars appeared in Cairo in 2003, on the model of Western bookshops such as Barnes and Noble that adopted a new marketing strategy: they held book-signing parties (*ḥafalāt tawqīᶜ*), literary events in which readers could meet the authors and have their books signed. Blogs and social networks played a crucial role in advertising these events and encouraging young people to buy and exchange books.

Blogging has also favoured the discussion and promotion of Arabic literature in English. While many Western publishing houses still seem reluctant to publish Arab authors in Western languages, unless they are accompanied by Orientalised titles and covers, we can see that a growing number of websites written in English and other languages have begun to show an interest towards Arabic literary production. An example of this is the blog *Arabic Literature (in English)* started by Marcia Lynx Qualey in 2009.[38] Qualey, who was based in Cairo until 2011, offers many contributions regarding literary events both in Arab countries and abroad, reviews of books, topical contributions, cross-references, links, and more.

Social networks also promoted print books by favouring the emergence of 'electronic readers' clubs' (*nawādī al-qurrā*ᵓ *al-īliktrūniyya*), for example, the Saudi-based Facebook group founded in 2009 and the Egyptian-run Facebook group 'Let's read a book monthly', also founded in 2009. As in traditional book clubs, readers would agree on reading the same book and discuss it simultaneously with readers from all over the Arab world, and sometimes even chatting with the author. Similarly, the website Goodreads allows readers to share their book reviews and ratings. One could wonder whether these strategies contributed to the phenomenon of bestsellers in the Arab world, a status achieved for the first time by the novel *ᶜImarat Yaᶜqubiyan* (translated into English as *Yacoubian Building*, 2004) by Alaa al-Aswany (ᶜAlāᵓ al-Aswānī), published in 2002.[39]

Besides, blogging contributed to the book market as more and more blogs were turned into books. From 2007, Egyptian publishers started monitoring the Internet in order to find new creative voices. They realised that the blogosphere was a fertile ground for new ideas and fresh voices. Additionally, on a more practical level, editors are interested in blog books because bloggers usually have an established audience, a connection with readers or ready-made fans (Nelson 2006: 10). In 2007, Malamih publishing house, founded by the blogger Muhammad al-Sharqawi, published the literary work of three bloggers, among which was the novel *Rogers* by Ahmed Naji. In 2008, Dar al-Shuruq, the largest private publishing house in Egypt, published three Egyptian blogs written by three female bloggers: *ᶜAyzah Atgawwiz* (*I Want to Get Married*) by Ghada Abdel Aal, *Aruzz bil-Laban li-Shakhsayn* (*Rice Pudding for Two*) by Rihab Bassam (Riḥāb Bassām) and *Amma Hadhihi fa-Raqsati Ana* (*This is My Own Dance*) by Ghada Muhammad Mahmud (Ghāda Muḥammad Maḥmūd).[40] They chose these blogs for both their popularity and their literary quality. These numbers are reflected in the number of books sold, as these book-blogs soon became bestsellers. The blogging community and their online fans visited bookshops and attended book-signing events and literary discussions. In particular, *I Want to Get Married* by Ghada Abdel Aal, a first-person account dealing with the theme of arranged marriage and written with a mordant humorous style, was translated into several languages. In 2010, it was turned into a television series broadcast during Ramadan, starring the renowned Egyptian actress Hind Sabri (Hind Ṣabrī).

Following Dar al-Shuruq's initiative, more and more Egyptian publishing houses adapted blog posts into books. A number of publishing houses, Dar Uktub (Write!) or Dar Dawwin (Blog!), as the names imply, were established with the specific intent of giving bloggers the possibility to turn their work into print.[41] Similarly, in 2009, the Arabic Network for Human Rights started the magazine *Wasla* (*Connection*), with articles entirely retrieved from blogs and including the readers' comments.

Vice versa, authors tried to emulate the style and form of electronic media in their printed novels, achieving a rejuvenating effect on both the form and content of novels. For example, the novel *Banat al-Riyad* (*Girls of Riyadh*, 2007, translated by the author with Marilyn Booth in 2008) by the Saudi writer Rajaa Alsanea (Rajāʾ Al-Ṣāniᶜ) is entirely written in the form of emails and includes some vernacular and English expressions (Ramsay 2007). In 2007, the author Ibrahim Abdel Meguid (Ibrāhīm ᶜAbd al-Majīd) published the novel *Fi kulli usbuᶜ yawm gumuᶜ* (*In Every Week There is a Friday*), which tells the story of nineteen Egyptians, coming from different social backgrounds, brought together by the desire to confess every Friday on an online forum. The novel borrows the format of websites, and includes dialogues and expressions in several language registers, and emoticons and symbols typical of the Internet writing style.

The number of books retrieved from blogs and of books reproducing Internet aesthetics has dramatically increased in the last few years and is almost impossible to track now, showing that Arabic literature continues to thrive between the online and the offline realm.

Notes

1 See *Arab Human Development Report 2003: Building a Knowledge Society*, http://hdr.undp.org/en/content/arab-human-development-report-2003 (last accessed

20 June 2017). The report was sponsored by the United Nations Development Programme (UNDP), providing leading Arab scholars a platform through which to analyse the challenges and opportunities for human development in the Arab Region. The authors conclude that despite the presence of significant human capital in the region, disabling constraints hamper the acquisition, diffusion and production of knowledge in Arab societies.

2 See, for example, 'Is the Arab World Ready for a Literary Revolution', *The Independent*, 15 April 2008, www.independent.co.uk (last accessed 20 August 2017); 'One Thousand and One Delights', *The Guardian*, 12 April 2008, www.guardian.co.uk (last accessed 20 August 2017).

3 An example of that is the controversy over the re-publication of the novel *Walima li aᶜshab al-bahr* (*Banquet for Seaweed*, 1983) by the Syrian author Haydar Haydar (Ḥaydar Ḥaydar) in the year 2000 by the Egyptian Ministry of Culture. The Islamist-oriented newspaper *as-Shaᶜb* launched an attack against the author and the Ministry of Culture, and asked the religious institution of al-Azhar to issue a fatwa against the book. As a result, the book was banned from publication. For more details of the Haydar Haydar affair, see Sabry Hafez (2000), 'The Novel, Politics and Islam'.

4 Data retrieved from https://data.worldbank.org/region/arab-world?view=chart (last accessed 20 May 2018).

5 The Egyptian author and scholar Sahar El-Mougy (Saḥar al-Mūjī), who started writing at this time, declared in an interview with the journal *al-Qahirah*: 'Naḥnu jīl bilā qurrāᵓ wa-riwāyātunā lā taṣluḥ li-sīnimā' ('We are a generation without readers and our novels do not suit the cinema [industry]') (27 April 2004). Similarly, Youssef Rakha told me in a personal interview in 2011 that 'until 10 years ago, the readers were also writers. We used to circulate novels among each other.'

6 http://www.jehat.com/jehaat/ar (last accessed 20 August 2017).

7 'Al-Turuq Intahat fa-li-Yabdaᶜ as-Safar' ('The roads are over, so let us start the trip'), paper presented by Qasim Haddad at the Bahreini Internet Association, 26 July 2003, http://www.jehat.com/ar/3naljehah/Pages/default.aspx (last accessed 20 June 2017).

8 'ᶜAn al-Jiha' ('About the Direction'), http://www.jehat.com/ar/3naljehah/Pages/default.aspx (last accessed 20 June 2017).

9 http://ofouq.com, website no longer available.

10 http://www.kikah.com (last accessed 20 June 2017). On the website, Shimon explains that *Kikah* is named after his father, 'a deaf and mute child who was born and grew up an orphan amid fierce wars between tribes, sects and groups

inhabiting the mountains of northern Iraq … I wanted to give his name to this journal, because he was born an orphan and without a language of his own, in an amorphous geography, redrawn differently from time to time. And because I was certain that in the end he would only be on the side of humanist values.'

11 In addition, Shimon is notable for his contribution to the selection and editing of the volume *Beirut 39: New Writing from the Arab World* (Shimon 2010), which introduces the works of thirty-nine emergent Arab authors below the age of forty to an English-speaking audience.

12 http://www.nashiri.net (last accessed 20 June 2017). On this website, see also N. Lenze (2012), *Telling Stories Online in the Gulf: Prolegomena to the Study of an Emerging Form of Arabic Literary Expression.*

13 http://www.kotobarabia.com (last accessed 20 June 2017).

14 http://www.neelwafurat.com (last accessed 20 June 2017).

15 http://www.alwaraq.net/Core/index.jsp?option=1 (last accessed 20 June 2017). For an overview of Classical and Medieval Arabic literary sources online, see Katia Zakharia (2012), 'Guide de la littérature arabe médiévale et classique-sur-Web'.

16 https://www.4shared.com (last accessed 20 June 2017).

17 http://www.arab-ewriters.com (last accessed 20 June 2017).

18 In 2007 the prize was awarded to the Moroccan literary critic Saᶜid Yaqin (Saᶜīd Yaqīn) for his literary criticism about Digital Literature. The prize consisted of 2000 USD.

19 http://www.alsakher.com/forum.php (last accessed 20 June 2017).

20 These blogs also soon became very famous in the West. Salam Pax's blog was published in book form in 2004 with the title *Salam Pax and The Baghdad Blog* (London: Atlantic Books), and enjoyed wide circulation.

21 Blogger's own transliteration of ᶜAmr ᶜIzzat used on social media.

22 'Eih da baᶜ' ('What is this, then?'), *Tayy al-muttasil*, 10 December 2003, http://zamakan.gharbeia.org/2003/12/10/153459 (last accessed 20 August 2017).

23 Hofheinz reports that the word *mudawwana* was coined by a blogger based in Abu Dhabi and then spread all over the Arab blogosphere (2007: 77).

24 This is how the blogger ᵓIhath reflects on this topic on his blog: 'Three weeks ago, I was feeling frustration because there were no blogs in Arabic. I have been blogging in English for one year and I have been following Iraqi blogs, but they are all written in English. I was feeling sorry for myself, for the state of the Arab nation and for the Arab language. Why are there no blogs in Arabic? Why do all the Arabs prefer to blog in English? Then I said to myself: "instead of cursing darkness, light a candle, even if it is weak". I decided to start blogging in Arabic

and after some days I found a number of blogs in Arabic that I like. After some days, the frustration turned into hope. I started dreaming big dreams. Maybe Ihath and others will become the pioneers of the phenomenon of blogs in the Arab world.': 'Auf … Aufayn … Thalatha' ('Uff … Two Uffs … Three'), *Ihath*, 30 October 2004, http://www.ihath.com/arabi/2004_10_01_archive.html (last accessed 20 August 2017).

قبل ثلاثه أسابيع كنت أشعر بالإحباط نتيجة عدم وجود بلوجات بالعربي. فقد مرت سنه علي بداية كتابتي للبلوج بالإنجليزي وأنا من متابعي البلوجات العراقيه بشكل مستمر ولاكن كلها بالإنجليري. كنت أشعر بالأسف علي نفسي وعلي حال الأمه العربيه وعلي حال اللغه العربيه. لماذا لايوجد بلوجات بالعربي؟ لماذا كل العرب يختارون الكتابه بالإنجليزي؟ وبعدها قلت لنفسي" بدل ما تلعن الظلام ولع شمعه ولو خافته». قررت أن أبتدئ الكتابه بالعربي وبعدها بأيام أكتشفت عده بلوجات عربيه أعجبتي. وخلال أيام تحول الإحباط إلي أمل. وأصبحت أحلم أحلام كبيره. لربما أصبحت إيهاث وغيرها من رواد ضاهرة البلوجر في العالم العربي

There were some Egyptian bloggers who continued to publish in English, like Zeinobia, author of the blog *Egyptian Chronicles* (http://egyptianchronicles.blogspot.no, last accessed 20 August 2017), or Mahmud Salem, author of *Rantings of a Sandmonkey* (http://www.sandmonkey.org, last accessed 20 August 2017). Lynch (2007a) defines them as 'bridge bloggers', in the sense that they aim to transfer their thoughts to a Western audience.

25 Likewise, in Lebanon, blogging became a widespread phenomenon in conjunction with the 2005 Cedar Revolution and the 2006 war with Israel (Jurkiewicz 2018: 52). In Kuwait, the high-water mark came in 2006 when a group of bloggers successfully launched an electoral reform campaign to prevent corruption (Nordenson 2010: 43). In his study of the Tunisian blogosphere, Mohamed Zayani reports that Tunisian bloggers first adopted blogging as personal diaries, and only later as spaces for political discussion (2015: 107).

26 Bloggers went out in the streets to cover the event and verify the integrity of the process. This is how Haytham reports it: 'Parliamentary elections were for me the biggest disillusion ever. I entered a small street in Alexandria and I found people selling their votes for food. My friends and me started to shout that it was unfair and we were beaten. Ingenuously I went to the police station to report the event and I was sent home humiliated. I realized that, no matter how fair the election process is, people do not want change and just care for today.' (Interview, December 2011.) Indeed, the result of the elections confirmed the frustrations of the blogger.

27 Data retrieved from Internet World Statistics, available at http://www.internetworldstats.com/af/eg.htm (last accessed 20 August 2017).

28 Ahmad Gharbiyyah maintains that bloggers' writing style was more clear and coherent than the one used by classical journalists. On their online pages, bloggers had trained themselves to write for an active audience. (Interview, April 2012.)

29 A group of bloggers were sitting at a café when a friend ran in to tell them what was happening, compelling them to go to the streets and take pictures and video of the crimes being committed against random women. These were posted and the bloggers wrote about what they saw. Yet for three days the attacks were unacknowledged by the authorities or the news media until the blogger Nawara Nijm (Nawwāra Nijm) was invited onto the popular talk show *al-ᶜAshira Masaᵓan* to talk about a different subject. Nijm asked the host, Mona el-Shazly (Munā al-Shādhlī), why there had been no coverage and el-Shazly decided to investigate, eventually leading to comprehensive coverage throughout the Arab and Egyptian news media. From there, the story migrated to the independent press. Consequently, the Interior Minister was forced to issue a report about the event. For more on the blogging responses to the assaults, see Otterman (2007), 'Publicizing the Private: Egyptian Women Bloggers Speak Out'.

30 http://ana-ikhwan.blogspot.no (last accessed 20 August 2017).

31 Lynch (2007b) reports that in one of his letters from prison, Mahmud described his blog as 'my message to myself, to the young Muslim Brothers and to society. I wanted to show that Brothers are humans who have the same dreams [as anyone else]. We have fun. We drink [tea and coffee]. We sit at cafés. We go to movies. We demonstrate … and we blog for freedom.'

32 The community of Bahaᵓi counted 2,000 members in 2010 according to ARDA (Association of Religion Data Archives). During the last half of the twentieth century they had gone through large-scale persecution after being denied all rights as an organised religious community. For more, see the Bahaᵓis page on the ARDA website: http://www.thearda.com/Denoms/D_1135.asp (last accessed 20 August 2017).

33 http://egyptianbahai.wordpress.com (last accessed 20 August 2017).

34 Muhamad Husayn (Muḥammad Ḥusayn), Personal Interview, March 2012.

35 www.alkalimah.net (last accessed 20 August 2017).

36 http://alketaba.com (last accessed 20 August 2017).

37

وأنه يسعى إلى أن يكون صوتا لكتابة مهمشة ، لكتابة جديدة ، لكتابة جادة ، أن يلقى
الضوء على أصوات لم يسمعها أحد بعد لكنهم يساهمون بقدر ما في تجديد دماء الكتابة

'Itlaq Mawqa[c] al-Kitaba' ('Release of *Al-Kitaba* Website'), retrieved from Muhammad Abu Zayd's personal blog, 1 April 2009, http://mohamedabuzaid.blogspot.no/2009/04/blog-post.html (last accessed 20 August 2017).

38 http://arablit.wordpress.com (last accessed 20 August 2017).

39 Jacquemond reports that total sales of the Arabic edition and of the English, French and Italian translations were estimated at over 300,000 at the beginning of 2007 (2008: 232). Translations in other languages followed after that. On Arabic bestsellers, see also Rooke (2011), 'The Emergence of the Arabic Bestseller: Arabic Fiction and World Literature'.

40 Hoda el-Sadda notices that the history and general direction of Dar al-Shuruq should be taken into consideration: its owner, Ibrahim al-Mu[c]allim (Ibrāhīm al-Mu[c]allim), was once president of the Union of Arab Publishers; it is hardly an avant-garde publisher and its publishing history is predominantly liberal Islamic; and the focus of its venture into the literary field has not been to discover new talent, but to republish the classics of Arabic literature (2010: 318). For a profile of this publishing house, see also Y. Gonzalez Quijano (1998), *Les Gens du Livre*.

41 '*Dawwin*' is the imperative form of the verb '*dawwana*', 'to register', that consequently acquired the meaning 'to blog'.

2

The Paratext of Egyptian Blogs

Thresholds of Interpretations

The investigation of the autofictional nature of blogs begins with the paratext. The term 'paratext' is borrowed from the literary theorist Gérard Genette (1997) and is usually associated with books. It indicates information that is secondary to the main text, for example, the name of the author, the book covers, illustrations, titles, dedications, forewords, epigraphs, the index or table of contents and other factors (such as interviews with the author, magazine reviews, recommendations by word of mouth, and so on). I am analysing the paratext because autofiction is partially inscribed there: indeed, autofictional critics place emphasis on the correspondence of the author's, narrator's and main character's name and the indication on the cover that the text is fictional. Moreover, Genette maintains that the paratext is 'a zone not only of transition but also of transaction: a privileged place of a pragmatics and a strategy, an influence on the public, an influence that is at the service of a better reception for the text and a more pertinent reading of it' (Genette 1997: 2). Therefore, the uncertainty of the reader regarding the ontological status of the work (that I have defined as the main feature of autofiction) can in most cases be ascribed to the paratext. In my discussion of the blogs below I will deal with paratextual features, focusing on choices of authorship, titles, and meta texts retrieved from the the blogs and interviews.

As for choices of authorship, Genette defines 'onymity', the case in which the name of the author corresponds to the real name of the author; 'pseudonymity', the case in which the author signs with a fictional name; and 'anonymity', the case in which the name of the author is left unknown

(1997: 39). However, the latter is not possible in blog-writing, as users have to register a user-name in order to create a blog.

Titles constitute another important element of the paratext. Studying literary titles is important because, as Genette states in his book *Paratexts: Thresholds of Interpretation* (1997), they are not just names. Rather, as the metaphor of the door threshold indicates, they are both an indication of what to expect from the text and an invitation for the readers.[1] Adams (1987) also believes that one of the major functions of the literary title is 'focusing', because it selects from among the main elements of core content one theme to stand as the forefront of the work.[2] All the studies done in the field of titology deal with printed book titles. There are some similarities and differences between the title of a print book and the titles of blogs. First of all, just like many print book titles, blog titles often consist of a main title and a subtitle. As for the location, while the title of a book is located on the cover, the title of the whole blog is usually displayed at the top of the page, often presented in a graphic banner across the top section. The date and sender of the title also differ in blogs. For print books, the choice of the title is usually made both by the publisher and the author and they share the responsibility for it. However, this decision may not meet with the author's satisfaction, and this dissatisfaction may persist after the submission of the manuscript and, indeed, the first publication of the work. At that point, the author has to deal with his publisher, the public and possibly the law. Since blogging is an act of self-publication, the blogger is the only party who can decide on and change the title. We encounter many blogs whose titles have changed, sometimes after a period of years. This does not seem to have caused any issues for the readers, who appear to be accustomed to the idea that blogs are continually modifiable, changeable and may vanish and be reborn from one time to another.

The interviews I conducted with the authors fit into the category that Genette defines as 'private epitext', within the confines of the larger paratext. The private epitext differs from the public epitext (interviews given to the media) because they are addressed to a first addressee (me) interposed between the author and the potential public. The author addresses this individual person for his or her own sake, even if the author's ulterior motive may be to let the public subsequently stand witness to this interlocution. Thus, we can use this correspondence as a certain kind of statement about the work (Genette 1997: 371). The aim of my interviews with the authors was to retrieve biographical information about the author, in order to sketch a physical profile of these authors; to identify markers of identity between the real author and his or her online character; and to investigate the reasons behind their forays into the blogosphere. Commentary about blog-writing can also be found in the opening post of the blog or scattered in successive posts in the comment sections, and these are also included in the analysis. This is not only a recurrent feature among Egyptian bloggers, as it will be shown later, but seems quite common with bloggers worldwide. Serfaty identifies it as a common theme in the American blogosphere (2004: 31). In his study of French blogs, Lejeune states: 'the beginning of a diary is nearly always emphasized. People seldom begin without saying so' (quoted in Serfaty 2004: 31).

Finally, Genette considers the cover another element of significance. For the blog, I will analyse the visual elements that can be found on the main page of the blog, such as the graphic banner (where usually the title is inscribed), the layout of the blog and the profile picture of the author.

The first part of the chapter focuses on the analysis of the paratext of the six blogs chosen as case studies: *Wassi^c Khayalak* (*Widen Your Imagination*) by Ahmed Naji; *Ma Bada Li* (*What Seemed to Me*) by Amr Ezzat; *Tanatif Ma^cat* (*Ma3t's Bits and Pieces*)[3] by Mona Seif[4] (Munā Sayf); *Yawmiyyat Imra'a Mithliyya* (*Diary of a Gay Woman*) by the writer who uses the pseudonym 'Emraamethlya';[5] *Al-Kanaba al-Hamra* (*The Red Sofa*) by Bilal Husni (Bilāl Ḥusnī); and *Yawmiyyat ^cAnis* (*Diary of a Spinster*) by Abeer Soliman (^cAbīr Sulaymān). In the second part, the data retrieved from these blogs will be analysed together with the larger sample of blogs selected for this study.

Case Studies

Wassi^c Khayalak (Widen Your Imagination) *by Ahmed Naji*

Figure 1 Header of the blog *Wassi^c Khayalak* (*Widen your Imagination*) by Ahmed Naji. The blogger changes the picture in the header frequently. I chose this one because it is also the cover of his novel *Rogers* (2007). Retrieved from http://ahmednaje.net, accessed 28 August 2013.

Naji was born in Mansura, Egypt, in 1985. He graduated in journalism at the Akhbar al-Yawm Academy in 2006 and shortly after started working as an editor in the state-owned literary journal *Akhbar al-Adab*, reflecting his primary interests in the fields of literature, new media and popular culture.

In our interview, Naji stated that he started blogging in January 2005, a decision mainly driven by his curiosity and excitement towards the new Internet medium. At the time, the Egyptian blogosphere was still in its early stages. Up to this point, Naji had been using forums to publish his literary attempts. However, the blog form appeared to him as 'more entertaining', as he could publish without having to undergo the approval of a moderator. The fact that he could receive feedback and comments from an unknown audience also attracted him to the form.[6] This is shown by his words written in one of his first entries entitled '*Tanwih*' ('Notice', 16 February 2005), in which he defines the blogs as a 'game' and the blogosphere as an unexplored 'universe' (*malakūt*).

Naji first entitled his blog *Yawmiyyat Khayal al-Zill* (*Diary of a Shadow Play*), a title influenced, as he stated himself in an interview, by his reading of the Portuguese poet Fernando Pessoa (1888–1935). More specifically, he seems to be influenced by Pessoa's use of heteronyms, namely, his multiplication of himself into three major fictional characters alongside a dozen lesser dramatis personae, each one endowed with a specific biography, psychology, politics, religion and physique. In a similar vein, Naji uses the Internet to turn himself into several fictionalised online characters. In this sense, blog-writing is the continuation of a fictional game that he had started playing before on chat sites and Internet forums. On the blog, he explains to his readers:

> Shadow Theatre was astonished at Pessoa's games in the beginning and considered him a gambler that plays with different parts of his body to amuse the reader … Oh God, I think I was superficial in this period, but I also saw in myself the sufficient ability to play and gamble – me too – I made up more than one life … more than one character … I saw myself as Odysseus who came home safe, Adam Na^cman, Ghabu 'Fayruz Haraz' and sometimes I visited Mr. Turbara. The Internet of course was an amazing theatre, for it only needs a chat room or a forum to start playing, choose an entire personality with all its vocabulary and its small and big life details to start the nonsense (*ᶜabath*). ('*Bisswa*', Pessoa, 11 March 2005)
>
> خيال الظل كان مندهشا من ألعاب بيسوا في البداية و رأى بيسوا كمقامر يلعب بأجزاء من جسده لمتعة القارئ .. يا الله ، اعتقد انى كنت سطحيا في ذلك الوقت ، لكن أيضا رأيت في نفسى القدرة الكافيه أن العب و أقامر أنا أيضا ، ابتكرت أكثر من حياة .. أكثر من شخصية .. رأيت نفسى ..أدوسيوس الناجى ، ادم نعمان ، جابو « فيروز حراز» ، و أحيانا كنت ازور السيد طوربارا
> النت طبعا كان مسرح مدهشا ، فالامر يتطلب فقط غرفة للشات ، او مساحة للمنتدى ليبدأ بعدها اللعب ، اخترع شخصية كاملة بكل مفرداتها و تفاصيل حياتها الصغيرة و الكبيرة ليبدأ العبث

In this light, the title *Yawmiyyat Khayal al-Zill* becomes highly significant. Firstly, the expression '*khayāl al-ẓill*', which translates literally as 'shadow imagination', reminds the readers that what they read may contain fictional elements. Secondly, the term brings us back to the medieval tradition of the shadow theatre, a form of popular entertainment achieved by moving cut-out figures between a source of light and a scrim, to create the impression of human figures and other three-dimensional objects.[7] As such, the title suggests that the blogger is using the screen of his computer as a puppeteer would use his scrim: he is using his entire body or projecting parts of it to create imaginary figures in order to entertain the audience. Additionally, the fact that Pessoa's 'drama of life' (Zenith 1993: 47) is turned into an interactive, multimedia 'shadow theatre' anticipates the blogger's intention in mixing his interest in Western literature with his Arabic literary heritage and his mastery of new media technologies. The reference to the shadow theatre might also be an indication that, just as in the medieval Egyptian tradition of the shadow theatre, the blog is also aimed at mocking social and political issues and making fun of certain Arab public figures.

Interestingly enough, Naji has chosen the devil as his online counterpart, as evidenced by the name of his shadow, 'Iblis'[8] ('The Devil'). Later, Iblis would become 'Beso' (Bēsō), its shorter and more sympathetic version. Naji clarifies that the choice of this name is meant to highlight his difference (*ikhtilāf*) from and opposition (*iᶜtirāḍ*) to his social community. Indeed, according to the Quran, Iblis was the only angel of God to refuse to bow to Adam.[9]

However, conscious of the negative traits that the nickname carries, Naji reassures his unknown online community that his contribution to the blogosphere is not driven by devilish intentions, rather by the need to write freely and to explore a new world. In a post celebrating his one-hundredth post 'Miᵓa Tadwina min al-Mahabba' ('One Hundred Posts from Love', 16 September 2005), Naji praises his online community for giving him a feeling of existence. Indeed, the act of reading and being read satisfies his curiosity, his self-exploratory spirit and his need to be heard, qualities that are ignored by the offline society. In his words: 'my chauvinistic instinct and sense of self-esteem are blown' (*gharīzatī al-shūfūniyya wa-iḥsāsī bi-dhātī infatakh*).

Naji is aware that he shares this feeling with many of the other young people gathered in the blogosphere. In the blog post 'ᵓArghab fī l-Buh bi-Lahazat al-Bahja' ('I Desire to Reveal the Moments of Joy', 29 July 2005) he describes the blogosphere as 'a swarm of migratory birds taking collective rest on a tree to feel [the warmth] of being-together (*sarb ṭuyūr muhājira yastarīḥ jamāᶜatan fawqa al-shajara li-yashᶜur bil-lamma*). The metaphor of the swarm signals that Naji envisions blogging as a collective move-away from state-owned culture and society as they can no longer satisfy their cultural and existential needs, and a search for new intellectual shores.

The most devilish aspect of Naji's personality consists of 'tempting' the readers with another reality that is carved out of his own imagination (*khayāl*). To emphasise this aspect, in 2006 Naji changed the title of his blog to *Wassiᶜ khayalak – ᶜish kaʾannak talᶜab* (*Widen Your Imagination – Live as if you were playing*).[10] As the title anticipates, Naji used the blog to develop something he claims to be a 'new' *adab*, a new kind of Arabic (literary) writing in which imagination plays a key role, and is intended by the author, and received/ understood by the readers, as a game.

This stress on imagination and fantasy is evidenced by the visual layout of his blog. The blogger changes the picture in the header frequently. The images include pictures of famous Egyptian stars, global art, comics and graffiti, fantasy portraits and explicit sexual images (see Figure 1). The profile section includes personal pictures of the author.

In 2011, Naji moved from the Omraneya platform (the blog aggregator created by Alaa Abdel Fattah and Manal, see Chapter 1), to an autonomous website, still entitled *Wassiʾ Khayalak*, but on the address ahmednaje.net. He also abandoned his pseudonym 'Iblis' and now signs his entries with his real name transcribed in Latin characters ('Ahmed Naje'). In the interview, he explains that since bloggers have ended up meeting each other in the real world, there was no need to continue using nicknames. Additionally, by dropping his pseudonym he could protect and claim ownership over his writing under his real name. The blog has turned into a professional writer's website that includes a biography section, written both in English and Arabic; a section entitled 'The Whale's Belly' that includes reviews of his books; a section that includes his articles in English and a section including his blog. The transformation of the website also reflects the global notoriety Naji has achieved through his blog, as the website is used as a platform for promoting his writing. The case of his imprisonment in 2016 is extensively documented on the website.

Ma Bada Li (What Seemed to Me) *by Amr Ezzat*

Figure 2 Header of the blog *Ma Bada Li* by Amr Ezzat, retrieved from mabadali.blogspot.no, accessed 17 August 2013.

Amr Ezzat is an Egyptian journalist and researcher from Cairo. He was born in Cairo in 1980 and grew up in the Imbaba suburb, one of most socially deprived areas of Cairo. In the interview he explains that his parents stressed the need for a good education as a means of social emancipation and had already planned their three sons' futures so that they would become engineers and physicians, the best potential careers according to the Egyptian family model.[11] Amr did not want to disappoint his family, so he graduated in Engineering at Cairo University and worked as an engineer for some years, in order to earn some money to cultivate his passion for the humanities. In 2009, he obtained a second degree in Philosophy and started working as a journalist for the Egyptian independent newspaper *al-Masri al-Yawm*. As far as his political interests go, Amr was influenced in his youth by the fundamentalist ideology that was then widespread in Imbaba: when he was sixteen, he joined the Muslim Brotherhood, and then a smaller Islamic Liberal organisation. In 2004, he approached the *Kifaya* movement, a grassroots movement that focused on government reform and change. For Amr, as for many young people, *Kifaya*'s strength was in its diversity, it being a wide umbrella under which various political currents were combined in the cause for democracy. Here Amr became acquainted with the blogging phenomenon, as many young people who joined the movement were already using blogs for political purposes.

What attracted Amr to blogging was the opportunity to publish any sort of writing without the need to classify it and without waiting for the moderator's permission to publish. In his first post 'Awwalan' ('First', 19 September 2005), the content of which is also inserted into the banner at the top of his online diary (see blog header in Figure 2), Amr quotes the German writer Goethe: 'I know nothing belongs to me / Except my thoughts, which constantly / wish to flow out of my soul / And every good moment / granted by Providence, / fills me with joy.'[12] This quotation affirms Amr's concept that his online writing is free, personal, independent from copyright and open to sharing.

For the title of his blog, Amr chose the expression *Ma Bada Li* (*What Seemed to Me*). This title suggests that he uses blogging to assert his personal perceptions of reality. It anticipates that Amr uses the blog to write about his own daily life, and to describe political, social and cultural issues through his own insights and feelings. The title recurs often in Amr's writing throughout the entire blog, as a musical leitmotif that contributes to the harmony of his writing. The title appears on a white banner, written in black. The entire visual layout is white in colour, without further decorations.

In his second post, 'Thaniya' ('A Second', 20 September 2005), Amr explains his reasons for writing his blog:

> Yesterday night it occurred to me (*badā lī*) that I had to start blogging, maybe because it seems to me (*badā lī*) – also – that I am at a critical moment in my personal history, where I am about to complete a quarter of a century in life.
>
> In this moment, I wished that I were an old blogger, so that now I could go through my blog and read myself two, three, five, ten years ago.
>
> How exciting it is to listen to all the people who I think I know well, while they are very different from me, just as I am different now [from myself before].
>
> How can I make out that thin line called 'I' that encompasses all those ['I's] … How can I make out what I was, but which was not 'I', but rather what I was pushed to do, like people are [often] pushed.

Is it absurd to say this … while I, all the time, keep thinking that I am 'this', or that I have to be 'this', or that I want to be 'this', or that I was actually 'this'.

How can you not make this out with sufficient clarity when you keep saying it to yourself or to the world insistently?

Those moments that I wandered between, those roles that I acted, those attributes with which I was described, those exploits that were attributed to me, those follies that I committed, those things that keep transforming in every moment. How can you say that I was there in all this, or that all this was mine, or was to me, by me, or from me.

In this blog, at least I can return to make sure that I was really 'there', because this signature that lies 'there' was mine!

بدا لي في ساعة متأخرة من مساء أمس أني يجب أن أبدأ التدوين!
ربما لأنه بدا لي - أيضا - أنني في لحظة حرجة من تاريخي الشخصي , اقتربت فيها أن أكمل ربع قرن علي قيد الحياة.
وددت في هذه اللحظة لو أنني مدون عتيق , يمكنني الآن أن أقلب في أرشيف مدونتي و أسمع نفسي من سنتين أو ثلاث أو خمس أو عشر سنين أو حتي أكثر.
كم هو مثير أن أستمع الي كل هؤلاء الذين أظن أني أعرفهم حق المعرفة , بينما هم مختلفون جدا مثلما أنا مختلف الأن.
كيف لي أن أتبين ذلك الخيط الرفيع المسمي « أنا « الذي يجمع هؤلاء جميعا .كيف لي أن أتبين ما كنته لكنه ليس « أنا « و إنما تورطت فيه مثلما يتورط الناس.
هل من العبث أن أقول ذلك ... و أنا طول الوقت أظل أفكر أني « كذا « او يجب أن أكون « كذا « أو أريد أن أكون « كذا « أو أنني كنت « كذا « فعلا.
كيف لا يمكن أن تتبين ذاتك بوضوح كاف و أنت تردد ذلك في سرك أو تقوله للعالم في إصرار.
تلك اللحظات التي تجولت بينها، تلك الأدوار التي قمت بها ، تلك الأوصاف التي وصفت بها ، تلك المآثر التي نسبت إليك ،،تلك الحماقات التي اقترفتها، تلك الأشياء التي تتحول كل لحظة، كيف لك أن تقول أني كنت هناك في كل ذلك، أو أن كل ذلك كان لي، أو بي،أو مني.
في هذه المدونة علي الأقل يمكنني أن أعود لأتاكد أني فعلا كنت « هناك « لأن هذا التوقيع الذي يذيل الـ «هناك» لي!

The confessional tone of this post sets the mood for intimacy and sincerity. The post clarifies that Amr's blogging is mainly driven by his need for self-identity and self-understanding. Amr feels the need for finding his own self and exploring his true personality, since he is hindered from doing so by an authoritative family and society. The blog helps him to search for this identity, thanks to the record it holds of 'snapshots' taken at a fixed point in time. By writing, and looking back at his older blog entries, Amr can assert his existence and can monitor the development of his identity. The blog helps him to build his character too, thanks to the life stories and comments provided by other bloggers. Therefore, his self-disclosure should not be understood as the simple unveiling of a pre-existent or perdurable self, but rather as a constitutive effort. The self that is disclosed is a construction, possibly an experimental one.

It is significant that Amr blogs with his real name. Additionally, he also uploads his profile picture in the 'About me' page of the blog. The interview confirms the reasons for blogging indicated by the words above. As he explained to me in an interview in May 2011,

> I used blogging as a way to affirm my individuality (*fardiyya*), because I had no need to create a fake virtual one. The military regime and society were trying to shut our mouths, so blogs were the only open channel in which we were allowed to express ourselves.

Amr stopped blogging in 2013. In the interview we had in March 2016, he attributed the reason to the changed political situation. He lamented a feeling of desperation (*yāʾs*) and nihilism (*ʿadamiya*) that prevents him from writing about himself. He prefers to focus on his academic writing. Nonetheless, in addition to continuing writing opinion pieces for *al-Masri al-Yawm* and *Mada Masr*, he manages Facebook, Twitter and Tumblr accounts.

Tanatif Maʿat *(*Ma3t's Bits and Pieces*) by Mona Seif*

Mona Seif was born in Cairo in 1985. She obtained a degree in Science at the University of Cairo, and currently works there as a researcher in the Cancer Biology Research Laboratory. Mona belongs to a family composed of outstanding political activists. Her father, Ahmad Sayf al-Islam (Aḥmad Sayf al-Islām), was an internationally known human rights lawyer.[13] Her mother, Layla Suayf (Laylā Suwayf), is a Mathematics professor at the University of Cairo who has always combined her academic career with political activism.

Mona's elder brother is Alaa Abdel Fattah, the founder of the Egyptian blog aggregator and a leading political activist.[14]

When talking about blogging during the interview, Mona first of all states her love for writing.

> I have always been writing. When I was a child I used to write letters to my imaginary friends. When I was fifteen, I lived abroad with my family and I wrote emails to my friends to tell them about my new life in a new city.

However, when asked about the reason that pushed her into publishing her writing online, she attributes it to the fact that in 2006 she felt that she was entering a crucial phase of her life, one that she aimed to resolve through online writing.[15]

It was in 2006 that Mona realised, through her own experiences, that the situation in Egypt was rapidly becoming a nightmare and that the Mubarak regime was revealing all its brutality. She realised that she had to develop her own political activism and strategies, not just to follow her family in demonstrations. Blogging could give her the ability to speak out, to document what was really happening in Egypt, and at the same time to join a community of people of her own age, who in the last year had distinguished themselves for developing a new political activism, taking advantage of the Internet. The same reasons are exposed in a blog post entitled 'Wa-Iktamalat ad-Daʾira' ('The Circle is Completed') published on 2 May 2010.

> In 2006, I started going to demonstrations by myself. I took part in the preparation for activities; I helped as much as I could. It was the start of a new path in my life. At this time, I met new friends, my guardian angel,[16] on a cold day on the pavement in front of the Judges' Club. And at this time, love struck me for the first time … In 2006 a new girl was born inside me. I discovered with her that I can draw, that I enjoy drawing childish sketches that looked much more mature in my imagination.

> في 2006 كانت بداية الفترة اني انزل اعتصامات بشكل مستقل تماما. اني اشارك بنفسي في الترتيبات لفعاليات، و اساعد باللي اقدر عليه. و كانت بداية طريق جديد في حياتي. وقتها اكتسبت أصحاب جداد، و اكتسبت ملاكي الحارس في يوم برد على الرصيف قدام نادي القضاة. و كمان وقتها خطفني الحب لأول مرة. ...

2006 كانت بداية بنت جديدة جوايا. اكتشفت معاها اني بارسم، و اني باستمتع بشكل مختلف جداً و انا بارسم رسومات طفولية كان شكلها أنضج بكتير في خيالي.

Significantly, the first post Mona writes in her blog is entitled 'Ana geit'[17] ('I've arrived', 6 October 2006) and it is written in Egyptian vernacular. In it, she declares: 'Today I enter a new world, one I've been longing to be part of, have always found excuses not to. Now, here I am.'

The fact that Mona uses the verb 'to arrive' when she describes her foray into the blogosphere shows that she is aware that the community is already there, and indeed she has watched it from outside with admiration. However, she is also aware that entering this 'new world' means redefining and reshaping herself anew, to show her nature to her lover and to establish new social relationships in a different society. This is challenging and exciting at the same time, which explains her hesitation to take this step. It is the urgency of the moment that sweeps away her initial reluctance.

Mona responds to this critical period of her personal life and the adverse Egyptian political situation by establishing a personal blog entitled *Tanatif Ma^{c}at* (*Maat's Bits and Pieces*).[18] In the title of the blog she turns her name into 'Ma3t', written in Arabic mixing Latin letters and numbers, to adapt it to current times and to the language of the Internet. The name '*mā^{c}at*' immediately links the blog to Ancient Egypt, where Maat (m3ʕt) was the goddess of harmony, justice and truth and, later, a representation of the concept of truth and justice itself.[19] Similarly, Mona chooses '*mā^{c}at*' to be not only her online persona but also the ideal that she aims to realise through her writing. In the title, she also declares her blog as '*tanātīf*', or 'bits and pieces' of herself, which suggests that she is only supplying snapshots of her life. The bits and pieces might also refer to the brevity of the texts that compose her diary. For her, blogging is not only an individual process of personal and political maturation towards the state of *mā^{c}at*, but also a way to reach and communicate with a different community, who aim to establish truth and justice in Egyptian political and social life.

As for her visual representation, she uploads her own drawing of a woman with loose hair in the header of her blog and on the profile page. In the header (see Figure 3), the woman (whom one assumes is a representation of herself/Maat) is in profile, in a seated posture, similar to the posture in which the Ancient Egyptian goddess is usually depicted, but amidst waves. Those parts of the body that are visible are uncovered. The water that surrounds her is red, dotted with flowers. Another element of difference is her hair: unlike the straight, disciplined hairstyle of the goddess, Maat emphasises her curly, rebellious hair. Her hair is also the most striking element of her blog profile picture, where she depicts the same character lying under the sun (see Figure 4).

Figure 3 Banner of the blog *Ma3t's Bits and Pieces*. Source: http://ma3t.blogspot.no.

Figure 4 Mona Seif's profile picture. Source: http://ma3t.blogspot.no.

In 2011, on the occasion of her brother's imprisonment, Mona comes out with her real name on the blog. Many bloggers who were taking part in demonstrations could certainly deduce who 'Maat' was, since she had uploaded pictures of her family. But after the revolution, on the occasion of her brother Alaa's imprisonment, Mona announces her real identity publicly on her blog with these words:

> In every new story dealing with injustices of the army I always look for some details that let me embrace the cause from a personal perspective. A small thing that can entangle their pain with my pain, and that can make our battle one.
>
> This time I don't have to search for details in order to make the case personal. This time the case belongs to me, and the sorrow is imprisoned inside me: I am Mona Seif, the sister of Alaa Abdel Fattah. My brother is unjustly in prison! ('ᶜAlaʾ ʾIlli Humma Ma-yiᶜrafuhush' ('The Alaa (whom) they don't know'), 7 November 2011)

في كل قصة جديدة عن ظلم العسكر دايما بأدور على تفصيلة تخليني أتبنى الموضوع
بشكل شخصي. حاجة صغيرة تشبك وجعهم بوجعي و تخللي معركتنا واحدة.

المرة دي مش محتاجة أفتش على تفاصيل لشخصنة القضية. المرة دي القضية مني، و
الوجع محبوس جوايا: أنا منى سيف أخت علاء عبد الفتاح. أخويا في السجن ظلم!

After the revolution, Mona came to the realisation that she does not need to conceal her true identity anymore. According to her, the revolution has brought the Truth (*māᶜat*) to Tahrir, to her people, has broken her fear of the public and the authorities. Additionally, it seems that the very act of disclosing her identity on the blog is a political act itself: by claiming her name, Mona is speaking the Truth louder.

Mona still blogs to the present day but with less frequency, as well as being active on Twitter and Facebook.

Yawmiyyat Imraʾa Mithliyya *(*Diary of a Gay Woman*) by Emraamethlya*

I interviewed this blogger by email in June 2010 and August 2012: she[20] provided me with some clarifications regarding her blogging activity, but she expressed her wish to remain anonymous. She informed me that she uses some precautions to hide her personal information, such as hiding the IP address of her computer.[21] She claimed that the anonymity granted by the online medium is the only means she has to express herself freely as a contemporary Egyptian gay woman and avoid the risk of identification by the Egyptian State and society.

In actuality, despite homosexuality not being in itself illegal in Egypt, many lesbian, gay, bisexual and transgender individuals and groups are still targeted by the Egyptian State under laws based on derogatory terminology, such as those that outlaw 'debauchery' and 'public immorality'.[22] Homosexuals are also strongly discriminated against by Egyptian society on religious grounds: both Islamic and Christian believers consider homosexuality to be sinful and refer to the story of *qawm Lūṭ* (The People of Lot) to elucidate their disapproval.[23] This sexual orientation is generally seen as a symptom of an illness, often deriving from a disturbing experience with the opposite sex in childhood; therefore it is believed that it can be healed through psychiatric support. Accordingly, the Arabic word that is usually used to define homosexual individuals is '*shādhdh*', which literally means 'deviant, abnormal'.

While much has been written by academic researchers and human rights activists about male homosexuality in Egypt, very little is known about female homosexuality.[24] Egyptian lesbian women are hardly ever represented in the media, cinema or literature, and the few existing images are mentioned as negative examples.[25] According to the scholar Iman al-Ghafari, in a predominantly patriarchal culture like that of Egypt, female sexuality is mostly seen as primarily heterosexual. Therefore, 'erotic relations among women are devalued as a temporary substitute for the love of men, and are considered of no real threat to the dominant heterosexual system as long as they remain undercover, or in the closet' (2003: 86). Egyptian society's attitude towards lesbianism is mirrored in the language used to define it. The Arabic word used to describe lesbians is '*suḥāqiyya*', which is a word that refers to the 'act of rubbing two bodies to reach sexual pleasure'.[26] The word also highlights society's tendency to reduce female homosexuality to a mere sexual practice, rather than acknowledge it as a specific sexual identity.

In the interview, Emraamethlya states that she started blogging in January 2006, as she felt that the blogosphere was the only place where she could express herself freely as a lesbian.[27] Since individuals cannot identify openly as homosexuals in Egypt for the reasons listed above, many of them tend to express their sexual identity online through chat sites, forums and blogs (Abou-Chakra 2008). These online tools allow them to find information about sexuality, health and identity, to talk freely about themselves under the shelter of a nickname, as well as to respond to their need for friendship. In particular, blogs have enabled lesbian women's first-person narratives that could not have found an outlet in traditional media.[28]

The profile page of her blog informs us that she is a woman from Egypt, while her nickname immediately confirms her sexual identity. The choice of the nickname is an active reaction to the fact that, in the Egyptian dialect, female homosexuality is either left nameless or defined negatively. The term '*mithliyya*' has been introduced only recently into the Arabic language as a loan translation (calque) of the English word 'homosexual' and is considered to be the most appropriate term by the blogger and many other homosexual online users.[29]

The profile picture, just like the nickname, fulfils the need to remain anonymous while reshaping the image of Egyptian lesbian women. It is the picture of a wall painting in the tomb of Queen Nefertari located in the

Valley of the Queen, in Luxor (Egypt). It portrays the ancient Egyptian goddess Isis (right) leading Queen Nefertari by hand (Figure 5).

Figure 5 Emraamethlya's profile picture. Source: http://emraamethlya.blogspot.no.

The blogger explains her choice of this picture by the fact that they represent two important female figures in Ancient Egyptian times: Nefertari was one of the most beautiful and powerful queens in Ancient Egypt; Isis was worshipped as the ideal mother and wife, patron of nature and magic.[30] The choice of two powerful female figures seems to emphasise her femininity and oppose the masculine attitude that is usually associated with lesbian women. Their act of holding hands in the picture suggests a feeling of tenderness and trust between the two women, which is often described in her blog. In the interview, the blogger states that she refers to pharaonic culture because she believes that homosexuality was practiced in Ancient Egypt without any form of repression.[31] True or not, the choice of referring to the pharaohs is significant because it suggests that the blogger wishes to distance herself from her Arab Muslim identity, to refer instead to an ancient idyllic past, where femininity, beauty and sexuality were celebrated without the taboos imposed by Muslim society. The emphasis on her female identity is also given by the choice of the blog's layout, which is completely pink.

In the first post of her blog, written on 20 January 2006, she introduces her diary to the Egyptian blogosphere with these words:

> I claim I am the first one to speak out but for sure I will not be the last one. Yes, I am a woman and I am lesbian. I advise those who will read my blog, and by that, I mean men, do not expect me to write about my sexual adventures and red nights or green.[32] I know that men have reveries about lesbians; however, it doesn't matter so I will not write about this, and don't expect things like this.
>
> I will write here about myself as a woman who chose to be herself instead of deceiving it. I have never felt any attraction for men, I don't hate

them, we could be siblings, colleagues but I can't love them, the love that is [romantic] love, and not because they have problems or I have a problem or deficiency, but because I am like this and this is natural and every woman is free in her choice.

I expect that some people will get shocked by my blog. Hmmmmm, no, they won't be shocked because my existence or the existence of any other lesbian woman is a reality which all of you know, although you may be afraid or embarrassed of it. Anyway, this is not important, what is important is that no matter how the people and the society deny it, it still exists. I hope for those who will read my words that nobody will try to erect gallows and start trying me, I hope also there are no pedantic people who pretend to be religious and preachers, and I hope there are no curses, or rudeness [in response].

This blog might be just a way to test the water [lit. to measure the pulse], which I may continue or stop, we'll see.

I am a very normal woman, I have experienced a struggle with myself, I tried to suppress it, circumcise it and censure it until I discovered how stupid I was, and how much time I wasted, and how many chances of happiness and love I missed by giving in to the pressure surrounding me and the admiring glances from the men and their attempts to get close. [My] moans in bed and the shivers [of pleasure] were just lies and acting.

My woman understands me just looking into my eyes and pronounces my words before I pronounce them, she listens to me, and she bears me up. I am amazed by how she knows exactly what I want. But enough for today, I will write to you tomorrow. ('Awwal Kalam' ('First Words'), 10 January 2006)

أزعم انني الأولى التي تتحدث و لن اكون الأخيرة أكيد نعم أنا إمراة و مثلية و نصيحة لمن سيقرأون مدونتي و أقصد من الرجال لا تنتظرون أن اكتب عن مغامرات جنسية و لا ليالي حمراء ولا خضراء أعلم أن الرجال يكون لديهم أحلام يقظة عن المثليات ما علينا لا يهم فلن أتطرق لهذا و لا تنتظروا شيئا كهذا.
سوف اكتب هنا عن نفسي كإمراة إختارت أن تكون نفسها و لا تخدعها لم أشعر يوما بأي إنجذاب للرجال و لست أكرههم بل ممكن ان نكون إخوات زملاء لكنني لا أستطيع ان أحبهم الحب اللي هو الحب و ليس لأن لديهم او لدي أي مشكلة او نقص لكن أنا كده و هذا طبيعي و كل إمرأة اختارت هي حرة.

أنتظر أن البعض تصدمه مدونتي هممممم لا مش حتصدمه لان وجودي او وجود اي إمراة مثلية اخرى هو واقع كلكم عرفينه بس يمكن خايفيين منه ولا يمكن مكسوفين منه ؟؟؟ على العموم مش مهم المهم ان مهما أنكره الناس أو المجتمع فهو موجود . يا ريت من سيقرأ كلامي ألا يحاول نصب المشانق و محاكمتي و بلاش كمان الناس اللي عيشه الدور و عمله متدينه وواعظه و كمان بلاش الشتايم و قلة الأدب.

يمكن تكون المدونة دي جس نبض و يمكن أكمل فيها و يمكن أتوقف حنشوف.

أنا إمراة عادية جدا عشت في صراع مع نفسي حاولت ان أكبتها و أختنها و امنعها حتى إكتشفت كم كنت حمقاء و كم اهدرت من الوقت و وأضعت فرص للسعادة و الحب و رضخت لضغوط من حولي و نظرات إعجاب ذكورية و محاولات منهم ليقتربوا و أهات في الفراش ورعشات كانت كذبا و تمثيلا.

إمراتي تفهمني من نظرة عيني و تنطق بكلامي قبل أن أنطقه تسمعني و تتحملني و اتعجب كيف تعرف تماما ما أريده الأن يكفي اليوم سوف اكتب لكم غدا

In this way Emraamethlya announces to the blogosphere that she is going to write about herself as a contemporary Arab lesbian woman. But while in offline society she is forced to pretend that she is heterosexual, on her blog she can dispense with this social mask and reveal her true self, letting out her own feelings, fears and passions. Self-writing gives her the feeling that she exists, against society's denial and rejection, and thus it produces a strong sense of relief and self-awareness. Additionally, by writing in a public space like a blog, she is able to communicate her existence, as well as promoting a new vision of homosexuality. Being marginalised in offline society, her writing is an attempt at testing the blogging community's reaction, and integrating herself as a 'normal individual' into this new social group that she imagines being different from the society outside, as it promotes values of social and political change. Indeed, among the several insults and negative comments that she receives in the comment section of the entry, one of the readers replies:

> Welcome to the blogging world. As one of the [female] bloggers said before. Here you will find all colours of the rainbow, the world here is not very different from the world outside, you will find those who will accept you and those who will reject you and curse you.
>
> But the advantage here is that you can reach people who are able to interact with human beings as humans and nothing else. The difference

here is that reaching them [the good people] happens in a simpler way than in the outer world …

Your appearance is a beautiful thing, because it completes the rainbow colours that [already] exist in the blogs. I think it is important that you help us to form a new and more humane view of the homosexuals, than the mere sexual view which is prevalent in talking about homosexuals.

مرحبا بك في عالم التدوين، وكما قالت احدى المدونات من قبل هنا تجدين كل اشكال الطيف.
العالم هنا ليس مختلفا كثيرا عن العالم الخارجي ستجدين من يقبلوكي ومن يلعنوكي
ولكن الميزة هنا انك تستطيعين الوصول الى اناس قادرين على التعامل مع البشر
بصفتهم البشرية وليس اي شئ اخر
الفرق هنا ان الوصول اليهم يتم بشكل ابسط من العالم الخارجي …
ظهورك امر جميل لانه يكمل الوان الطيف الموجودة على المدونات، واعتقد انه من
المهم ان تساعدينا في تكوين نظرة جديدة اكثر انسانية عن المثليين من مجرد النظرة
الجنسية البحتة الشائعة عند الحديث عن المثليين

Over the years, the blogger alternates the writing of her past tribulations, fears and despair, with stories written mainly in the third-person and occasionally in first-person revolving around lesbian characters and themes. The blog is still active to the present date (May 2018).

Al-Kanaba al-Hamra *(*The Red Sofa*) by Bilal Husni*[33]

Bilal Husni is a filmmaker from Alexandria. Born in 1981, he graduated from the University of Alexandria's Faculty of Economics in 2002, where he majored in International Economy. In 2005, he enrolled in a two-year workshop on film-making that was offered by the company SEMAT at the Jesuit Cultural Centre in Alexandria.[34] Since then he has written and directed several independent movies: *Min ba^c^id* (*From Faraway*, 2004), *Maxim* (2006), and *Bayt* (*House*, 2007), all of which were produced by the Jesuit Cultural Centre in Alexandria, and *Sitta fi Tis^c^a* (*Six Times Nine*, 2009), produced by Bibliotheca Alexandrina, Egypt.

In the interview, Bilal explains that he started blogging in January 2007, at which point blogging had already reached the height of its notoriety in Egypt. In Alexandria, a number of young people were using blogs primarily as a platform for self-expression and to connect with each other.[35] Encouraged by his flatmate Bahz and by one of his friends, who were both active in the blogosphere, Bilal established his blog *The Red Sofa*, and in the profile page of his blog he introduces himself with his real name and these words:

> Last year my mom suddenly departed (lit. achieved death), without any justification; she took everything with her as a souvenir from Earth and only left me her red sofa, so now I wander among rented houses carrying her sofa … or maybe being carried by it …
>
> العام الماضي قامت ماما بالموت فجاة وبدون مبررات واخدت كل حاجه معاها كتذكار ارضي تاركة لى كنبتها الحمرا وها انذا اجوب البيوت المؤجرة حاملا كنبتها … او تحملنى هى …

Thus, Bilal introduces his blog as the story of his journey with the red sofa. Noticeably, while his mother 'achieved death' (*qāmat bil-mawt*), that is, died, Bilal describes himself as 'carried by the sofa'. As he explained in the interview that we had in Alexandria in March 2012, his mother's death had changed his life completely. Left alone, broke and without a place to stay, Bilal felt carried away by a flow of events that were both real and incredible (*ᶜajība*) at the same time, events that were worth recording and sharing with an online audience.[36] After wandering around several places in Alexandria, the sofa eventually takes Bilal to live with his friend Bahz (Bahẓ) in a flat near the sea, which is where we join him in the narrative. He writes about this in his first post entitled 'Bayt Muwarab' ('Half-Open House', 9 January 2007):

> I live with Bahz in a flat near the sea in Alexandria. We are both escaping from two different places and after several struggles with other shared flats, but the idea is that I decided to start blogging to record the life events that I share with Bahz without violating any privacy, as if the house door were ajar, not completely open.
>
> Mr. Bahz and I live in a flat composed of three rooms and a stupid living room, but we only occupy one room where there is the sofa next to the mattress.
>
> Oh, I forgot to mention that I own one red sofa and supposedly, in a fabricated way, I imagine it was inherited from my mom, and on which I sleep, eat and write short movies. The sofa is next to Bahz's mattress on which he sleeps, eats, smokes and hosts his friends from Cairo to sleep

with him temporarily. Since we come from decent families, we decided to dedicate the room with the balcony for the dirty socks; we are too lazy to wash them so we buy new ones.

Bahz works in a field of pure metaphysical, developmental field [sic] and I write movies. Ok? After many years I will be back to read this strategic stupidity so that the freshness of these words will bring me back to these times. Imagine Bahz, this time will turn into nice memories. How, I don't know. We start an important blog of the history of the flats in which Bahz and I have lived before.

باسكن اناو بهظ فى شقه قرب البحر باسكندريه انا وهو هربنين من مكانين مختلفين وبعد صراعات مع شقق مشتركه تانيه بس الفكرة انى قررت اعمل مدونه اسجل فيها تاريخ مشترك بينى وبينه من غير ماانتهك خصوصيه ما نسبيا كما لو ان البيت موارب مش مفتوح
انا والسيد بهظ عايشين ف شقه من 3اوض وصاله هبله فى نفسها لكننا لسه قاعدين فى اوضه واحده الكنبه جنب المرتبه
اه نسيت اقول انى املك عدد واحد كنبه حمرا يفترض بشكل مفتعل انى واهم نفسي انى وارثها من امى والى بنام عليها وباكل وباكتب افلام صغيره بجوارها يوجد مرتبه بهظ والى بينام عليها وبياكل وبيدخن وكمان بيعزم صحابه من القاهرة ينامو معاه عليها مؤقتا حيث اننا ولاد ناس نضيفه قررنا تخصيص الاوضه ال بتطل على البلكونه للشربات المستعمله ده لاننا بنكسل نغسلها فنشترى جديد
بهظ بيعمل فى مجال تنموى ميتافيزكى بحت وانا باكتب افلام
اوك
بعد سنين طويله هبقى ارجع اقرا الهبل الاسترتيجى ده لان طزاجه الكلام هترجعنى تانى للوقت ده
تصور يا بهظ
الوقت ده هيبقى ذكريات حلوة
ازاى مش عارف
نبتدى مدونه مهمه فى تاريخ الشقق ال سكنتها انا و بهظ قبل كده

As we can see from this passage, Bilal's intention is to use the blog to recollect the events that took place after his mother's death, and to provide a regular account of the present, the time he spends living with his friend Bahz. Writing down his feelings offers him relief from his mother's death. Additionally, since he feels unable to control events surrounding him, writing helps him to fix them on the screen, in order to try to make sense out of them.[37] In addition, by writing them down, Bilal is able to record the present and the past in order to turn them into 'nice memories' for the future. As he writes later:

> The idea of 'The Red Sofa' itself lies in the fact that one day, when I will be completely old, I will enjoy reading [it], you can call it 'paranoia or a complete diabolic stupidity'. ('Burwaz fīhi lamba' ('A Light Bulb Inside a Frame'), 28 August 2007)
>
> فكرة الكنبه الحمرا نفسها قايمه على تسليتى لما اكبروابقى عجوز تماما
> انى اقعد اتسلى فى قرايتى
> سميها برانويا او هبل شيطانى محكم

However, the blog is not only meant as a personal record, but also as respite from loneliness. The metaphor of the half-open house suggests that Bilal is willing to let outsiders sneak into the flat, listen to and participate in his stories. Additionally, his flatmate Bahz replies and adds his own version of the facts. Through blogging, Bilal intends to meet and connect with other people, people who may possibly share his own interests and lifestyle, to receive feedback on his writing and his life. As he writes:

> Once I found a place like the blog I thought
> I could publish my poems, my self-writing, and cinema [projects],
> to convince people who might be interested, or preoccupied with the same thoughts,
> that through the blog we can connect with each other and I can find
> other very normal people willing to discuss [things], and we interconnect with each other through a different medium.
> It is awful to talk to yourself while nobody is expecting anything from you.
> And as I said I start a blog honey-colored and one with pretty stripes or red just like …
> Anything red
> You can understand it as the [red] sofa.[38] ('al-Kalb al-Ajrab al-Hazin' ('The Sad Mangy Dog'), 1 July 2007)
>
> انا افتكرت انى اول ماهلاقى مكان زى المدونه
> انى انشر فيها شعرى او كتابات ذاتيه او سينما

هقدر اقنع المهتمين او المشتغلين على نفس الموضوع
اننا نتواصل من خلال المدونات والاثى[39] ناس تانيه
عاديين جد ا بس بيجادلوا وبنحتك ف بعض كده عبر وسيط تانى
حاجه تقرف انت بتكلم نفسك ومحدش مستنى منك حاجه
. ...وزى ماقلتلك اقوم اعمل مدونه عسلى وواحد مخططه حلوة او حمرا زى
زى اى حاجه حمرا
ممكن تفهمها على انها الكنبه

Like the other bloggers, Bilal laments a feeling of loss and solitude. By choosing *The Red Sofa* as the title of his blog, Bilal turns the sofa from being a simple object on which he spends his days sitting, to a space where he can construct his online counterpart and build a new community of friends. By fictionally linking the sofa to his mother's death, fabricating a story that he inherited it from her, Bilal renders it as the element that connects his separation from his mother to the beginning of his new life.

The outline of *The Red Sofa* reveals Bilal's passion for visual arts. Both in the header of the blog and in the right-hand margin, Bilal uploads pictures of Jennifer Garant's paintings showing whimsical chefs riding bikes and mopeds and carrying food and wine (Figure 6). The profile picture also depicts a chubby chef clumsily serving two bottles of wine (Figure 7). By choosing this picture, the blogger is highlighting the corpulence of his body which, as we shall see later, is also depicted in his writing. Additionally, he informs his audience of the possibility that his blog may contain some elements considered '*ḥarām*' (forbidden by Islamic law) by more conservative readers. To more liberal readers, however, the illustrations can be seen as an invitation to pour a drink, sit on his red sofa and enjoy his stories.

Figure 6 Header of the blog *Al-Kanaba al-Hamra* by Bilal Husni, retrieved from http://knbahmra.blogspot.no/, accessed 8 October 2013.

Figure 7 Bilal Husni's profile picture, painting by Jennifer Garant. Retrieved from http://knbahmra.blogspot.no/, accessed 8 October 2013.

Bilal stopped blogging in 2009, as he felt that his relationship with the sofa had come to an end. In the interview, he states that he left it on the Cairo-Alex road, 'in the middle of nowhere', letting it continue its travels alone, starting a new set of stories. After closing his blog, Bilal established a Facebook page called *al-Futih al-Ahmar* (*The Red Armchair*), on which he published his poems. However, he found that Facebook does not allow him to recreate the same interaction with his readers and closed it after several months.

Yawmiyyat ᶜAnis (The Diary of a Spinster) *by Abeer Soliman*

Abeer Soliman was born in 1979 in Qina, Upper Egypt. She wrote as a columnist for the independent Egyptian newspaper *al-Dustur* until 2009. She also worked as a spokeperson for the Arabic Network of Human Rights, and here she became acquainted with many online political activists, who introduced her to blogging.

Abeer explained to me that she started blogging in 2008 mainly as an act of personal catharsis, to express her anger about being an over-thirty-year-old single woman in Egypt. She wanted to vent her feelings about the social discrimination directed toward unmarried women in Egyptian society. Despite many Egyptian women delaying marriage until their mid-to-late twenties, society still looks at them in a critical, disapproving light.[40] She had already introduced this subject in her columns published by the newspaper *al-Dustur* and she had received private emails from a number of readers who praised her writing. Later she opted to start a blog because it gave her the opportunity to share her writing with a wider audience and to get direct feedback on her writing. This is how she introduces the topic to her readers:

> I will talk to you about our generation … about our reality … we have seen the generation before us and we have witnessed divorces reaching up to one every six minutes. A strong feeling remained with us that marriage is not the happy ending that we have seen in Arab films … So, we decided to search for happiness inside ourselves … because it is not logical to search for happiness in others before it is realized in ourselves. (1 June 2008)

> سأحدثكم عن جيلنا ..عن واقعنا.. فقد شاهدنا الجيل السابق لنا وعاصرنا حالات
> طلاق وصلت الى حالة طلاق كل ستة دقائق فترسب داخلنا إحساس قوى بأن الزواج

ليس هو النهايات السعيدة التى شاهدناها فى الأفلام العربية .. فقررنا البحث فى
داخلنا عن السعادة.. فليس من المنطقى أن نبحث عن السعادة فى الآخرين قبل أن
تتحقق بداخلنا

As shown by the passage above, Abeer intends to write about her life story to demonstrate that contemporary young Egyptian women and men are disillusioned by the traditional rules and customs imposed by society. Many women still accept marriage to get rid of the stigma of the title of spinster, only to find themselves later carrying the title 'divorcee'. But others, like her, have come to the conclusion that, rather than relying on 'the others' – that is the family, marriage and religious traditions – they need to focus on their own self in order to succeed. Blogging is a means of representing these other lives, in order to legitimise their existence and to change the way society perceives them.

> I decided to take a brave step forward … I will write my diaries as a spinster from the point of view of society … and as a free woman from the point of view of my generation … my goal is not to bemoan my luck as a woman who did not marry, but rather to open a window to my generation (women and men) overlooking the society around us so that those surrounding us can see our situation and can relieve us from the worn-out titles which do not suit any more the time we live in.

> ... فقررت اتخاذ خطوة جريئة الى الأمام ... . سأكتب يومياتى - كعانس من وجهة
> نظر المجتمع ... . وكامرأة حرة من وجهة نظر أبناء جيلى ... ليس الهدف منها هو
> ندب حظى كامرأة لم تتزوج و لكن الهدف هو فتح نافذة لجيلى (نساء و رجال)
> على المجتمع من حولنا كى يرى المحيطين بنا حالنا و يرفعوا عنا الألقاب البالية التى
> أصبحت لا تناسب العصر الذى نحيى به.

The home page of her blog contains the painting *Woman at the Window* (1926), by Salvador Dalí, in which we see a dark-haired woman standing and leaning against a windowsill as she looks out onto a bay (Figure 8). The blue of the sky and sea of *Woman at the Window* sets a reflective and peaceful mood. However, the focus of the painting is not on what is through the window, but on the woman herself. This might indicate that rather than talking about the outside world, Abeer desires to talk about her life and show her personal view of the surrounding reality. At the same time, the fact that the woman is viewed from the back foreshadows a 'now you see me, now you don't' narrative strategy, with which she reveals some aspects of her life, while letting the reader wonder whether the narration is true or fictional.

Figure 8 Cover image of the blog *Yawmiyyat ᶜAnis.* Source: http://yawmiyat3aness.blogspot.no.

It is important to notice also that, unlike Brāyd (Arabic transliteration of the English word 'bride'), who became known as Ghada Abdel Aal only after the publication of her blog, Abeer signs the blog entries using her real name and has uploaded a personal picture in the 'About me' page. Her blog was brought out as a book of the same title and published by Al-Dar in 2010. In the book, Dali's painting is replaced by a glamorous cover in pink, silver and black (see Figure 9).

Figure 9 Cover of the book *Yawmiyyat ᶜAnis* by Abeer Soliman, 2010. Source: http://yawmiyat3aness.blogspot.no.

In 2012 Abeer stopped blogging and decided to focus exclusively on fictional writing and other cultural projects she had started. She told me: 'I felt the personal nature of the blog constitutes a limit on my creativity, as anything I write is attributed to my own life. I turned to the novel, where I can disguise autobiographical elements under the clear fictional nature of the genre.'[41]

The Egyptian Bloggers

As it is evident from the case studies, the majority of the Egyptian bloggers are 'young'. Their ages range between the early twenties and the early thirties. The case studies and interviews also show that blogging is primarily an urban phenomenon. Some of the bloggers do originate from other provinces – Ahmed Naji is from al-Mansura, Abeer Soliman from Qina (Upper Egypt) – however, the majority of them moved to Cairo or Alexandria to complete their education or to find a job. Indeed, from the interviews it emerges that the blogosphere evolved into two social groups that mainly evolved around these two cities.

From the family sketches provided in the blogs analysed and from the interviews, it also emerges that most of the bloggers come from a middle-class family background (in the interviews some of them use the English expression 'middle class').[42] Indeed, their parents' occupations include schoolteachers, doctors, public-sector employees and engineers. As Walter Armbrust argues, in Cairo being middle class was figured primarily in terms of education. To be middle class meant having an education, being acquainted with modern institutions, and enjoying a 'clean' life, removed from Cairo's lower classes. It did not necessarily imply a certain minimum life standard, as incomes ranged from a few hundred to tens of thousands of pounds per month (Armbrust 2003: 107). Some of the bloggers told me that their families were part of the large number of Egyptian people who migrated to the rich oil-producing Gulf countries to improve their social status. This was a very common phenomenon in Egypt in the 1980s, as reported by Galal Amin (2011: 95). Indeed, some of them, for example 'JarelKamar' and Nael Eltoukhy, spent their childhood in the Gulf. According to some of them, this is the reason why their writing in Arabic is sound (*salīm*), as they received a high standard of education in Arabic.[43] Others maintain that spending their childhood in the Gulf has left them with a strong feeling of social exclusion. When they returned to Egypt, they found it difficult to establish social interaction with their peers in Egypt. The Internet helped them to establish social relationships from behind the screens of their computers by accessing forums and chat rooms.[44]

As for their education, all the bloggers interviewed have university degrees in a range of disciplines. Only a small number of bloggers have obtained degrees in the field of Humanities (eleven), with more coming from a scientific or technical background (eighteen). Before blogging, they worked in or were engaged in study towards a wide range of professions: nine of them were studying or working in healthcare (medicine, pharmacy, psychology, biology), four of them in information technology, two in engineering, five as journalists, four in cinema or film-making, four as writers and one as a translator. Some of the bloggers have used the skills and contacts gained and developed through their online activity to change their career entirely.

Their level of education can also be seen through their linguistic skills. Most of the bloggers mixed both English and Arabic in the interviews. According to de Koning, this English-Arabic vernacular is popular among younger generations, who were educated in language schools, and use a mix of Arabic and English both at leisure and at work. Speaking a mixture of colloquial Arabic and English has become part of a distinctive upper-middle-class normalcy as well as an expression of distance from less privileged Cairene realities (de Koning 2009: 64).

Like Amr Ezzat, some of the bloggers found it important to disclose their affiliations to particular religious or political movements in their interviews and blogs. For Amr and his brother Mahmud ᶜIzzat (Maḥmūd ᶜIzzat), joining a fundamentalist religious group like the Salafists, and then the Muslim Brotherhood, was quite natural, since they were influenced by the religious conservative culture spread in the populous area of Imbaba, a district regarded as the nest of terrorist groups.[45] For others, this was due to the fact that their families had strong ideological ties with the Muslim Brotherhood. The scholars Moaddel and Karabenick link the tendency of Egyptian young people to embrace religious fundamentalism to fatalistic attitudes and feelings of insecurity, deriving from political authoritarianism and economic difficulties (2008: 1681). These feelings led them to take refuge in traditional social institutions that encourage a strong attachment to social norms. Other bloggers, like Nirmin Nizar (Nirmīn Nizār), participated in the political activities that spread after 2004, mainly coinciding with the rise of the anti-globalisation movement, the American invasion of Iraq and the birth of the *Kifaya* movement. The others admit that they became interested in politics only after having joined the blogging community, and many of them only found themselves participating in demonstrations after 25 January 2011.

Bloggers have entered the blogosphere in different ways: some of them were already familiar with other Internet media; others became acquainted with blogs from political activism, after joining movements such as *Kifaya* which, as I have already explained, used blogs to organise and promote political demonstrations. Some of them were encouraged by friends who were already blogging. Others became acquainted with blogs through the newspaper *al-Dustur* that, in 2005, began to publish blog entries in its print edition.

Finally, another element from the interviews that I consider worth mentioning is the locations where I met the bloggers for the interviews. In most cases it was the bloggers themselves who chose the place where they felt most comfortable to talk, away from the crowds. With them, I moved around the traditional street cafés (*ahāwī baladī*) located in the area of Downtown Cairo or on the Corniche in Alexandria and new coffee shops like Beanos, Café Costa and Cilantro located Downtown or in the more elitist areas like Mohandiseen, Zamalek or Dokki. According to Peterson, these places are an indication of the bloggers' social status and their cultural background. While Downtown sidewalk coffeehouses tend to be frequented by young artists and intellectuals, these new coffee shops are frequented mainly by upper-middle-class people, as they serve Western types of food and drink and allow for public gathering of both women and men (Peterson 2011: 138). This indicates that the Egyptian blogosphere may be comprised of both a young intellectual scene and a more professional upper-middle-class group.

Thus, if we were to sketch a profile of 'the Egyptian blogger' we might say: he or she is young, belongs to a middle- or upper-middle-class milieu; he or she is a graduate, and possibly employed, in either a humanistic, scientific or technical field, and speaks a foreign language. Their upper/middle-class status is also indicative of their digital skills and of the language style they use in blogs. This information supports Doubrovsky's claim that while autobiography is reserved for the important people of the world, autofiction may be written by anyone. Blogging, like autofiction, allows for a 'democratization' of self-writing and thus the appropriation of a more prestigious genre by 'ordinary people'. It democratises speech and writing, usually reserved for intellectuals, and allows everyone, especially young people, to express their aspirations and views on society.

It Ain't Me: Onymity and Pseudonymity

One of the main features of the autofictional genre is the identity of the author, narrator and main character (Gasparini 2008: 300). The case studies above have shown different choices regarding the indication of the author's name. Out of six blogs, three are signed with real names, and this is what Genette defines as 'onymity'. The other three are signed with a name that is not the legal name of the author, which Genette defines 'pseudonymity'. Among these three pseudonymous blogs, in two of them the bloggers later reveal their legal names. After a certain time, it appears that these bloggers felt that they should 'come out' with their 'real' identity. This pattern of onymity/pseudonymity correlates with that found in a larger sample of blogs encountered by myself. Indeed, on one side, we have a greater number of bloggers who sign their blogs with their real names (29 out of 40, i.e. more than 70 per cent, some of whom also upload a personal picture) than those who write pseudonymously (11 out of 40, less than 30 per cent).

The choice of onymity is motivated by several reasons. For Amr Ezzat, as for other bloggers interviewed, it is a response to the political situation: revealing their full identity online is a reaction to society's attempts to silence his generation's voice. By indicating their names, some bloggers aim to push the boundaries of what can be said in public. This political stance is also confirmed by the fact that Mona Seif (Maat) reveals her name after the 25 January uprising to attribute a stronger political meaning to her writing. Others use their names to attribute more authenticity or sincerity to their life-writing. Additionally, some bloggers who already work as professional writers (journalists, for example) or aspire to do so use their name to claim authorship of their writing and, eventually, to enlarge their readership.[46]

Some bloggers became known by their real name once their blog was published in book form. Others, like Ahmed Naji or the film director Ahmad Abdalla (Aḥmad ᶜAbd Allah), who were relatively anonymous in the beginning, decided to reveal their name later because they realised that there was no need for retaining their anonymity, since their identity had been disclosed both online and offline. This disclosure also came after they acquired notoriety in the cultural field, respectively as a writer and as a film director.[47]

We can also see that several bloggers sign their blog entries with a pseudonym. This was very common, especially in 2005, when the blogging community was still emerging. For many of the bloggers I interviewed, using a nickname was a means of playing with the medium, of trying out a new personality while accessing a different social setting. For others, like Emraamethlya, it was a means of protecting their anonymity while dealing with highly sensitive topics. The identity of author-narrator and main character fulfils a contractual importance; as stated by Lejeune, in a form of autobiographical writing, by stating his name the author establishes a factual contract with the reader. In a work of autofiction the identity of the author-narrator and the character combined with the label 'novel' establishes the 'oxymoronic pact' (as defined by Laouyen 1999) that forms the very essence of autofiction. But Lecarme (1993: 227) also suggests that there might be versions of autofictions in which the proper name is masked by the use of a pseudonym. Viviane Serfaty (2004) points out that the use of pseudonyms does not really go against the trend towards greater self-revelation. Pseudonyms are often chosen to actualise some of the psychological traits the writer cannot express anywhere else and may thus acquire considerable expressiveness. Adopting a pseudonym may therefore signal that one is entering a distinct universe in which different rules apply and where one's personality may develop to the full (Serfaty 2004: 93). For example, given the association of the word *ḥaddūta* with folklore, Bassam's nickname 'Ḥaddūta' can also be said to emphasise the feminine, as well as the unpretentious, perhaps even naive and childish, trait of the blogger's online personality, mirrored in the pink layout of her blog. It is interesting to notice that often readers also carry pseudonyms. Thus, bloggers create themselves as central characters in a fictional theatre, populated by a large supporting cast of minor characters and readers (Sorapure 2003: 13).

What's in a Title?

In the Egyptian blogs analysed, most of the titles point out that the blog is meant as a form of self-writing. This is indicated by including the name or the pseudonym of the blogger in the title, like *Tanatīf Maᶜat* (others include Bint al-Qamar, JarelKamar, Africano and Bint Misriyyah). The bloggers who have already gained exposure as writers, due to the publication of one or more books, tend to name their blogs after their legal name. This is the case for the blogs *Na᾽il al-Tukhi, Ibrahim Farghali, Tariq Imam, Muhammad Salah al-ᶜAzab, Ahmad al-ᶜAyidi* and *Nuha Mahmud.* The autobiographical subject of the blog may also be indicated by including a first-person pronoun in the title itself. This is true, for example, in the blog *Ma Bada Li* (*What Seemed to Me*) by Amr Ezzat, *Hakadha Ana* (*I am Like This*) by Radwa Usama (Raḍwā Usāma), *Maᶜa Nafsi* (*With Myself/On My Own*) by Ghada Mahmud, *ᶜAyzah Atgawwiz* (*I Want to Get Married*)[48] by Ghada Abdel-Aal and *Wa-ana Ma-li* (*What Have I Got to Do with This?*) by al-Baraa Ashraf (al-Barā᾽ Ashraf). In particular, in this last title, we can see that the focus on the self is also achieved by indicating the blogger's disdain towards bigger issues. Indeed in the subtitle of his blog he adds, 'If I got distracted from my homeland by the thought of eternal life, my homeland would be stolen', and 'It's [part] of the good Islam of a person that he/she leaves behind that which does not directly concern him'[49]: quoting a *ḥadīth*, he expresses the paradox that even religious sources claim that citizens should not direct their interest towards big issues.[50] Similarly we have *EgypToz*, written by 'WS', a portmanteau composed of 'Egypt' (the English name reflects the fact that several posts are written in English) and '*Toz*', a slang expression that can be translated as 'so what?!', 'who gives a damn?', indicating the blogger's derision of national issues. The same disengagement and scepticism towards big issues is indicated by Salma Anwar's (Salmā Anwar) blog title *Allah, al-Watan, Amma Nshuf* (*God, the Nation, Well, Let's See*).[51]

Titles also reflect the form and genre of the written entries. Titles like *Yawmiyyat Khayal al-Zill* (*Diary of a Shadow Play*), *Yawmiyyat ᶜAnis* (*Diary of a Spinster*) by Abeer Soliman and *Yawmiyyat Imra᾽a Mithliyya* (*Diary of a Gay Woman*) announce that the blog is meant as a diary (*yawmiyyāt*), an autobiographical form of writing. The latter two examples also clarify that the bloggers focus their writing on a precise and maybe peculiar aspect of their identity. A more metaphorical indication of the genre is in the title *al-Koftah Tuday*[52] (*Meatballs Today*) managed by the *koftajī* (the one who prepares *kofta*), as the author, Muhammad Husayn (Muḥammad Ḥusayn), defines himself in the 'About me' section of his blog. The blog, according to Muhammad, is like *kofta*, because, like meatballs, it can be made of everything, it can vary in quality, recipes, price and taste. Accordingly, the blogger, just like the *koftajī*, is ready to experiment with a number of ingredients and serve the dish to his clients. In the title, the word *kofta* is combined with the English word 'today' (transliterated in Arabic characters), which elevates the tone of the title and makes it more original.[53] In this sense the title has also a connotative function, as it recalls titles of Egyptian newspapers like *Al-Masri al-Yawm* or the satirical news website *Koshary Today*.[54] Some titles also announce a scattering or fragmentation of the narrative form. Mona Seif defines the form of her diary as '*tanātīf*' or 'bits and pieces'. Likewise, we find titles like *Mulahazat Basita* (*Simple Notes*) by 'M. El-Hajj', or *Shakhabit* (*Scribbles*) by Mahmud Hasan (Maḥmūd Ḥasan). These titles also reflect a certain modesty expressed by the writers towards the narrative of their blogs. Similarly, for Muhammad Mursi (Muḥammad Mursī) his blog is just a *Taq Hanak*, 'blah blah blah', an Arabic Levantine colloquial expression with '*ḥanak*' meaning 'jaw' and '*taq*' indicating the sound the jaw makes moving up and down.

Some titles also suggest that the blog might contain fictional elements. This has already been pointed out in the analysis of blog titles like Ahmed Naji's *Yawmiyyat Khayal al-Zill* (*Diary of a Shadow Play*), which later became *Wassi*^{c} *Khayalak* (*Widen Your Imagination*). Probably inspired by him, Ahmad al-Fakharani (Aḥmad al-Fakharānī) calls his blog *Tiyatru Sahib al-Sa*^{c}*ada* (*His Excellency's Theatre*). Just like Naji, al-Fakharani conceives the blog as a theatre, a stage where he can try out several personalities and modes of self-writing by experimenting with different literary styles. The fictional nature of blog-writing is also reflected by the title of the blog written (in English) by Muhammad Aladdin: *Writing is a Green Dragon with Purple Mustache*. In the interview, the author explains: 'I chose this title to mean that blog writing is anything, is whatever you want to do with your imagination and creative spirit.'[55] Ramiz Sharqawi (Rāmiz Sharqāwī) names his blog *Ghawaya, Mujarrad Ghawaya* (*Seduction, Just Seduction*), suggesting that his writing drags you away from the physical world and daily life. A further example is given by Rihab Bassam's blog title, *Hawadit* (*Children's Stories*).[56]

Many bloggers also elaborate the title to create a metaphor of the blog as a gathering place where the blogger can relax and host his readers. For example, the title *al-Kanaba al-Hamra* (*The Red Sofa*) indicates not only the 'main character' of the narrative, but also stands as a spatial metaphor of the blog.

The blog is conceived as a space where the readers are welcomed to sit down, listen and participate in the stories. The blogger Jimmi Halim (Jīmmī Ḥalīm) entitles his blog *ᶜArabiyyat Ful*, after the mobile cart used by street vendors to sell fava beans (*fūl*).[57] For Jimmi, the fava beans cart is a metaphor for his blog: it is authentically Egyptian, flavourful, and is a place where people gather, start discussions and exchange small talk with people they may not know. The same concept is expressed in the title *al-Banika*, by 'sham3on'.[58] '*Banīka*', a term used only in Alexandrian dialect, indicates a temporary place arranged illegally by Alexandrian street vendors for any kind of activity, as for example a temporary café. Like the *fūl* cart, the *banīka* stands for the blog as it is a quick, temporary, transitory place for gathering and relaxing.[59] The blogger 'Zubayda' introduces her blog as *al-Haramlik*, a word that indicates the quarters of upper-class houses reserved for women. Indeed, the blog is conceived as an intimate, secure place, a closed compartment reserved for an insider group. The film-director Ahmad Abdalla named his blog *O7od* (i.e. *Uḥud*, according to standard transliteration). *Uḥud* in Arabic is the name of the mountain that gave the 'Battle of Uhud' its name, and where the Prophet Muhammad and his companions suffered a humiliating defeat by the infidels of the Qurayshi tribe. The name of the blog is thus meant to mock the religious establishment and provoke religious conservative groups: it suggests that it is a space where Islam might be defeated. Another interesting spatial metaphor may be found in the title *Akhir al-Hara*.[60] For the blogger ᶜAbd al-Rahman Mustafa (ᶜAbd al-Raḥmān Muṣṭafā) the *ḥāra* represents the Egyptian blogosphere, a virtual space where he can take refuge from ordinary life and meet and interact with different types of people. However, in the interview the blogger explains that when he entered the blogosphere in 2007, he felt that the blogging community had already become a closed society; bloggers were expected to be engaged in politics, to be leftist in their ideology, and they all tended to use vulgar language and an aggressive tone. Thus, the title suggests that the blogger wishes to take refuge in the very end of the alley. This is supported by his statement on the main page of the blog under the main title:

> Far from the crowdedness of spacious streets and the stray cars, I chose the alley as an escape from a desolate society, but then I soon had to escape

again … I escaped to the best place in the alley … faaaar from eeeeevery-body … to the end of the alley.[61]

بعيدا عن زحام الشوارع الفسيحة والعربات الطائشة، اخترت الحارة كي أهرب إليها
من مجتمع موحش، لكن سرعان ما اضطررت إلى تكرار هروبي مرة أخرى.. هربت
إلى أفضل مكان في الحارة.. بعيييدا عن الجميييع . إلى آخر الحارة

To sum up, the titles chosen by bloggers reflect a number of interesting issues that are significant with regard to the question of genre (fact, fiction, autofiction, oxymoronic writing, and so on) raised at the beginning of the chapter, but also, and related to that question, to their content. The blog is conceived as a form of self-writing. This is expressed in some blogs by naming the blog after the author, whether legal or pseudonymous, or including a first-person pronoun in the title. The focus on individualisation can also be highlighted by expressions that indicate the blogger's lack of interest in, or disdain for, higher causes. As for a genre specification, the titles also anticipate that the blog is meant as a diary or as a literary attempt. Some titles suggest that the blog will include fictional content. In their titles, many bloggers use metaphors to indicate that the blog is a secure, intimate place where the blogger and readers can feel at home and be themselves. Indeed, even if the subject of the diary is the blogger's identity, the medium can still be used as a meeting place. Titles also reflect the blogger's inspiration from a number of fields: street life, popular culture, Arabic and Islamic history, but also songs, journals or romantic expressions. From a linguistic standpoint, they also show that bloggers mix Egyptian dialect (*ᶜāmmiyya*), formal Arabic (*fuṣḥā*) and English to form catchy, attractive titles. While some of them write the title in Arabic letters, others transliterate the title with Latin letters and numbers.

The Pursuit of an Original Form

The interviews with the authors and the statements exposed in the opening paragraphs of the blogs have illustrated the bloggers' reasons for blogging. Their motivations are by no means mutually exclusive and may come into play simultaneously.

As in the case of Abeer Soliman and Mona Seif, many of the young bloggers, especially women, were driven by the need to speak out in order to achieve a personal relief. Abeer used the blog to vent out against discrimination towards unmarried women in Egypt. Mona Seif felt the need to make public her anger and fear towards the regime and the society. Similarly, many young people used the blogosphere as a free, uncensored space where they could vent their frustration, anger, love and other emotions deriving from daily life. At the same time, by publishing them on the blog, they were able to find support from other bloggers who share the same feelings. In their words, this is due to the fact that they live in a society where they are not allowed to express their voice freely, both in traditional media (for religious and political reasons) and in public (because of social pressures).

The words expressed by Mona Seif, Amr Ezzat and Bilal Husni also highlight another reason for blogging, which is the need to record personal experiences. Indeed, many young people started blogging at a crucial phase of their life, often coinciding with the passage from adolescence into adulthood. In this sense, blogging gave them the ability to assess important events of their life, in order to try to make sense of it. It also allowed them to record important events of their life and to go back to read them again after some time, in order to monitor the development of their personality.

Blogging is also driven by the need for self-assertion and self-affirmation in a new, unexplored society. Emraamethlya uses the blog to assert herself and communicate her existence as a lesbian woman. Abeer Soliman writes about herself to affirm that she is a 'spinster' because marriage is not a priority in her life. As expressed by their words, mainstream society tends to reject or deny the existence of people who are different by nature or who do not conform to existing social norms. By contrast, the online community is imagined by many bloggers to be more inclusive, as it is mainly composed of a diverse range of young people who share the frustration against society and the regime. In this sense, blogs are used as a way to effect changes in society. By using their lives as examples and participating in discussion with the readers, bloggers hope to change the way society perceives them.

Others, like Ahmed Naji, as well as Ahmad Gharbiyya or Mahmud ʿIzzat, who were already familiar with other Internet tools such as forums, started their blogs simply for 'entertainment', to try out a new Internet medium. Blogs were just another spot where they could 'have fun' on the Internet. Additionally, since they had been following blogs in foreign languages, they were willing to contribute to the rise of an Arabic/Egyptian blogosphere, to produce and read content in Arabic.[62]

A common reason given for blogging is also the love of writing and the desire to be read. Many of the bloggers make it clear that they did not start blogging to get published or to become a writer, even if blogging eventually proved an inroad into print literature. What drove them to blog was mainly the will to cultivate their passion for writing and receive feedback. Indeed, some of them had written before but had kept their notes, memories or short stories hidden from anyone else. The blog medium perfectly suited their love for writing and encouraged them to publish their writing for a number of reasons. Firstly, online publication was easy and cost-free. Secondly, it gave them the opportunity to publish anonymously or pseudonymously, and to address an unknown audience (namely, one that did not include their family or close friends). Thirdly, it allowed them to receive immediate feedback from their online audience. Finally, it was easy to revise. For Mona Seif, Amr Ezzat, Mohammad Rabie and 'Sham3on', who work in scientific or technical fields, blogging was a way to cultivate their passion for writing in their free time. For young people who have been educated in foreign languages, like Mona, it was also a means of improving their written Arabic. Others, who already wrote professionally, like Ahmed Naji and Abeer Soliman, approached the blog in order to develop a new writing style. They were attracted by the idea that, unlike Internet forums or other traditional print literary genres, blog-writing was free, independent, uncategorised and not regulated by a topic or a moderator. Additionally, it gave them the possibility to insert their own points of view or personal life details, and it combined writing with other media, such as music, videos and pictures.

The blog is also used as a publishing platform, to reach a wider audience or to validate stories that could not be published in traditional media. Abeer Soliman stated that she started blogging in order to reach a wider audience, as blog readers were more numerous than newspaper readers. Others used it to publish stories that could have been censored in print (for example, 'Emraamethlya'). Others, like Mahmud ᶜIzzat, were willing to publish stories and poetry written in dialect, which is hard to publish in print form.

From the reasons highlighted here, it appears that bloggers resorted to blogging in pursuit of an unexplored territory (the blogosphere) and an 'original form' of writing that could allow them both to speak freely about themselves and at the same time to exercise their imagination and try their hand at writing.

These reasons illuminate two main aspects of blog literature. The first is that even though these blogs may be classified as 'personal' (Walker 2005), they are political, in the sense that the political situation does not act as a background, but every individual matter is immediately plugged into the political (Deleuze and Guattari 1983: 16). Indeed, the bloggers mentioned above write about their life to tackle issues of the political and social exclusion of youth, fear and anger towards an authoritarian regime, sexual harassment and discrimination, questions of marriage, and unemployment, to name a few. The second aspect is that even though the blog is understood as a 'personal' space, the bloggers use it as a way to get in contact with people with whom they do not make contact in daily life, but may possibly share their own interests and lifestyle. Mainly frustrated, alienated and marginalised in offline society, bloggers entered the blogosphere to find a new place to assert their identity and socialise with different people. Deleuze and Guattari consider these two features, that is the political and collective, as two main attributes of 'minor literature'. The third main element of 'minor literature', that is its 'deterritorialized style', will be the object of analysis in the following chapter.

Notes

1 By analysing an impressive list of book titles published in the Modern period, in this book Genette provides academics with terms, definitions and categories with which they might discuss titles. Viviane Serfaty has also hinted at the importance of blog titles in her book *The Mirror and the Veil* (Serfaty 2004: 23).
2 According to Genette, titles aim to achieve several functions: (1) to identify the work; (2) to describe the subject matter (descriptive thematic function); (3) to describe the formal feature, the genre (descriptive rhematic function); (4) to link the text to another text (connotative function); and (5) to incite the reader to purchase or read the book (temptation function).
3 Blogger's translation of the blog title as indicated on her website.
4 Blogger's own transliteration used on social media.
5 Blogger's own transliteration of ʾImraʾa Mithliyya.
6 Interview, March 2011.

7 On Egyptian shadow theatre, see Francesca Corrao (1996), *Il riso, il comico e la festa al Cairo nel XIII secolo: il teatro delle ombre di Ibn Dāniyāl.*

8 Transcription of the Arabic word *iblīs* as used by the blogger himself. The Arabic *iblīs* is a loanword from Greek *diábolos*, i.e. the one who turns things upside down, spreads chaos. Iblis is also one of the main characters of the most famous shadow play written by Ibn Daniyal (d. 1311), deemed the father of Egyptian shadow theatre, *Ṭayf al-khayāl* (*Shadow of Imagination*). See Cyrus Ali Zargar (2006), 'The Satiric Method of Ibn Daniyal: Morality and Anti-Morality in *Ṭayf al-Khayāl*'. Iblis is also important in the Sufi tradition, see Peter J. Awn, *Satan's Tragedy and Redemption: Iblis in Sufi Psychology* (Awn 1983).

9 See *The Holy Quran*, The Battlements, 7, 11–12.

10 The title is an expression suggested to him by the blogger Muhammad Khalil Khalfat (Muḥammad Khalīl Kalfat). This shows how the members of the blogging community exchange and transform their mutual writing.

11 Personal Interview, March 2011.

12

> ”أعرف أن لا شيء ملكي و لكن الفكرة تتدفق سيالة من روحي و كل لحظة طيبة يجود بها قدري السمح ..تملأ أعماقي فرحا“!
>
> The German original is: 'Ich weiß, dass mir nichts angehört / als der Gedanke, der ungestört / aus meiner Seele will fließen / und jeder günstige Augenblick, / den mich ein liebendes Geschick / von Grund aus lässt genießen.'

13 Ahmad Sayf al-Islam (1951–2014) was arrested in 1983 and held in prison for five years for his communist beliefs. After his release, he dedicated himself to fighting torture and injustice, speaking publicly about the torture he received in prison. Ten years later, he founded the Hisham Mubarak Law Centre, one of Egypt's top human rights centres. He died in Cairo in August 2014.

14 Since 2005, Alaa has campaigned against the growing abuses by the Mubarak regime. He was arrested at a demonstration in 2006 and imprisoned for forty-five days; upon his release, he and his wife moved to South Africa, where they continued their campaigns and criticism. Shortly before the outbreak of the revolution, he went back to Egypt and was arrested again, accused of inciting violence in the Maspero events, and has been in prison ever since.

15 Interview, Cairo, April 2011.

16 Here the word 'angel' is hyperlinked to the blog written by the Egyptian blogger Malek Mustafa writing under the nickname 'Malek-X' that actually translates as 'angel'.

17 Author's own rendering of *anā gēt* (Egyptian dialect, 'I arrived').

18 Title translated by the blogger.

19 See Robert S. Ellwood (ed.) (2007), *Encyclopedia of World Religions*, New York: Facts on File, 132. Mona Seif explained in the interview that she learnt about this concept from her aunt, the Anglo-Egyptian writer Ahdaf Soueif. In her words: 'She was speaking about this concept that she would develop in her next novel. She told me that if there was Maat, we would not live this present situation. Then I started to see this symbol everywhere and I decided to use it for my online character.' For Ahdaf Soueif's conceptualisation of Maat, see her interview with Nehal al-Sherif (2008), 'On the Thresholds of Maat'.

20 I am giving credit to the blogger and thus stating the assumption that she is a woman. However, her online identity could also be completely fictional. See, for example, the case of the blog *Gay Girl in Damascus*, whose author was found out to be a middle-aged American man living in Edinburgh, mentioned in the Introduction.

21 Interview, June 2010. The blogger decided to use these precautions following the advice of the more experienced bloggers Ahmed Naji and JarelKamar, given through the comment section of her blog.

22 This is shown by the significant episode of repression of male homosexuality known as 'Cairo 52' or the 'Queen Boat trial' that took place in Cairo in May 2001, when fifty-two gay men were arrested and tried during a police raid at the nightclub 'The Queen Boat', which at the time was a known meeting place for Cairene gay men. See the report by *Human Rights Watch* (2004), http://www.hrw.org/sites/default/files/reports/egypt0304_0.pdf (last accessed 15 September 2012). See also Serena Tolino (2012), 'Identità omosessuale in tribunale tra l'Egitto e il Libano contemporanei'.

23 According to both the Quran and the Bible, Lūṭ/Lot was the Prophet commanded by God to go to the land of Sodom and Gomorrah to preach to his people on monotheism and to stop them from their lustful and violent acts. Lūṭ's messages were ignored by the inhabitants and Sodom and Gomorrah were subsequently destroyed. It is written in the Quran: 'Then, again, remember Lot, when he said to his people: "Do you commit an indecency that no people anywhere have ever committed before you? You go lusting after men rather than women. You are indeed a people depraved"' (*Quran* 7: 80–1). In another verse, Lūṭ advised them: 'Do you cohabit only with males among mankind, and abandon what your Lord created for you of wives? You are a people who have truly overstepped the limit!' (*Quran* 26: 165–6). The biblical account of

Sodom and Gomorrah is recorded in the *Book of Genesis* in the Hebrew Bible in chapters 18–19.

24 Samar Habib's book (2007) *Female Homosexuality in the Middle East* is an attempt at filling this gap by providing evidence of female homosexuality from the Islamic medieval era to the present. See also H. Al-Samman (2008), 'Out of the Closet: Representation of Homosexuals and Lesbians in Modern Arabic Literature'. For a discussion of homosexuality in Arabic Literature, see F. Langrange (2000), 'Male Homosexuality in Modern Arabic Literature'.

25 Few examples can be found. The anthology of short stories *Arab Women Writers*, edited and translated by Dalya Cohen-Mor (2005), includes a short story by the Egyptian writer Nura Amin entitled 'My Mother's Friend' that recounts the lesbian relationship between the mother of a young girl and an unmarried woman, narrated from the perspective of the girl. In 2009, Egyptian movie *Bi-dun riqaba* (*Without Censorship*, 2009) portrayed a female character, Shirin, as having sexual desires for women. In one scene she has sex with a man. Later, she is shown trying to sexually harass another woman. As Emraamethlya points out in her blog, the movie still shows lesbians as deviants that are reliant on men. See her blogpost: 'Bi-dun Riqaba, Thaqafat al-Muʾakhkhirat' ('Without Censorship, The Culture of Buttocks'), 8 February 2009. Outside Egypt, the Lebanese movie *Sukkar Banat* (*Caramel*, 2007) portrays a lesbian character without a moralistic approach.

26 The root *s-ḥ-q* means 'grinding, or rubbing something'.

27 Interview, June 2010.

28 As an example of how homosexual voices are silenced in the Egyptian publishing market, Emraamethlya reports the story of the Egyptian journalist Mustafa Fathi (Muṣṭafā Fatḥī). In 2009, he wrote the book *Fi balad al-awlad* (*In the Boys' Country*), recounting his personal encounter with a group of Egyptian male homosexuals. Since he could not find a publisher willing to publish a book about homosexuality in Arabic, he was obliged to self-publish it. However, he was forced by the Security Forces to add a disclaimer that the 'novel is a product of the writer's imagination'. Thus, the existence of homosexual identities was justified in terms of fiction, imagination, and therefore not in real life.

29 The term '*mithliyya*' is an abbreviation of '*mithliyya jinsiyya*', which literally means 'sameness in sex' and thus is a translation of 'homosexuality'. This, according to Joseph Massad, is proof that, just like the linguistic expression, the whole idea of Arab homosexual identity is borrowed from the West. See Joseph Massad (2007), *Desiring Arabs*. Massad's argument is disputed by Samar Habib who,

relying on her analysis of Islamic medieval texts, argues that a lesbian identity existed before the term was adopted from the West. Like Emraamethlya, other bloggers define themselves as *mithlī* or *mithliyya*. This can be seen in the nicknames chosen by many users commenting on her blog. Additionally, the blogger Karim Azmi (Karīm ᶜAzmī), in his blog *Yawmiyyat Karim ᶜAzmi*, claims to be '*shakhṣ mithlī fī mujtamaᶜ ᶜarabī*' ('a homosexual person in an Arabic society'), http://kareemazmy.blogspot.no/2006/11/blog-post.html (last accessed 26 June 2017).

30 Interview with Emraamethlya, August 2012. Joyce Tyldesley confirms that Nefertari played a major role in state affairs behind her husband Ramses II, which is evidenced by the fact that her tomb is a 'particularly fine one' (1995: 350). As for Isis, Tyldesley points out that her cult travelled beyond the Egyptian empire and she became a universal symbol of motherhood (1995: 345). See Joyce Tyldesley (1995), *Daughter of Isis: Women of Ancient Egypt*.

31 She refers to the figure of the Queen Hatshepsut, the female pharaoh who ruled Egypt from 1479 to 1458 BC who was known for wearing male attire, including the pharaoh's headdress, kilt and false beard, and was depicted in statues and texts without female traits. She claims that this is just her 'belief'; therefore, she cannot support it with any scientific evidence. However, some researchers have speculated on the nature of homosexuality in Ancient Egypt. Thomas A. Dawson (2008), for example, refers to the duo Khnumhotep and Niankhkhnum, manicurists in the palace of King Niuserre during the Fifth Dynasty of Egyptian pharaohs, circa 2400 BC, based on a representation of them embracing nose-to-nose in their shared tomb (see 'Queering Sex and Gender in Ancient Egypt').

32 In Egyptian dialect, the expression 'red nights' indicates 'nights of sexual license'. The blogger makes a pun of 'red and green nights' that does not make the same sense in English.

33 For a literary review of the blog, see also Nael Eltoukhy (al-Tukhi 2008), 'Al-Kanaba al-Hamra: Muhawala li-Rtifaᶜ Daraja Fawqa al-Waqiᶜ' ('The Red Sofa: An Attempt at Getting One Degree Beyond Reality').

34 The Jesuit Cultural Centre has played a key role in the development of independent art in Alexandria. Aside from the film-making workshop, the institution also organises music concerts, exhibitions, theatre shows and functions as a meeting place for young Alexandrians. On the movie-making collective experience started by the Centre, see http://www.bibalex.org/alexcinema/revival/an_account_of_the_revival.html (last accessed 15 April 2018).

35 Bloggers from Alexandria agree that the blogging community in Alexandria was not involved in as much political dissent as the Cairo community. A couple of Alexandrian bloggers used blogs as a political tool (for example Taq Hanak and 'JarelKamar'), but later they moved to Cairo.

36 Interview, March 2012.

37 Interview, March 2012.

38 Here Bilal alludes to the insult used in Egyptian dialect: طيزك حمرا (*ṭīzak ḥamrā*, i.e. your arse is red, i.e. like a monkey's).

39 Probably typos for الائي, (*ʾalāʾy*, English 'I find').

40 An Arabic proverb, reiterated by mothers, aunts, grandmothers and even friends, says: 'Better a man's shadow than that of a wall', meaning that having any man is better than remaining single. From 'Egyptian Spinsters and Old Maids Sitting Happily on the Shelf', post published on *Muslimah Media Watch* by Ethar el-Katatney (2007).

41 Interview, March 2012.

42 Interview with Haytham Yahya (Ḥaythām Yaḥyā, mentioned before as 'JarelKamar'), December 2011; Ahmad Abdalla, December 2011.

43 Interview, Ahmad Abdalla, December 2011.

44 Interview, Haytham Yahya, December 2011.

45 Interview, Mahmud ᶜIzzat, March 2012.

46 Al-Baraa Ashraf uses his real name to claim the authorship of his writing. In the interview, he affirms: 'When I was writing on the website *Ishrinat* (20s) I could use my name to sign only three or four articles, I had to sign the rest of them with a nickname. I felt very disappointed when readers were praising the writing I signed with my nickname because I could not reveal it was me.' It is not just onymous bloggers who care about the protection of their copyright. Several bloggers, even though they write under a pseudonym, indicate that their blog is protected by 'Common Creative Rights' and that 'readers are free to share, modify it', but on the condition that they indicate the original source.

47 Ahmad Abdalla is the director and screenwriter of the movie *Heliopolis* (2008), who won the Best First Screenplay Award of the Sawiris Foundation in Cairo 2008. He reached global notoriety with the movie *Microphone* (2011), released shortly before the 25 January uprising. The film has been screened in film festivals worldwide and has received prizes in Egypt and abroad (Toronto, Dubai, Istanbul, Cairo).

48 This title is also very provocative for readers, as very rarely would an Egyptian woman declare this in public.

49 وطني لو شغلت بالخلد عنه.. هيتسرق. The first part of the sentence is extracted from a poem by the Egyptian poet Ahmad Shawqi (Aḥmad Shawqī) that he dedicated to Egypt on the occasion of his exile to Andalusia, in 1914. The blogger here mocks the poet's longing for his homeland.

50 من حسن إسلام المرء تركه ما لا يعنيه

51 The title is a parody of the old slogan 'God ... the country ... the King' that was – and still is – used in Arab countries ruled by a monarch (Morocco and Jordan), as an expression of obedience and loyalty to the ruler. It is used also in popular culture, but people generally change the third element to express a personal preference, like the name of a beloved, or football team, or meal, etc. The blogger chooses as a third term the expression *'ammā nshūf* (e.g. dialect: 'Well, let's see'), that indicates that she does not give any loyalty to religion nor to the State, but only waits to see the unfolding of life events.

52 *Kofta* is an Egyptian meat dish made by mixing minced meat with spices and rice and can be cooked in a number of ways.

53 Interview, February 2012.

54 The contents of the website are written in English. The website's description says: 'In case you haven't noticed, *El Koshary Today* is not a "real" news site. Our philosophy here is to use sarcasm and imagination to raise awareness of some of the serious (and not so serious) issues plaguing our nation. It is not intended to relay any factual information or credible circumstances, though where possible readers will find news links to the actual issues being satirized herein.' Significantly, the site stopped being updated after the return of the military regime in July 2013: http://www.elkoshary.com (last accessed on 15 April 2018).

55 As explained by the writer in the interview held in April 2012, this title may designate both blog-writing and the new literary writing developed by young Egyptian authors in the past ten years. Indeed, both bloggers and young writers (himself included) tend to experiment with several styles, the blurring of fiction and non-fiction, the presence or absence of plot, snapshots and memories to create new literary forms.

56 This is also the title of a famous album by the Egyptian pop singer Mohamed Mounir (Muḥammad Munīr).

57 Usually this cart appears on Egyptian street corners at breakfast time (from 7 am until 1 pm): it serves sandwiches filled with fava beans and soup, which are easy and quick to eat, and considered generally more delicious and authentic than the ones served in a shop. In the morning, in every Egyptian street, it is possible

to see Egyptians from every social class gathering around the vendor and eating their sandwiches, standing around the cart or leaning on cars parked nearby.

58 Original spelling of the nickname chosen by the blogger.

59 The title also reflects that the stories told in the blog deal with characters and situations that are truly Alexandrian and are set in the most populated and poorest neighbourhood of the city. Indeed, they differ from the conventional romantic accounts in which Alexandria is depicted as a cosmopolitan coastal city.

60 The *ḥāra* indicates a small street in the residential areas of the Arabic city, far from the big streets of the city centre. For the Egyptian writer Naguib Mahfouz (Najīb Maḥfūẓ), the *ḥāra* represents the main source of inspiration and the main setting of his novels. For example, in his novel *Zuqāq al-Midaq* (*Midaq Alley*, 1947), besides being a topographical element, the *ḥāra* stands as a microcosm of Egyptian society, where different human types live close to each other. See Rasheed El-Enany (1993), *Naguib Mahfouz: The Pursuit of Meaning*.

61 http://abdoubasha.blogspot.no (last accessed 20 August 2017).

62 Interview with Ahmad Gharbiyya, February 2012.

3

Mixed Arabic as a Subversive Literary Style

The Reception of (Book-)Blogs

In his preface to the novel *Fils*, Doubrovsky clarifies that language occupies a central position in his definition of autofiction. His idea was to subvert the formal style in which traditional literary autobiographies are usually written and to allow new, more experimental styles into the realm of autobiographical writing. The expression 'adventure of language' that he used to describe his novel has come to describe his innovative style, described by Sarah Pitcher McDonough (2011: 15) as 'self-referential, paradoxical, and linguistically complex'.

Gasparini notices that Doubrovsky's 'adventure of language' has inspired autofictional writers who have followed him to experiment with a range of styles from the oral to the baroque, the epic, and also to a more stripped down, bare style, to the point where it is not possible to attribute to autofictional writing a definite, precise literary style. 'Nonetheless' – Gasparini claims – 'we expect an autofictional work to present a minimum of originality, innovation, creativity in terms of language and style' (2008: 302).

Egyptian autofictional blogs are indeed characterised by an original, innovative style that I define here as 'Mixed Arabic'. This style has been an object of debate among the Egyptian literati (*al-udabāʾ*). Shortly after the publication of the best-selling Shuruq blog-books in 2008, the renowned Egyptian author Gamal al-Ghitani (Jamāl al-Ghīṭānī), founder of the state-owned literary magazine *Akhbar al-Adab*, published an article in the same magazine in which he claimed that, 'in these days strange titles are published and out very quickly. They are like Kleenex tissue because you use them only once and then throw them in the rubbish' (19 August 2009). In particular, al-Ghitani shared with other literary critics the concern that bloggers were tainting Arabic literary production by writing books in poor language, and 'they even express ideas making fun of language' (*arāᶜ taskhar min al-lugha*), ignoring the fact that 'language (*al-lugha*) is the main essence of literature (*adab*)' (ibid.). By defining 'blog literature' as 'Kleenex literature', he labelled it as popular, 'disposable' literature, as opposed to high literature that stands out due to its high quality.[1] Bloggers' writing style was dismissed as the linguistic expression of youth who have insufficient command of proper *fuṣḥā*, and who take the opportunity of the democratisation allowed by the media, and the lack of gatekeepers, to get their work published.[2]

On 22 January 2009, a seminar entitled 'Bloggers' Literature – The screams of youth or Kleenex tissue?' was held at the annual Cairo International Book Fair, in which bloggers were invited to respond to al-Ghitani's article. That year, bloggers had taken the fair by storm, as more than fifteen book titles had been retrieved from blogs, and Facebook swarmed with invitations to groups and events promoting these books and the book fair. The seminar was organised by the prominent writer Yusuf al-Qaᶜid (Yūsuf al-Qaᶜīd) and hosted the bloggers Ghada Abdel Aal, Shadi Aslan (Shādī Aṣlān) and Mayada Midhat (Mayāda Midḥat). Against the accusations of some of the old-guard literati, the best-selling blogger Ghada Abdel Aal defended blog literature as 'the expression of youth who do not need to show off their lexicon, since their aim as writers is to deliver the message in the most comprehensible form' (Rakha 2009).[3]

A new chapter to this debate was added in April 2011, when the renowned academic and literary critic Hoda Wasfi (Hudā Waṣfī), editor of the literary journal *al-Fusul*, dedicated a special issue to blogs. The journal validated the use of the term '*al-mudawwanāt al-adabiyya*' (literary blogs) to indicate blogs that 'share with literary texts of the highest quality the voyage of self-discovery, but depart from them for their special rhetoric' (Wasfi 2011: 6).[4] The issue includes an article entitled 'Al-Mudawwinun Yatahaddathun: Shahadat min Qalb Mujtamaᶜ al-Tadwin al-Misri wa-l-ᶜArabi' ('The bloggers remember: Testimonies from the heart of the Egyptian and Arab blogging society') in which fifteen bloggers were asked to write about their experience concerning their blogging practice, and the relation between blogging, *adab* and Arabic language. Most of the bloggers interviewed agree on the fact that blogging is a breaking point in the history of Arabic literature, and that freedom (*ḥurriyya*) is the key word for it (al-Abd 2011: 238), as the medium allows young authors to connect to each other, away from the control of linguistic authorities (censors, proofreaders, editors) and to break together the rules of literary writing (*qawāᶜid al-aᶜmāl al-adabiyya*, ibid.: 255). By blogging they want to create a style aimed at conveying the truth, the immediacy/spontaneity (*'afawiyya*) of their feelings, convey ideas (*tawṣīl al-afkār*) and forge connections (*taḥqīq al-tawāṣul*) (ibid.: 236). The words expressed by these bloggers explain that their linguistic and literary practices should be understood as attempts at 'subverting' or reversing established rules and values in the literary field embodied by al-Ghitani and the other writers of the previous generation, and specifically the fact that literature should be written in a beautiful, embellished style. By blogging, they set themselves at the margin of the literary field, and from there they subvert hegemonic discourses and the conditions of the literary system.

In this chapter I use Deleuze and Guattari's theory of 'minor literature' (1983) to illuminate the subversive nature of bloggers' literary practices.[5] The concept of 'minority' sheds light on the collective and political value of this literature, as it is produced by writers who publish their personal life-stories on the Internet to distance themselves from mainstream, state-owned media, and to connect with each other and push the boundaries for freedom of expression. Besides, 'minority' allows us to understand the use of mixed varieties of Arabic as a 'deterritorialized language' (ibid.: 16), that is, a new, subversive literary style coined by a young generation of writers who feels alienated in respect to the national standardised written language. In particular, it shows that these writers aim at questioning the sharp distinction between the two main varieties of Arabic, *fuṣḥā* (FU, high variety) and *ᶜāmmiyya* (AM, vernacular), and the exclusive use of FU as the variety for prose fiction. Rather they opt for the mixing of elements drawn from high and low varieties (Mixed Arabic) and foreign languages to develop new literary styles.

This chapter is based on the analysis of the six blogs chosen as case studies, but it includes examples drawn from the larger sample of blogs. It builds on previous studies on language choice in literature and combines theories drawn from sociolinguistics and literary studies.

The Influence of Diglossia on Arabic Literature

The issue of language has been debated in the Arabic/Egyptian literary field since the nineteenth century. The Arabic language has often been described as an example of diglossia, in which a high variety, *fuṣḥā* (FU), is opposed to the vernacular *ᶜammiyya* (AM), which is the ordinary, native spoken variety of the general population, linguistically related to the 'high' variety but very different from it (Ferguson 1959). The two varieties are supposed to accomplish two different functions: FU is the variety used in formal, written discourse, while AM is used as an informal, oral variety. Meanwhile, recent studies of both oral and written practices in Arabic have shown that this sharp distinction between the two varieties does not represent the real language use.

In oral discourse, Badawi (1973) and Mejdell (2006a) opt for a description of a diglossic continuum, in which FU and AM are at extreme poles.[6] Speakers mix the two varieties according to context and level of formality of the linguistic situation (using what Mejdell defines 'mixed styles of Arabic', or Arabic: *al-lugha al-wusṭā*).[7]

For the written discourse, the situation is slightly different. Research in the history of Arabic has shown that mixed varieties that combine standard and colloquial features have been in use since early times (called 'Middle Arabic', MA); authors would write in MA because they found it appropriate, usually in less formal genres or sometimes simply because they were not fluent in Classical Arabic (Lentin 2012: 209). Then, in the nineteenth century, the period of social and cultural reform that is known as the Nahda (renaissance), Arab literati stressed the need to revive the Arabic language and preserve the beauty and purity of FU linked to the historical tradition and intellectual splendour of ancient times by coining a modern version of it, which could be used at the same time as a pan-Arab national language (Suleiman 2003). Since then, *faṣāḥa* (adherence to exemplary FU) has become a criterion for determining the artistic quality of a work of literature (Somekh 1991: 67). Somekh explains that the language form/variety that was selected to be the written medium for the modernising Egyptian society was the existing, although archaic, literary norm with no native speakers. Those literati took the challenge to make this functionally rather restricted language form functional for new domains – by simplifying its elaborate stylistic conventions, by expanding its vocabulary, by diversifying its syntactic and phraseological means. Nonetheless, the written variety remained consistently different from the spoken one.

Throughout the twentieth century, Arab writers have attempted to find creative solutions for this linguistic divide. Some authors have tended towards the use of a simple FU infused with vernacular flavour.[8] With the emergence of a realist trend in literature, it became commonly accepted to write dialogue in AM, while the narrative remained in FU. Others have nonetheless chosen to write their works in vernacular, for a variety of reasons, but their works have mostly been considered to be lacking in value, or 'illegitimate', therefore not included in the literary canon.[9] Recent studies on language choice in literature (Eid 2002; Bassiouney 2010; Mejdell 2006b; Abboud-Haggar 2010) regarding Egyptian literary works written in the last fifty years seem to show that the position of FU remains unchallenged in the literary field, especially in narrative.[10]

However, some new tendencies could be detected in recent literary production, especially since the 1990s, favoured by the emergence of private publishing houses, which allowed authors to publish their work at their own expense and thus to keep away from state-controlled publishing houses. Rosenbaum (2000) provides examples of a mixed or alternating style in fiction and journalism, under the label *fuṣḥāmmiyya* to achieve entertaining, humorous purposes. Also, Madiha Doss finds an increasing number of novels written exclusively in Egyptian dialect and she points out that the novel *An Takun ᶜAbbas al-ᶜAbd* (*Being Abbas el Abd*), by the Egyptian author Ahmed Alaidy, is written in a mix of written Arabic with spoken Cairo dialect, youth language and Egyptianised English, sometimes written in Roman letters and numbers (Doss 2004: 66).[11] In her survey on language choice in literature, Mejdell also notices a different approach among poets of the 1990s generation in Egypt, in the sense that they refuse the labels of FU and AM and they claim to be simply writing 'poetry' (2006b: 203).

Doss ascribes this phenomenon to a change of attitude towards language, coupled with the diversification of means of publication, and suggests a serious study leading to a better understanding of the changes taking place among authors, writers and publishers. Indeed, previous studies carried out in the field of contemporary Arabic/Egyptian literature give evidence that these language choices should be viewed in the light of a gradual aesthetic break with the previous traditional narrative discourse taking place in the 1990s, at the hand of a young generation of authors who felt more and more disconnected from society and its intellectuals' nationalist views.[12] In light of these findings, Mejdell expects substantial changes brought by uncensored media, namely the Internet, at the hand of a young generation of writers, as she notices a general tendency to disdain the beauty of the Arabic language in favour of the vernacular and English, especially among the Arab youth. In her words, these new media represent 'a challenge to our beautiful language that promises vitality, variation and change' (2008: 123).

Strangers in their Own Land

In the previous chapter, we have seen how blogging emerged as a young, urban phenomenon. We have also seen how it has brought together a highly disparate group of people. However, even though they carry different life stories, their blogs share the expression of a feeling of estrangement and alienation from the surrounding society. This is well evidenced by the words of the blogger Ahmad Mihanna (Aḥmad Mihannā) in the conclusion to the book *Misr Fi Qitᶜat Gato* (*Egypt in a Piece of Cake*), an anthology of blog posts published in print.

> In my search among these creatures that are alive with our words, entities that we metaphorically call blogs ... I found many views that are absent from society and its limited values, works that do not beg at the feet of the state or its famous intellectuals (*muthaqqafūhā al-mashhūrīn*)[13] ... I found the death of hope (*mawt al-amal*) in the words of those who were failed by a nation (*waṭan*) that did not satisfy their sense of belonging (*intimāʾ*) ... I found expatriates (*mughtaribīn*) living inside the nation (*waṭan*). (Mihanna 2008: 231, quoted and translated in el-Sadda 2011)[14]

The expression '*mughtaribīn*' used by Mihanna explains that these writers perceive themselves as a minority because they live as marginalised/alienated, in a state of exile and alienation in their own country.[15] This is related to their political values, as well as their cultural and educational background.

Even though youth represents the demographic majority of the population, they occupy a minor status in Egypt, in the sense that 'they are excluded from full participation in the life of society, and may even be objects of contempt, hatred, ridicule and violence' (Wirth 1945: 348). In fact, their ages imply that most of them have spent the majority of their lives under Hosni Mubarak's authoritarian rule (1981–2011) and, as such, under the grip of the emergency law that was imposed by the Egyptian government after the assassination of President Sadat by religious fundamentalist groups.[16] This generation grew up in a society where a multiplicity of political voices was absent (the two options available were either the ruling party or, ironically enough, the 'forbidden' Muslim Brotherhood), where the political system did not involve them (except under the umbrella of the ruling party), where the liberal voices who intellectually enriched the Egypt of the 1960s were hushed, emptying the scene for the unchallenged and increasingly clamorous voices of conservative thought (El-Mougy 2011: 164). Additionally, the Egyptian State under Mubarak failed to supply its citizens with satisfactory public services, such as education or health, nor did it treat the Egyptian people with dignity.

While the previous generations of writers and intellectuals who still dominate the canon of Arabic literature and are at the forefront of major cultural institutions in Egypt have stressed the need for using literature as a means of contributing to the modern process of nation-building and for using FU as a pan-Arab national language (Jacquemond 2008), these young authors feel themselves alienated in respect to the national community and the idea of the *waṭan* (nation). Despite the fact that they all carry Egyptian citizenship and feel an emotional link to their country, many cannot reconcile this with an Egyptian State that can be at turns both cruel and entirely indifferent to their needs.[17]

Their alienation from Arabic national culture and literature is widened by the fact that these writers have grown up in a time in which the use of digital technologies has completely changed their approach to knowledge and culture. Since most of them were born after 1980, they belong to the first generation of so-called 'digital natives' (Palfrey and Gasser 2008: 1) as they are the first Egyptian generation to have access to networked digital technologies and have the skills to use them. The anthropologist Linda Herrera argues that the access to new media and communication technologies has facilitated a significant generational rupture, as 'it has opened their cultural frontiers in unexpected ways' (2012: 342). She explains that the Internet, and the arrival of torrent peer-to-peer file sharing in the early 2000s, has provided writers with exposure to and interaction with global cultural and scientific repertoires, that is, ideas, people, images, virtual spaces and cultural products outside their everyday environments. This led to a substantial change in their mentality and worldview; they experienced 'a veritable cultural revolution' (ibid.: 342).

While the Internet has turned them into 'citizens of the world', the educational background of these writers is also significant to understanding their minor relation to the Arabic language. Most of these writers come from a middle-class family background, as their parents' occupations include schoolteachers, doctors, public-sector employees and engineers.[18] Therefore, most of them have attended language schools (also called *madāris tajrībiyya*) or private schools.[19] Some of them have even attended private universities, where the education curricula are taught in foreign languages (generally English). Interestingly, most of these writers are educated in scientific or technical subjects, like engineering and medical sciences, and cultivate a passion for humanist subjects in their spare time. This implies that they speak a mixture of colloquial Arabic and English, both at leisure and at work. They might have studied FU at school, but it is a variety that they rarely use in daily life. For most of the bloggers I interviewed, the FU variety, which is expected to be used in literary works, is a dead, foreign language, or what Deleuze and Guattari define as a 'paper' language (Deleuze and Guattari 1983: 16) that is not apt for expressing their own feelings.

This feeling of alienation from the nation and its literary language explains these writers' 'impossibility of not writing, the impossibility of writing in the major language and the impossibility of writing otherwise' (ibid.: 16). Minor writers are conscious of their minor positions, and nonetheless they write because they have something important to say. Indeed, for many of these writers, writing is a means of speaking out about their marginalisation in society, and at the same time connecting with a community of peers who might share their feelings of estrangement. From their minor position, they coin a new 'minor' literary style that sets them on the margin and, from there, 'makes them able to express another potential community' (ibid.: 17).

Mixing Arabic on the Blog

As these bloggers perceive themselves as a minority in their own language and society, they choose to write in a major language, but in a way that expresses their estrangement and alienation from it. Deleuze and Guattari define this style as a 'language affected by a strong co-efficient of deterritorialization' (1983: 16) and consider it an important attribute of a minor literature.

For example, in the blog *Yawmiyyat Imraʾa Mithliyya* (*Diary of a Gay Woman*), the narrator/main character Emraamethlya makes a parallel between her being a minority both in terms of sexual identity and in terms of language skills. She explains that since female homosexuality is completely silenced in mainstream discourse, she has learnt the ABC (*alif bāʾ*) of herself through the Internet in another language. So, she is ignorant of the 'grammar' (*naḥw*) and 'deflection' (*ṣarf*) of the bed in her mother language (*al-lugha al-umm*). On the blog she wants to find (*ajid*) and create (*ūjid*) words that could describe herself (*taṣifūnī*), her feelings (*mashāʿirī*) and parts of her body (*ajzāʾ jasadī*) in her own language, 'to say them, repeat them, publish them' ('Hubb bi-l-ʿarabi' ('Love in Arabic'), 4 August 2009). In her blog, she discusses her rejection of other Arabic terms, and offers motivation for her readers. For example, she writes about the word '*suḥāqiyya*' thus:

> Long ago I could not stand hearing this heavy-sounding, bad word *suḥāq*/*suḥāqiyya* but lately I have learned the meaning and I realized that I am not a *suḥāqiyya*. The word '*saḥaqa*' indicates the action that takes place between two women by rubbing their bodies together. I don't do that, I am not *suḥāqiyya*. I think it is stupid to reduce the love and intimate relationship between two women by describing it as '*suḥāq*'. Any male or female can practice this rubbing of bodies in order to achieve pleasure without knowing anything, but only for the sake of experimenting. The word *suḥāq* does not express any sexual or sensual orientation. This word does not represent lesbians [*mithliyyāt*]. ('ʾAna mish Suhaqiyya' ('I am not "*suḥāqiyya*"'), 20 August 2008)

منذ وقت بعيد كنت لا أطيق أن أسمع تلك الكلمة ذات الوقع الثقيل السيء على
اذني «سحاق» سحاقية و منذ وقت قريب عرفت
معنى الكلمة و أدركت إني مش سحاقية

و كلمة سحاق هي الفعل الذي قد تقوم به أنثى مع اخرى من سحق أو حك
أجسادهن معا
انا بقى مش بعمل كده انا بقى مش سحاقية و ارى أن من الغباء إختصار علاقة
حب و موده بين إمراتين ووصفة بانه سحاق
حك الأجساد من اجل لذة ده ممكن تعمله أي واحدة و أي حد مش عارف
حاجة بس عايز يجرب
كلمة سحاق لا تعبر عن اي توجه جنسي او حسي
الكلمة لا تعبر عن المثليات

As for the term '*shādhdh*', in one of the early entries of her blog she rejects its use with its meaning of 'deviant, abnormal':

> Why do people think that they are the natural ones (*ṭabīᶜiyyūn*)? Why do the others consider themselves normal (*ᵓaswiyāᵓ*) and consider us as deviants? Is this because they all do the same thing? People who believe that they are right and those who are different from them are wrong are either conceited, or stupid and narrow-minded. ('Al-Shudhudh' ('The Deviants'), 1 March 2009)

> لماذا يعتقد الناس أنهم طبيعيون؟ لماذا يعتبر الأخرون انفسهم أسوياء و نحن شواذ
> هل لانهم جميعا يفعلون الشيء نفسة؟غرور أم غباء و ضيق عقل أن يعتقد
> الأخرون انهم على حق و المختلفون عنهم على باطل

In this way she aims at creating a language with which Arab lesbian women can become aware of themselves. Similarly, in the blog *Yawmiyyat ᶜAnis* (*Diary of a Spinster*), the author/narrator/main character Abeer explains that she wants to write in Arabic (as opposed to English) to change the language of society on women and marriage. In the blog entry 'ᶜAnis … wa-ᵓEih Yaᶜni' ('[Yes, I am a] Spinster … So what? / what does it matter?', 1 June 2008), she explains that she defines herself as a 'spinster' in order to change the meaning attributed by society to this term. In her words, 'in the dictionary *al-Muhit* the word stands for both woman or man that has reached maturity and has not married yet, but the popular understanding (*al-mafhūm ash-shaᶜabī*) attributes the word only to the woman, not the man'. In another entry she explains that her marginalisation in society, as an unmarried thirty-year-old woman, is linked to 'the vocabulary' (*mufradāt*) of our blessed/Mubarak age[20] ('Itnayn fi-l-Hawa' ('Two in the Air'), 9 September 2008), and this is what she aims at changing through writing.

The language that both Abeer and Emraamethlya, and other bloggers, write on their blogs is 'deterritorialized' in the sense that it is based on their mother-tongue (*al-ᶜarabiyya*) but it undergoes a process of reinvention and creativity, as a minority would do in a major language. Deleuze and Guattari explain 'deterritorialization' in terms of language functions, where each language function in turn is divided and involves multiple power centres. It is a language that 'play[s] one function against the other, bring[s] the coefficients of territoriality and relative deterritorialization into play' (1983: 27). As I explained before, in the case of Arabic literature, FU is preferred for narratives in literary works, because it is the high variety apt for expressing an educated and refined discourse, while AM is reserved for dialogue, according to a realistic mode of narration. The examples found in the blogosphere demonstrate that blog authors opt for a 'mixed style' or what Mejdell defines as *al-lugha al-wusṭā*[21]: an 'intermediate/medium language production in terms of being both a) functionally intermediate, serving a middle position between formal and informal, and b) structurally, i.e. linguistically, intermediate between standard and vernacular' (2011). For example, Abeer usually uses very short sentences, often interspersed with questions asked directly to the readers. She tends to use a simple FU, made of very short sentences. However, sometimes she switches from FU to AM in the same text. In the blog post 'Yawm Batiᶜ' ('A Slow Day', 11 May 2008), written in first person, Abeer, the narrator-author-main character, describes a day in which she has decided to ignore the everyday social struggle and to focus only on her own happiness. Here is an excerpt of the text by way of illustration:

> I opened my eyes this morning and I found I was in a wonderful mood. I smiled at the world … and I said to my spirit: 'Good Morning' [*ṣabaḥ al-full*] …
>
> I woke up my lazy cat sleeping next to me … I played a bit with her and gave her a bit of 'bssss' … I jumped out of bed full of life and energy … I ran to the CD player and played Fayrouz … There is always a relationship between Fayrouz's voice and the morning … especially those mornings that hug a human being and welcome them to life … I started preparing my Nescafe, I went to the bathroom …

> I left the bathroom feeling like a rose open to life, sweet-smelling and enraptured with the sunshine of the morning … I drank the Nescafe while putting on my clothes; I chose a dress that resembles my new morning … nice, simple and short … I wore my favorite shoes … I paid attention to detail … I picked my bag and I said bye to my cat who did not give me any attention: she was standing at the edge of the bedroom window, watching in amazement a world to which she did not belong … I filled my lungs with air, opened the door and laughed to the day … I looked at the lift mischievously and ran down the stairs … I emerged into the street. I said good morning to Muhammad the doorman and Umm Mahrus the grocer … I hailed a taxi … the driver was discontented because of the traffic and heat … I did not want to ruin my day … I took out the novel *Slowness* by Milan Kundera and I immersed myself into reading.

> فتحت عيونى الصبح و لقتنى « مودي" لطيف. إبتسمت للدنيا.. وقلت لروحى «صباح الفل».. صحصحت قطتى الكسلانة اللى نايمة جانبى.. ولاعبتها و بسبست فيها شوية.. نطيت من السرير و كلى طاقة للحياة.. جريت على ا CD Player وشغلت فيروز.. دايما فى علاقة بين صوت فيروز و الصبح.. خصوصا الصبح اللى بيحضن البنى آدم ويرحب بيه فى الحياة.. علقت على النسكافية.. دخلت الحمام.. [...]
> خرجت من الحمام وكأنى زهرة متفتحة للحياة .. يفوح منها العبير.. تنتشى من شمس الصباح ..شربت النسكافية وأنا أرتدرى ملابسى.. أنتقيت فستان كثير الشبه بصبحى الجديد.. جميل و بسيط وقصير.. إرتديت حذائى المفضل.. أعتنيت بتفاصيلى.. حملت حقيبتى وودعت قطتى التى لم تعرنى أى إهتمام يذكر فقد كانت تقف على حافة شباك غرفة النوم تتطلع بدهشة وترقب الى عالم لا تنتمى إليه.. ملأت رئتى بالهواء وفتحت باب الشقة وضحكت للنهار.. بصيت للأصانصير بلؤم .. وأخدت السلالم جرى.. نزلت الشارع .. صبحت على محمد البواب.. وأم محروس بياعة الخضار.. ووقفت [sic] تاكسى.. وكان السائق يتأفف من الزحمة والحر .. كنت لا أرغب فى إفساد يومى.. فأخرجت رواية البطء ل»ميلان كونديرا» واستغرقت فى القراءة.

In the first part, Abeer writes mainly in AM, as shown by the insertion of the relative pronoun *illī*, *bi*+verbal form, the negation *mish*, and the adverb as *shwayya*. The narrative also includes vernacular expressions, like *ṣabaḥ al-full*, onomatopoeic verbs, like *ṣaḥsaḥt* (I woke up), *basbist fihā* (to call a cat), which give a playful tone to the narration. One can also notice the term *mūdī*, where the English noun 'mood' is used and adapted to Arabic grammar by keeping the original word and adding the pronominal possessive suffix, 'ي' (*ī*, first person sing.), indicating 'my mood'; the English expression 'CD player' instead is left in English and written in Latin characters. This section is apt for describing her morning routine, by setting a joyous, light and intimate tone of narration. Then, the main character puts on Fayrouz's music and starts to get dressed. Here the narrative switches to FU syntactical structure (as indicated by the use of the relative pronoun *allatī*, the use of *lam* and *lā* for negation, and other lexical items like *ḥaqība* for 'bag' instead of AM *shanṭa*) with AM lexical items (such as *baṣṣēt*, 'I looked') and focuses on the details of the dress, the perfume, shoes, drawing attention to the character's femininity and to her refined taste. The code-switch gives the idea that Abeer is moving from a natural stage of cuteness, freedom, into a more 'intellectual stage' that she wants to display in society. Indeed, in the final scene, she rides in a cab and the taxi driver starts talking to her, but she immerses herself in the reading of a book pretending not to hear him. It seems that the mix of these two styles contributes to give the reader a peek into Abeer's private life, while also portraying her as a refined, intellectual woman. Indeed, in the blog, the author aims at showing that she is not married not because of personal deficiencies, but because the 'Oriental man' (*al-rajul al-sharqī*) cannot stand a woman that is beautiful (*jamīla*), educated (*muthaqqafa*),[22] independent (*mustaqilla*), intelligent (*dhakiyya*), religious (*mutadayyina*) and artistic (*wa fannāna*) ('Shillat Banat ᶜAwanis' ('A Group of Spinsters'), 4 March 2008).

Similar strategies of mixing and code-switching are adopted by the author of the blog *Yawmiyyat Imraᵓa Mithliyya*. In many entries the writer chooses to write narrative in FU and dialogues in AM, according to the canon of Arabic literature. However, often the dialogue is not signalled to the reader through punctuation, creating a flow between FU and AM. In some cases she switches from FU to AM in the same sentence in order to change the tone of narration. For example, in this passage drawn from the story 'Mudarrisati' ('My Teacher', 22 January 2006):

> I want to be free I want to shout my love for her that fills my heart I want to let everybody know that she is my lover I am forbidden from doing this because I live in a society that does not understand this … or rather understands it but denies it maybe I am lucky because here I can walk by her side hand in hand I can hug and kiss her without worries but maybe I

look worried because I know that I am doing it with different feelings not the ones that other people expect [them to be] well what are the feelings that come over any woman when she hugs and kisses another woman when they greet each other for example when they meet? This is a complicated question to which I cannot give an answer.

أريد ان أكون حرة أريد ان أصرخ بحبها الذي ملأ قلبي أريد أن يعرف الجميع أنها حبيبتي انا محرومة من أن أفعل ذلك لأنني أعيش في مجتمع لا يفهم هذا ... بل هو يفهمه و لكنه ينكره يهمله لا يريده يمكن اكون محظوظه لاني هنا ممكن امشي جنبها و ويدانا متشابكتان و يمكنني أن أحتضنها و أقبلها دون قلق بس يمكن القلق يبان علي لاني حكون عرفه أني بعمل كده بمشاعر أخرى غير اللي الأخرين متوقعينها طيب و هي إيه المشاعر اللي بتيجي لاي إمراة عندما تقبل أو تحتضن أخرى في السلام مثلا عند اللقاء؟؟؟؟ سؤال محير مقدرش أرد عليه

The first part is written in FU variety, as indicated, for example, by the use of the verb *urīd an*, the relative pronouns *alladhī*, the demonstrative pronouns *dhālika* and *hādhā*. The part that follows the conjunction *bass* ('but') is written in AM, as indicated by the use of *ḥ*– for future tense, the relative pronoun *illī* and the use of *mish* for the negative, and other items. As we can see, the narrator starts by expressing her idealised view of lesbian love, imagining herself and her partner walking hand-in-hand in the street; however, suddenly, the narration switches to vernacular to express collapse, weakness, an intimate fear of being recognised as lesbian by someone out there. In many entries, the author leaves misspellings untouched and uses almost no punctuation, endowing the autofictional narrative with a sense of authenticity: in this way, the reader tends to believe that a homosexual author is hiding behind the computer screen and writing in a hurry, fearing that somebody could find out her real identity.

In the blog *al-Kanaba al-Hamra* (*The Red Sofa*), Bilal Husni writes using a mix of standard and vernacular styles. He also experiments a lot with expressions drawn from youth slang,[23] for example, '*brustityūt, brustityūt yaᶜnī*', where the English word 'prostitute' is transliterated into Arabic characters and repeated twice to emphasise its meaning, a practice quite widespread in oral discourse; use of the same adjectives both in negative and positive ways (*faẓīᶜ mōt* meaning 'very horrible'); and other original expressions such as *al-banāt al-bitsh* (the bitchy girls), *ghanī shwayyetēn* (a bit rich) and *kunt musattab* (my brain was set up).[24] The language also undergoes 'a deterritorialization of the mouth, teeth and tongue' (Deleuze and Guattari 1983: 19) as it reproduces the articulation of sounds. For example, we find expressions such as اه (yes), اوك (ok), الواد (the guy), اوبس (that's it), اوووووه (aww), اااااااااااااااه (yeeeesss), لالالا (nonono), كده كده (so and so)[25] where the excessive lengthening of the vowel imitates the lexical stress. An added aspect of this kind of lengthening can be seen in the use of conversational interjections in narrative, such as *yā raaaaabb* (O Lord!), *allaaaah* (Gooood), *yā salām* (Oh boy!), and so on. We can also see that punctuation is often used in erratic ways, to make the text more expressive. Short sentences are combined with the use of very long passages, with a heavy use of ellipses, which may indicate the flow of thoughts, indeterminacy, pauses or moments of hesitation. The narrative abounds with metaphors alluding to sexual practices, sometimes with funny, subtle expressions, sometimes with more sophisticated terms. In some cases, FU syntactical constructions are mixed with vernacular elements, as in this passage:

> At dawn the room is lit by the light that comes from the closed shutters of the balcony. I am completely naked, standing on a few books and sheets of paper scattered on the floor, and the thin layer of dust that covers the carpet that is not Persian at all.
>
> قرب الفجر والاوضه بينورها بس نور البلكونه ال مقفول شيشها، واناعارى تماما واقف على حبة كتب وورق [sic]متبعتر وطبقه تراب خفيفه بتكسو السجاده ال مش ايرانى خالص (8 November 2007)

In this passage one can see that the FU structure of the '*iḍāfa* adjective' (*iḍafa ghayr ḥaqīqiyya*) is composed once of FU lexical elements (*al-balkuna al-maqfūl shīshuhā*), while in the next occurrence it includes the negative particle, *mish*, typical AM (*al-sijjāda al-mish īrānī khāliṣ*). The use of AM elements in the second *iḍāfā* is apt for downplaying even further the value of these objects, stressing the bohemian, impoverished lifestyle of the main character. Overall, we can see that the use of this style is functional to the meaning of the entire blog. Since the days of Sigmund Freud, the sofa has been viewed as an important component of psychoanalysis (Lable *et al.* 2010). Thus, it could be argued that for Bilal, the act of blog-writing is akin to lying on a shrink's couch: through each blog post, the author is able to describe his inner thoughts, to delve deeply into his psyche, much like the sofa allows a patient to open up to their therapist. The oral expression and the misspellings seem to contribute to presenting the narration as an immediate, untouched confession, a stream of consciousness.

Further examples of the use of Mixed Arabic as a literary style can be seen in the blog *Wassi^c Khayalak* by Ahmed Naji. Like Bilal, Naji deterritorialises language, making extensive use of youth slang. For example, the blog search tool is entitled '*baḥth al-tinnīn wa-natā$^{\circ}$ij al-sinīn*', evoking an expression broadly used by Egyptian youths to indicate a positive exaggeration.[26] In the narrative, the author mixes FU and AM in many creative ways, as in the post entitled 'Idhak Li$^{\circ}$annaha Baykha' ('Laugh, Because it is a Trite Joke', 4 November 2009), an excerpt of which I report in the following:

> And then what?
>
> I have lost my ability to dream since a long time. *Tozz* (Go to hell).[27] Your arm came unstuck and you haven't picked it up … *Tozz*. Everything around you has become boring and rotten. The news that is supposed to be fresh exudes a smell of rottenness. Lies have become too many for you to point at [one of them] and say this is a lie. *Tozz*. …
>
> This is not important, motherfucker (*kossommak*). Yes, I am saying it to you again, this is not important, motherfucker. It's not important that all around you sucks balls (*biḍān*), is trite and boring. Not important. *Tozz*. I mean, what are you going to do, because the joke has turned out to be trite, are you going to make a problem because of a trite joke? No, motherfucker … Laugh. Laugh. Because it is trite.

ثم ماذا؟
فقدت القدرة على الحلم منذ زمن طويل. طظ. سقطت
ذراعك ولم تلقتطها. طظ. أصبح كل ما حولك مملاً عطناً. الأخبار التي يفترض فيها
الطزاجة تفوح منها رائحة العفونة. الأكاذيب أصبحت أكثر من أن تشير بيدك وتقول
....هذه كذبة. طظ
مش مهم يا
كس أمك. ايوه بقولها لك تانى. مش مهم يا كس أمك. مش مهم أن كل اللى حواليك
بضان

وبايخ وممل. مش مهم. طظ. يعنى هتعمل أيه يعنى علشان النكتة طلعت بايخة. هتعمل
مشكلة علشان نكتة بايخة. لا يا كس أمك.. اضحك. اضحك لأنها بايخة

The passage builds on a verse of poetry by the Palestinian poet Mahmud Darwish drawn from the poem 'Madih al-Zill al-ᶜAli' ('Praise of the High Shadow', 1982) which says '*saqaṭat dhirāᶜuk fa-ltaqiṭhā*' ('your arm dropped off, pick it up!') but it subverts its meaning ('you didn't pick it up'). Indeed Iblis is affected by strong disillusion. In the first part of this passage, using lexical and syntactical elements from FU, the narrator complains about the rotten Egyptian reality. A number of words that compose the passage are hyperlinked to news websites, in which the reader can get the reasons and the context of the author's disillusion. The FU narrative is also interspersed with a slang word, '*ṭazāga*' ('freshness', from '*ṭāza*', 'fresh'). However, at the end of each sentence, the vernacular expression '*toẓẓ*' is repeated as a leitmotiv. The sound of the repetition resembles a snake hiss that expresses anger and frustration. In the second part, the narrator addresses the reader directly and switches to AM. The tone is aggressive, and carries marks of bitter disillusionment. This tone is reinforced by the use of vulgar expressions that the author addresses directly to the readers. These are used as a means of awakening the readers from their limpness. The use of this language reinforces Iblis' self-portrait as an evil, provocative individual, an image reinforced by the satanic cynical sneer he invites the reader to join in with.

Mona Seif deterritorialises Arabic language by creatively playing with a mix of Egyptian dialect, Modern Standard Arabic and English, and with an orthography composed of English letters, Arabic letters and numbers.[28] This form of transliteration is already evident in the title of her blog, *Tanatif Ma3t*, and in her first post entitled '*Ana Geit*'. In her post written in English about the G-spot, she writes:

> Sexuality and sex are regarded as taboo subjects, although I have noticed a lot that the very traditional families coming from *manate2 masreya sha3beya* [my emphasis],[29] actually talk about Sex & sexuality, very openly, something that is at first quite embarrassing and shocking, but then u realize how acceptable and insightful it is. The majority knew about the clitoris,

probably because of the *7'etan*[30] [my emphasis] issue, but none of the girls at university with me knew about the G-spot.

Interestingly, Mona switches between English and Arabic also as a way to filter her audience. When she deals with subjects that concern an Egyptian audience, as for example sexual harassment, she writes in Arabic. But interestingly, when it comes to the G-spot issue, and complaining about sexual education in Egypt, she writes in English to restrict the discussion to a more open-minded, well-educated upper-class readership. When she talks about the breakdown of her relationship, she uses English as a way to restrict the description of her feelings to her community of peers who, like her, are fully bilingual in English and Arabic, while keeping out older generations (her boyfriend's mother used to read her blog, she says in the interview). Mona also used English in 2010 when she joined the Women Bloggers campaign, an initiative that involved bloggers from Denmark, Tunisia and Egypt, in order to address and interact with an international audience. Since the 25 January uprising, Mona has written in English more often. Indeed, she knew that the blogging community was already in Tahrir Square, thus she took it upon herself to use her language skills to inform the foreign public.[31] Accordingly, during this period, we can see that more and more readers from several countries comment on her blog and praise her for her writing.

Mona also deterritorialises Arabic by inserting into her writing childish expressions and sounds, like *ya*^{c}*aaaa*, *lulululuu*. In addition, she often writes Arabic with a childish and clumsy handwriting, with the help of computer graphic tools, as shown by Figure 10. This adds an air of 'cuteness' or 'naivety' to her self-representation.

Figure 10 Mona Seif writes Arabic with childish handwriting. Source: http://ma3t.blogspot.no.

Amr Ezzat is among the few bloggers analysed in this study who exclusively uses FU in their blog. In some passages, he embellishes the texts with metaphors, symbolism and alliteration to elevate the style of the text. In the following passage, for example, he describes Cairo as the setting of an old Arab movie. The feeling of dissatisfaction and frustration with his country are expressed in a high literary style: the author uses frequent alliteration and combines words coming from the same root, words that consequently have similar sounds but different meanings:

> Does this have a relation to the fact that in these weeks Cairo is turning into a décor for a popular café that is hosting the shooting of a tacky old Arabic film, where two people start to argue for a superficial reason, and then they both stand up and grapple with each other, while two seconds before they were sitting at the same table exchanging friendly accounts …
>
> Suppressed rage and useless violence, tiny spaces and distressed souls, cursing and gestures, mistrust and outraged looks, ugly scenes and rotten smells, compliance without satisfaction, domination without trust, arrogance without pride, gatherings without encounters and separations that do not make a difference. Being used to filth and wretchedness, and insults, obtrusive and discordant sounds, scattered and uncovered waste lands, talking without connecting, hurrying without making it, scattered piles and unconsequent numbers, crowds without masses, enemies who get to know each other only at the hour of confrontation, that starts with no reason and ends with no meaning. ('Humula Zaʾida' ('Overload'), 10 November 2009)

> هل لذلك علاقة بأن القاهرة هذه الأسابيع بدت وكأنها ديكور مقهى شعبي يشهد تصوير مشهد مبتذل في فيلم عربي قديم، يتشاجر اثنان لسبب تافه فيهب كل اثنين ويمسكان بخناق بعضهما ولو كانا جالسين على طاولة وحدة يتبادلان الحديث الودي قبل ثوان…
>
> غيظ مكبوت وعنف بلا طائل، مساحات ضيفة ونفوس ضائقة[32]، فظاظة في اللفظ والإيماءة، سوء ظن وانتهاك نظر، قبح منظر وعفن رائحة، إذعان بلا رضا وتسلط بلا ثقة و كبر بلا كبرياء، تجمع بلا اجتماع وافتراق لا يصنع فارقا. اعتياد على القذارة والدناءة والإساءة، أصوات نافرة ومتنافرة وخرائب متناثرة وسافرة، كلام بلا تواصل وسعي بلا وصول، أكوام بلا تراكم وأعداد بلا نظام، زحام بلا حشود وأعداء لا يعرفون بعضهم إلا ساعة مواجهة تبدأ بلا داع وتنتهي بلا معنى

It is noteworthy that he always switches to AM in the comments section. In some cases he opts for blog titles in vernacular even when the post is written in FU. Vernacular might have a more appealing affect, reader to reader, as it recalls the language of advertisements, songs and movies.

It is interesting that Amr Ezzat never uses vulgar or vernacular expressions in his writing, aside from a post addressed to Ahmed Naji, written after the 25 January uprising:

> In this message I am trying with major difficulty to get closer to your style, especially because I never use expressions like 'sons of bitches'. Still what I feel, Naji, and I thank you for giving me the opportunity to talk about that, is that the revolution and all that happened was nothing to me but an expression of our contempt towards the sons of bitches.
>
> أنا هنا في هذه الرسالة أحاول بقدر من المراوغة الاقتراب من أسلوبك، خاصة إنني عادة لا أستخدم عبارات من نوع: ولاد الوسخة.
> ولكن ما أشعر به حقا يا ناجي، وأشكرك على إتاحة الفرصة هنا لي لأقول ذلك، أن الثورة وكل ذلك الذي حدث لم يكن – بالنسبة لي – إلا تعبيرا عن احتقارنا لولاد الوسخة.

Here it is evident that the use of vulgar expressions assumes a political, subversive value. For Amr, the dissent against political authorities starts from the liberation of the tongue, and a reformulation, a reinvention, of the major language.

It is difficult to determine how and why the bloggers choose a certain style in their blogs. For the majority of the bloggers interviewed, the choice of the style is entirely spontaneous and depends on the subject. For Ghada Abdel Aal, for example, it is an artistic choice, as it attributes more credibility to the narration.[33] For Bilal Husni, too, his pieces on quotidian issues require the use of a daily language. Mahmud ᶜIzzat writes poetry in AM, as an act of protest against a literary establishment that devalues poetry written in AM as folklore, but switches between AM and FU for prose texts (quoted in al-Abd 2011: 257). One would think that the colloquial style would be more appropriate to entries about private issues. Indeed, ᶜAmr Mustafa says that he uses AM for personal, light notes or to report dialogues with others, while using FU for political or public issues (quoted in al-Abd 2011: 254). Additionally, the novelist Muhammad Aladdin, when he started to blog, initially decided to write in AM in order to show '*ᶜAlaᵓ al-insān*' ('the human side of ᶜAla°") but then gradually switched to FU to write about more general issues.[34] Ghada Mahmud prefers simple FU that is very close to AM, inserting words and expressions in AM to add flavour to the text, and in some cases she writes posts entirely in AM, as she feels it is the only way to convey her feelings (quoted in al-Abd 2011: 259). Conversely, Nirmin Nizar uses FU to write about her private feelings, as she feels more confident with it, while she mixes FU with her native dialect (Alexandrian Arabic) to write about things foreign and internal Egyptian affairs (quoted in al-Abd 2011: 255).

The style aims to emphasise specific traits of the blogger's personality. The use of FU with specific stylistic devices (dialogue, metaphor, alliteration) attributes literariness and fictionality to the text, and contributes to the representation of the author as a writer and intellectual. The use of the vernacular sets the tone for intimacy, authenticity, honesty, liberal thought, accessibility, pragmatism, closeness to ordinary people, and a leftist and anti-traditional attitude; often it also has a humorous effect. The use of youth language is also a sign of playfulness, creativity and originality; it softens the intellectual/elitist image of the blogger, and emphasises their image as young and 'cool'. Additionally, the use of English is quite significant. In Egyptian society English is a sign of being well-off, educated and belonging to a globalised upper middle class. Thus, the use of English attributes more prestige to the writer.

Therefore, it seems that bloggers opt for one style or another to privilege or emphasise certain aspects of their personality or because they think it is more apt for delivering their message, irrespective of existing language rules.

Another aspect worthy of attention is the fact that in blogs, orthographical and grammatical errors are rather common. According to Deleuze and Guattari, this is another common trait of minor literature that 'exposes the inner tensions of a language' (1983: 22). In some cases, bloggers openly reflect about the presence of these mistakes in their texts. For example, in her blog *Hakadha Ana* (*This is me*) Radwa Usama writes that her husband Amr tells her to avoid linguistic mistakes.

> I write now with extreme difficulty ... This is the fourth time that I write and then I delete all I wrote with a simple push on the button at the top far right of the page, so all that I wrote is deleted ... Now I want to write ... I

> don't have in mind a precise subject … writing anything just sitting down and writing in a way free from everything … I remember Amr's words: 'You make horrifying grammar mistakes … You have to take care and revise what you write.' I say to myself: language mistakes don't matter … I want to write freely. I know that now he will say to me in his kind and tolerant tone: 'You are free (Do what you want).'

> اكتب الان بصعوبة شديدة ..هذه هى المرة الرابعة التى اكتب فيها وامحو كل ما كتبته بضغطة واحدة على تلك العلامة فى اقصى يمين الصفحة فيمحى كل ما اكتبه ..الان انا اريد ان اكتب ..ليس فى ذهنى موضوع معين ..الكتابة فى اى شيء مجرد الجلوس والكتابة بشكل متحرر من كل شيء ..اتذكر كلمات عمرو " عندك اخطاء نحو فظيعة ..لازم تاخدى بالك وتراجعى وانت بتكتبى " اقول لنفسى مش مهم اخطاء اللغة ..عايزة اكتب براحتى ..اعرف انه الان سيقول لى بلهجة طيبة ومتسامحة " انت حرة "

In this passage, Amr might stand for any masculine authority attempting to regulate and correct her tongue, while she wants to break free from these constraints. According to Serge Tisseron (quoted in Serfaty 2004: 68), the keyboard makes it easier for the author to disregard the rules of proper spelling because it frees them from the rigours of our early training. When writing with a pen on paper we are bound by the rules we were taught as children, rules which we have internalised. The keyboard, on the other hand, is often a self-taught skill and is free from any painful association with red ink, low grades or punishment. Writing with the help of a keyboard may thus relieve the writer from the fear of the school teacher. Additional reasons why bloggers rarely correct their spelling mistakes might be because they are attempting to preserve the appearance of spontaneous speech and immediacy, or simply because they do not know the correct spelling.

When it comes to print publication, different choices have been made concerning these language irregularities. For example, when writing about his experience as an editor for *Wasla* (Connection), a print journal entirely derived from blogs, Ahmed Naji states that 'published material does not undergo any correction of spelling, syntactical or grammar mistakes, because this random language of some blog posts is an essential element of the spontaneous spirit of blogging'.[35]

In an article published in the journal *Fusul*, the scholar Ahmad ᶜAbd al-ᶜAzim (Aḥmad ᶜAbd al-ᶜAẓīm) analyses the blog post 'Latkha Bayda'' ('White Blot') from the blog *Shakhabit*, and underlines that he has chosen this post despite the fact that it contains linguistic mistakes (2011: 175). Nonetheless, one section of his article is dedicated to a list of all the grammatical mistakes found in the blog (*hamzah* orthography, pronouns referring to masculine/feminine nouns, paragraph delineation, punctuation). Still, he decides to leave them as they are because they are part of the blogging experience and they do no harm to the creativity and artistic effect of the narration. He ascribes the mistakes to the spontaneity (*'afawiyya*) of blog writing; according to ᶜAbd al-ᶜAzim, they express the bloggers' desire to express themselves, to get in contact with others (2011: 176). In an interview given to *Fusul*, Nirmin Nizar (author of the book-blog *Iskandariyya/Bayrut*) says that when she was writing her blog, she did not notice the presence of mistakes, nor did her readers draw her attention to it. However, when her book was printed by Shuruq publishing house, without revision, as a choice of the editor Muhammad Salmawi (Muḥammad Salmāwī), they became clear to her eyes. 'If I would have known that my blog would be turned into a book, I would have written in FU and without language mistakes' (quoted in al-Abd 2011: 255). This shows that according to her, language mistakes are acceptable as long as they are part of the blog, but they cannot be left uncorrected when the blog is published in print.

Becoming Minor?

Overall, blogs have facilitated the birth of a new written language that mixes FU and AM and includes expressions borrowed from English and from youth language, as well as slang. This language expresses the freedom afforded by the medium and has become the voice of a generation that does not recognise themselves in the language of mainstream media and discourse.

Madiha Doss (2004: 67) suggests interpreting this language in terms of an attitudinal change. On their own blogs, Egyptians are free to write as they want, using the language that seems most suitable to them, to convey their feelings and message. Since the blog is self-published, it is not necessary to follow grammatical, syntactical and orthographical rules; it is more important that the message 'gets through' and reaches the readers' hearts. According to the blogger ᶜAmr Mustafa (ᶜAmr Muṣṭafā), this language is an expression of the freedom of blogging, because 'every blogger has his own rule, and this is one of the benefits of blogging that cannot be found in any other writing medium' (quoted in al-Abd 2011: 259). The fact that typographical errors and 'wrong' grammar often remain uncorrected, even in print editions such as the journal *Wasla*, does not seem to derive from forgetfulness; rather, it shows that breaking established rules and a disobedience vis-à-vis linguistic normativity are the results of a deliberate choice rooted in an anti-authoritarian attitude.

The psychologist Shihatah Zayyad argues that the growing use of *ᶜāmmiyya*

> is a willed and conscious denial (*rafḍ*) from the younger generation of what is happening around them in society, and which they in the present situation have no possibility to change … the individual's act of protest against oppression, trying by all means to escape his uneasiness and to create a code of mutual understanding among his peers who, just like him, suffer from unemployment and the economic situation of the country. (Quoted in Mejdell 2008: 116)

Nonetheless, the examples provided in this study show that the linguistic convention is not totally rejected. Several bloggers imitate the stylistic trend prevailing in print literature, opting to present the narrative in FU and dialogue in vernacular. Others show that while the texts are published online, language does not have to follow conventions, but when they are published in print, they should be revised to fit the standard. This shows that bloggers are aware that they need to create a certain literariness and formality in their style in order to acquire a certain position within the cultural field. The other option is to remain minor and keep blogging an independent, revolutionary literary movement.

Notes

1 In this sense blogs would fit in the category that Jacquemond defines as 'para-literature' as opposed to 'legitimate literature'; this includes satirical literature but also more commercial fiction such as romantic, erotic and detective novels (Jacquemond 2008: 154).

2 Muhammad Abd al-Muttalib (Muḥammad ᶜAbd al-Muṭṭalib), for example, argued that the success of the Dar al-Shuruq blogs derived from the popularity of the medium, because authors can publish their writings and reach out to their readers immediately, without undergoing any critical evaluation. If they were to enter the print literature circle, they might 'falsify' the creative literary process (quoted in Ibadah 2008). The novelist Miral al-Tahawi (Mīrāl al-Ṭaḥāwī) declared that the success of the authors of blog-books derives from the fact that they write about topics that are familiar to the reader; moreover, their writing engages the readers directly, through the use of comments and simple literary language. She claimed that these publications respond to a need of the public for 'easy writing' and expressed her concern that this type of writing might become a surrogate for literary production. 'They don't add anything new to the Egyptian literary scene, as Ghada's book follows the trend of the satirical books written by Anis Mansur (Anīs Manṣūr) and Mustafa Mahmud (Muṣṭafà Maḥmūd)' (quoted in Ibadah 2008).

3 Pictures of the event can be found on Ahmad al-Sabbagh's blog http://ahmedelsabbagh.blogspot.com/2009/01/blog-post_23.html (last accessed 26 June 2017) while a translation of Ghada's words can be found on http://globalvoicesonline.org/2009/01/28/kleenex-literature-at-the-cairo-international-bookfair (last accessed 26 June 2017).

4 ببلاغتها الخاصة لقد شاركت بعض تلك المدونات أرقى الأعمال الأدبية في رحلة الكشف عن الذات ولكنها فارقتها

5 Deleuze and Guattari's (1983) central example of 'minor literature' is Kafka. Indeed, Kafka was a Jew who grew up in Prague, which at the time was part of the Austro-Hungarian Empire, and like most of the Jews at the time, he was speaking German. German was a 'language of the paper' or artifice, and so much more so for Jews who were a minority and excluded from it. At the same time, he felt distant from the Czech community. For him 'people are missing' and his literature sets out to summon those people.

6 Badawi (1973) identifies five language levels in contemporary Egypt and analyses each of them according to phonological, morphological and syntactic features.

7 In her book *Mixed Styles in Spoken Arabic in Egypt*, Mejdell (2006a) shows that a number of highly educated Egyptians use 'mixed styles of Arabic' during panel presentations at a public seminar (*nadwa*). See also Mejdell's (2011) entry on 'Luġa wusṭā', in *Encyclopedia of Arabic Language and Linguistics*.

8 The author Yusuf Idriss (Yūsuf Idrīs, 1927–91) has tended towards the insertion of vernacular lexical items in the FU narrative to give a local flavour to the

text. Naguib Mahfouz (1911–2006) instead has striven against the use of any colloquial elements, even in the dialogues, tending towards a 'conversational FU'. The novelist and play-writer Tawfiq al-Hakim (Tawfīq al-Ḥakīm) has even invented a *lugha thālitha* (third language), a purely artificial variety that he employed in two of his plays in the 1950s and 1960s to 'bridge the gap' between the written and the spoken text, as explained by him in the postscript, '*lughat al-masraḥiyya*' for the play *al-Warta* (1966). However, this experiment did not prove successful (Somekh 1991).

9 For example, Luwis Awad's (Luwīs ᶜAwaḍ) memoir *Mudhakkirat Talib Baᶜtha* (*Memoirs of a Student Overseas*) written in the early 1940s or the novel *Laban il-Asfur* (lit. *The Milk of the He-Sparrow*) by Yusuf al-Qaᶜid (1994). On this novel, see Liesbeth Zack (2001), 'The Use of Colloquial Arabic in Prose Literature: *Laban ilᶜasfūr* by Yusuf al-Qaᶜid'. For an overview of dialectal literature, see Humphrey Davies's (2011) entry on the subject in the *Encyclopedia of Arabic Language and Linguistics*.

10 Soha Abboud-Haggar illustrates some innovations in Egyptian literature, however only in dialogue. In her study of the novel *Banat ar-Riyad* (*The Girls of Riyadh*, 2005) by Rajaa Alsanea, she claims that while the narration remains in FU, the Saudi writer has enriched her novel through other peculiarities of Arabic-speaking societies, bilingual code-switching and the multidialectal reality of the Arabic language (2010: 210). Similarly, Alaa al Aswany opts for a practical application of the diglossic code-switching in the dialogue of his novel, *ᶜImarat Yaᶜqubiyan* (*Yacoubian Building*, 2002).

11 Aside from literature, Doss (2004) finds similar experimentation with vernacular and English in other private, independent media, such as advertisements and youth magazines (e.g. *Party*).

12 The novel *An Takun ᶜAbbas al-ᶜAbd* (*Being Abbas el Abd*) by the Egyptian author Ahmad Alaidy is read by Tarek el-Ariss (2010) and Samia Mehrez (2008) as the manifesto of a generation of urban, street-wise and tech-savvy youth that aims at subverting the nation with all its icons and therefore opens up new literary imagining and linguistic possibilities. For an overview of the ruptures introduced by the 1990s generation of writers in Egypt, see also Hafez (2011), 'The Aesthetics of the Closed Horizons'.

13 In correct *fuṣḥā* it should be '*muthaqqafūhā al-mashhūrūn*' or '*muthaqqafīhā al-mashhūrīn*'.

14 El-Sadda points out that these words indicate 'a conscious attempt to regain and revise the meaning of a nation, or a national project, by foregrounding

the unheard and unmediated voices, which are historically sidelined by state discourses and official points of view' (2010: 315).

15 In her reading of the blog *Kubri Imbaba* (*Imbaba Bridge*) written by Mahmud ᶜIzzat, Sahar El-Mougy also describes the Egyptian blogger community as 'a community of expatriates in their own country' (2011: 159). This expression is taken from the slogan of an Egyptian Internet radio station called 'Radio Teet', proclaiming itself as '*ṣawt al-jālīyya al-maṣriyya fī miṣr*' ('the voice of Egyptian expats in Egypt').

16 According to an Amnesty International report issued in 2010, this law had become a norm rather than an exceptional measure, http://www.amnesty.org/en/region/egypt/report-2010 (last accessed 20 August 2017).

17 This is evidenced by the words expressed by the blogger 'Malekx': 'Really, what does the word "homeland" (*waṭan*) mean? What does "Love for Egypt" (*hobb maṣr*) mean? And, indeed, who is Mrs. Egypt (*al-sitt maṣr*)? What does it mean that we should not ask what Egypt has given to us? Has she given me anything? Well, explain to me, what is Egypt? And which Egypt of them? Who, how, why? What does the word "homeland" (*waṭan*) and the word "belonging" (*intimāᶜ*) mean? I don't belong to the homeland, I don't know what "Egypt" means, it is not important for me to know and I don't want to know. I know people and I love them.' My translation, from MalekX, 'Yaᶜni eih Kilimit Watan' ('What does homeland mean'), Malcolm X blog, 5 April 2006, http:malek-x.net/node258 (link no longer available).

18 Interviews Haytham Yahya, December 2011; Ahmad Abdalla, December 2011. In the interviews, they use the English expression 'middle class'.

19 This type of school is a hybrid public-private school, which teaches certain subjects in English and others in Arabic. The choice of private over public education has become a common aspiration in middle-class circles, as the governmental educational system had undergone a significant decline in quality (de Koning 2009: 50).

20 Pun on *mubārak* as 'blessed era' (in a humorous sense) and President Mubarak's era (1981–2011).

21 Bloggers do not use this term. They describe their practice as *mazg* and *khalīṭ* (mixing) of *fuṣḥā* and *ᶜāmmiyya*.

22 The term '*muthaqqaf*', which literally indicates 'somebody cultured, educated' has been used in Arabic as an equivalent of the English noun 'intellectual' since the 1940s. However, its meaning currently oscillates between 'intellectual',

'educated' and 'cultured'. I analyse this conceptual issue in my article 'Critics, Moralists and Intellectuals: The Transformation of the (*udabā*[c]) in the Arab *nahḍah*: A Historical-Conceptual Approach' (Pepe 2019).

23 For more on youth language, see Rizk (2007), 'The Language of Cairo's Young University Students'.

24 The blogger even explains: '*musattab jāya min sītab*' (the word *musattab* is formed from 'set up'). The English verb 'set up' is used and adapted to Arabic morphology and formulated by keeping the original word and adding the appropriate prefixes and/or suffixes that make it sound like Arabic. More of these examples can be found in Daoudi (2011), 'Globalization, Computer-Mediated Technology and the Rise of E-Arabic'.

25 I have inserted them in Arabic to show the orthography used by the blogger.

26 The expression '*al-tinnīn wa al-sinīn*', literally meaning 'of the dragon and of the years', is drawn from Ahmed Mekky's movie *H Dabbour* (2005).

27 The word is used in Egyptian dialect to say 'Go to hell', but also in the sense of 'I don't care' (Badawi and Hinds 1986: 539).

28 This way of transliterating Arabic using Latin letters and numbers was introduced by Arabic-speaking Internet users who did not have an Arabic keyboard, and it is still very often used on social networks and mobile phones. It has been defined by Palfreyman and al-Khalil (2007) and Bjørnsson (2010) as 'Romanized Latin Arabic' or 'ASCII-ized Arabic'. The French scholar Gonzalez-Quijano calls it 'Arabizi' (2012). Egyptian bloggers define it 'Franco-Arabe'. Generally, it seems that bloggers dislike this kind of writing in the main entries of their blogs. Nael Eltoukhy ironically criticises it in his entry 'ba7bk' ('I love you'), 13 February 2009, http://naelaltoukhy.blogspot.no/2009/02/ba7bk.html (last accessed 20 August 2017). In his article in the journal *al-Fusul*, Sharif Darwish (2011: 93) reports that the blogger Tariq Amira started the campaign '*Lughati huwiyyati*' ('My language is my identity') inviting bloggers to use simple FU and avoid using 'Franco-arabe'. Many bloggers joined this campaign and put that banner on their blogs. Additionally, Rasha Abdullah reports the presence of a Facebook group called 'Those who are fed up to see Arabic written with a Western Alphabet' and aims at convincing users to use proper English when writing on a global forum such as Facebook (2008: 131).

29 That is, *manāṭiq miṣriyya sha*[c]*biyya* 'popular Egyptian neighbourhoods'.

30 That is, *khitān* '(here, female) circumcision'.

31 Interview, February 2012.

32 This is probably a misspelling of *ḍayyiqa*.

33 Interview, June 2010.

34 Interview, April 2012.

35 Interview, May 2011.

4

When Writers Activate Readers

The Autofictional Blog: An Interactive Adab (*Adab Tafā*[c]*Ulī*)

Autofiction is a hybrid genre that stands at the intersection of autobiography and fiction. This hybridity poses a particular challenge to the readers. The relationship between authors and readers operating in autofiction is such that, in order to obtain an understanding of the written self, readers must participate with a more creative and active way of reading. Doubrovsky's vision of the reader's role contrasts with the passive position that the reader of autobiography usually occupies. According to Chloé Delaume, the traditional autobiographical pact involves the author's sincerity and the audience's trust. The autobiographer is the definitive authority on the subject of himself, to whom the reader should defer and take as a source of inspiration. The corollary of the author's authority may be the reader's passivity: if the author provides a definitive account, the reader's function is not to question anything, but rather to assent to the autobiographer's authority and passively consume the account of the self that is offered.

Autofictional authors tend to produce narratives that obstruct this kind of passive reading. Obstacles placed in the path of this kind of reading include refusing narrative integrity by adopting several narrative strategies, such as alternating between first- and third-person narration; inserting a self-conscious narrator; indicating on the cover that the text is a novel; and denying a linear progression of the narrative by disrupting chronological narration or by organising it anachronistically. As a result, the reader has to abandon the idea that textual self-representation allows them to gain knowledge of the author, since self-writing does not guarantee any truth. Just as the writer's imagination is freed from the constraint to refer to a genuinely existing self, the reader is free to construct whatever fantasies or imagination of the self they choose.[1] Egyptian bloggers share with Doubrovsky and other autofictional authors the attention towards the active role of the readers. Just as Doubrovsky was driven to 'invent' an original form of writing because of his dissatisfaction with 'traditional' autobiography, so also some bloggers turned to blogging to change the traditional notion of literature as *adab* (useful, entertaining, and written in a high variety of language) and to innovate the practice of writing the self in Arabic literature.

This point is made explicit in a post entitled 'Mulahazat Hawla al-Adab' ('Notes about Literature', 2 November 2005) published on Ahmed Naji's blog *Wassi*^{c} *Khayalak –* ^{c}*ish ka*$^{\circ}$*annak tal*^{c}*ab* (*Widen Your Imagination – Live As if You Were Playing*), in November 2005:

> We have to produce a new opium-free *adab* … an *adab* that does not give rest to the reader but rather arouses anxiety, and that cracks the peace of his spirit and wounds his feelings.
>
> يجب أن نخلق أدب جديد خالى من الأفيون... أدب لا يقدم الراحة للقارئ بل يقدم له القلق و يشرخ له سلامه الروحى و يجرحه في مشاعره

Naji is revolting against a classic understanding of *adab* (literature) as 'education through entertainment' that dates back to the Classical period, and that has informed the formation of the Arabic modern literary imaginary.[2] Since the Nahda, this idea of *adab* has resulted in many authors adopting literature as an educational form of art, and not as a product of imagination. Samah Selim (2004) and Hoda el-Sadda (2012) have shown how nationalistic modern writers adopted the realistic novel to forge the idea of a nation and national identity. Later, the idea of *adab* as instruction through entertainment resulted in *adab* taking the form of committed literature (*adab multazim*). According to Jacquemond, this idea of *adab* continues to define what legitimate literature is and what it is not (2008: 10), as good literature is supposed to be both useful and entertaining. This approach to *adab* is reflected in the development of the autobiographical genre, a genre that was assimilated into the corpus of *adab* during the Nahda. Indeed, conventional autobiographies written in the first half of the twentieth century were to offer a retrospective literary account of the author's life describing – often in an educational manner – the intellectual path of the autobiographer (Anishchenkova 2014: 26) that could serve as an example for the readers.

As shown by the passage above, Naji and his peers want to transform this notion of *adab* and revolt because they think that its aesthetics and ideology resulted in a complete exclusion of the reader. The metaphor of the opium shows that they accuse their literary fathers of having used *adab* as a means of sedating the readers and making them accept a political and ideological project that was doomed to collapse (as shown six years later by the popular uprising that culminated in the fall of Mubarak's regime). For bloggers, *adab* should instead make itself useful by delivering a highly irritating, discomforting, rebellious message that the readers have to interpret by themselves and can contribute to shaping.[3]

The adoption of the digital medium is crucial in this respect. In his article 'A Four-Sided Model for Reading Hypertext Fiction', Hans K. Rustad (2009) claims that electronic literature might produce 'frustration and vertigo in the readers' and demands a more active engagement.[4] He writes:

> It seems fair to say that these texts set up the reader to experience frustration and subversion. They seem to pursue vertigo because they consist of an attempt to momentarily destroy the stability of perception and inflict a kind of voluptuous panic on an otherwise lucid reader.[5]

The autofictional pact, on which the blog is based, becomes a real means of involving the reader actively, both in the interpretation and composition of the text. The identity of the author-narrator-main-character might lead readers to attribute referentiality to the literary work. However, the use of certain narrative strategies complicates the distinction between factual and fictional information and provokes the readers' hesitancy regarding the ontological status of the narrative. Consequently, it engages them in a more active reading.

This chapter looks at the ways in which the blog transforms *adab* and in particular the autobiographical genre in Arabic literature. Drawing on theories of autofiction, digital literature and Arabic print literature, I will explore the innovative features of autofictional blogs resulting from the adoption of Internet technology. These are (1) interactivity, (2) the blurring of the author/main character, (3) the multimedia, open nature of the blog texts, and (4) their stylistic features. I argue that the combination of these elements transforms the practice of writing the self into an interactive game to be played among authors and readers, away from the gatekeepers of the literary institutions. By depicting modes of interaction between readers and writers in the Egyptian blogosphere, I will show how the autofictional blog requires the readers to be active participants in the interpretation of the text by discovering the blurred identity of the author/main character; to find their way in the open, multimedia text; and to contribute actively to the plot and style of the narrative.

In a blog, the author establishes their authority on the text to some extent. Authorship is identified with a real name or pseudonym that appears at the end of each entry and on the blog's profile page. Individual ownership could be established through the customisation of various elements of the journal's appearance, through the use of colours, fonts, headers and personal icons. Blog authors are also able to exercise direct control over access to their territory by others. The majority of interactions takes place on the personal territory of one individual and are initiated, centred around and regulated by that fact. Bloggers have the ability to restrict readership of their entries, to regulate the posting of comments, either by screening submissions prior to their display or by deleting unwanted comments subsequent to their appearance (Amir-Ebrahim 2008). The blogger is the only 'manager of the site' who decides what content can be displayed.

However, the most innovative aspect of Internet diaries and weblogs is that they not only make intimate writings potentially accessible to a multitude of readers, but that they also afford the reader the opportunity to respond directly to the text. The narrative created through the blog is essentially interactive and, as such, turns the literary text into a collaborative effort (Serfaty 2004: 465). Through its continuous updating over time, the weblog becomes a text that is constantly transformed through the input of both readers and writers (Himmer 2004).

In the following, I will show Egyptian bloggers' literary strategies of reader-activation, while in the next paragraph I will show that one of the tasks attributed to the reader consists of discovering the blurred identity that hides behind the events narrated.

The Blurred Identity of the Author/Main Character

In an autofictional blog, the narration is made in first person and it deals mainly with the main character's inner life. The author is driven by a 'quest for truth' (Cusset 2012) that consists of speaking out, revealing their innermost emotions and feelings. These in fact are considered to be the essential traits of one's 'true' subjectivity. Autofictional bloggers often write about feelings of alienation, love, fear and desire for freedom. Bloggers often address 'hot' issues in society such as sexual harassment, police brutality, homosexuality and religion, by describing how these issues affect their emotions and bodies (as will be further elaborated in Chapter 5).

However, usually in a work of fiction the 'I' of the narrator corresponds to an imagined character. In the case of autobiography, it corresponds to the author of the narrative. Autofiction, instead, 'has logic of its own, and uses autobiographical experience consciously, explicitly and sometimes deceptively' (Alberca 1996: 11). On the blog, the 'I' corresponds to a character that exists in real life, interacts with the readers in the comment section, and yet fictionalises his/her identity in several ways.

Pseudonyms

One way of fictionalising one's identity on the blog, for example, consists of adopting a pseudonym. In Chapter 2, we have seen how, for most of the bloggers analysed in this study, using a nickname was a means of playing with the medium, of trying out a new personality while accessing a different social setting, and not really a means of keeping personal security, as it is often believed.

According to Genette, 'the use of pseudonyms unites a taste for masks and mirrors, for indirect exhibitionism, and for controlled histrionics with delight in invention, in borrowing, in verbal transformation, in onomastic fetishism' (1997: 54). The media scholar Clay Calvert, in his famous study *Voyeur Nation*, argues that, on the Internet or on TV, the corollary of exhibitionism is voyeurism, that he defines as 'the consumption of revealing images of and information about others' apparently revealed and unguarded lives, often simply for purposes of entertainment' (2009: 2). In fact, we can see that when the entries are signed with a pseudonym, readers tend to read more actively to discover who the person hiding behind the false name is and then eventually tell it to others. In order to do so, they might navigate the blog looking for further markers of the author's identity or investigate in real life. This is evidenced by the words written by the blogger Nirmin Nizar:

> I opened this blog as a space for chatting without restrictions or fear. I wanted to hide behind a different name; although I knew that many people who know me in real life could easily guess it was me. But my dear friend decided to remove the curtain and reveal my identity to the world. ... This is not a farewell, not an excuse for leaving; it's just another nonsense talk. (*Iskandariyya/Bayrut* (*Alexandria/Beirut*), 2008: 64–5).
>
> فتحت هذه المساحة لتكون فسحة للفضفضة بدون تحفظات أو مخاوف. أردت أن اختفي خلف اسم آخر حتى لو كنت أعرف أن الكثير ممن يعرفوني في الحياة الحقيقية يستطيعون بسهولة استنتاج أن هذه هي أنا .و لكن اصدقائي الأعزاء قرروا أن ينزعوا الستار ويكشفوا هويتي للعالم. ... هذه ليست رسالة وداع ولا حتى إستئذان في إجازة. انها مجرد فضفضة أخرى.

Self-conscious Narrator

Another device often used to blur the line between the author and main character in the narrative comprises the fact that the author often acts as a self-conscious narrator. It means that while telling an intimate, confessional account, the authorial voice intrudes into the narrative and questions its authenticity, breaking the verisimilitude of the work.

For example, from the first entry of *al-Kanaba al-Hamra*, Bilal Husni alerts the reader that the blog may contain fictional elements. In the early entries of his blog, after introducing the house and his flatmate, Bilal writes, 'I forgot to mention that I own a number one red sofa and supposedly, in a fabricated way, I imagine it was inherited from my mom' (9 January 2007). In more than one entry he highlights his 'amazing ability of making up, creating details' (12 January 2007). In our interview, Bilal acknowledged that his tendency to manipulate life and reality is so ingrained that he often cannot distinguish between what is true and what is invented. Indeed, the word that he uses for 'fiction' is '*ifti*ᶜ*āl*', that is, 'pretence, fabrication'.

Nael Eltoukhy, instead, presents his blog as 'a lie' (*kidhb*). Indeed, the first thing we notice on accessing the blog is the title, *Na*ʾ*il al-Tukhi* (his own name) in the header, next to a picture of Pinocchio watching his nose grow long. The lie, embodied by Pinocchio, is also supported by the first post published on the blog (May 2006), entitled 'Iwᶜa Tsaddaʾ' ('Beware of Believing'). When asked in the interview about the significance of the Pinocchio picture, Nael confirms: 'Writing is a lie (*kidhb*), and blogging even more so, as you have even more freedom, so you can fool (*tishtaghal* ᶜ*alā*)[6] people more.'[7] Here again, the fictional element is presented as an element of playfulness, as also theorised by Ahmed Naji in his blog (see Chapter 2).

In some cases, the fictional cover might be used as a means of protecting the blogger's social respectability while revealing personal stories. In some entries, Al-Baraa Ashraf adopts a third-person narrator, inserting a central character called Mutawᶜi (Muṭāwᶜi). In the book adapted from his blog, Mutawᶜi's stories are introduced as such:

> Until recently, writing was a joint project between Mutawᶜi and me, and the project produced several pages, including this chapter, some of them are written by Mutawᶜi, some of them by me, and for technical problems, it became difficult to separate Mutawᶜi's production from mine, so I decided to publish the texts as they are, and the reader has the right to choose. Instructions for reading: Those who know Mutawᶜi in person are prevented from reading.
>
> حتى وقت قريب، كانت الكتابة مشروعا مشتركا بيني وبين مطاوع، وقد أنتج المشروع عدة أوراق، يتضمنها هذا الفصل، بعضها كتبه مطاوع، بعضها كتبته أنا، و لمشاكل تقنية، أصبح من الصعب التفرقة بين ما أنتجه مطاوع وبين إنتاجي، وقد رأيت أن أنشر النصوص كما هي، و للقارئ حق الاختيار.
> إرشادات القراءة: تمنع قراءة هذا الفصل للذين يعرفون مطاوع معرفة شخصية.
> (Ashraf 2011: 111).

Thus, Mutawᶜi is clearly presented to his readers as his own persona or his fictional alter ego.

Similarly, Mahmud Hassan, author of the blog *Shakhabit* (*Scribbles*), inserts a disclaimer for the readers before or at the end of several posts:

> (Note for those who have bad intentions)
> There is no personal relationship between this post and the author of this blog, nor is there a relationship, be it far or close, with his personal life.
> My greetings.[8] ('Mirsal', 6 December 2008)

The technique of adopting a self-conscious narrator can be often found in autofictional novels. E. H. Jones believes this strategy may have the reverse effect of enhancing the readers' belief (2009: 180). It may increase the readers' confusion regarding the 'truthfulness' of the blog. In fact, I will show later how this leads some readers to inquire about the factual nature of the account by asking the writers directly.

Other readers enjoy it as a fictional story and point out that the story addresses their feelings and fosters identification. The recurrence to the self-conscious narrator might be a means of protecting one's social respectability while revealing aspects of the self. But more significantly, it might signal that by presenting it as fiction, by temporarily removing themselves from the story, the authors aim at generalising and objectifying their feelings: their story becomes the story with which any young Egyptian may identify, and this is also one of the tasks generally attributed to literature and *adab*.

*Hoaxes (*Ishtighālāt*)*

Bloggers also tease the readers in a game that they call '*ishtighāla*', an expression in Egyptian vernacular that could be translated as 'hoax'. It consists of deliberately fabricating fictional stories and presenting them as truth by using an intimate, confessional tone of narration, with a call for readers' support.[9]

An example of this 'game' can be found in the blog post written by Naji entitled 'Li-Kulli Awwal Bidaya, li-Kulli Akhir Nihaya' ('In Every First There is a Beginning, in Every Last There is an End', 6 August 2005). On this day the narrator announces to his audience that on waking up one morning he realised that he had lost his sight. Dictating to his sister, he announces the news to his readers and asks them whether they could advise him where to get a keyboard with Braille fonts.

Several readers seem deceived by the nature of the medium and assume that what Naji writes is true.[10] They inquire how this could have happened and wish him a good recovery. Others seem to understand the game and participate in it following its rules: 'Look at the Kafka man, he woke up and found himself a cockroach (sic)! At least you still have your family; the other one was left to rot away!'[11] After several comments, the blogger reveals that this post is an 'unrestrained excess of imagination, an extravagant fantasy' (*shaṭḥ khayāl*). In response, a reader writes: 'Put a note saying that this is fiction, do you think we have a machine to distinguish fiction from reality?'[12] Another reader writes: 'You made me feel stupid, as usual!'[13] Thus, in this post the blogger achieves his goal of using the Internet medium to write a literary text that provokes the readers' discomfort. The literary text turns into an interactive game, a joke almost, played between readers and writers.

Once the readers realise that the story is fictional, they understand that the story is meant to expresses feelings of helplessness and vulnerability. By staging himself as blind, the character expresses his incapacity to see and understand reality. In addition, writing about blindness is also a means of writing about the act of writing itself. By pretending to be blind and therefore attributing the blame for these mistakes to his sister, he mocks the strict adherence to language rules on which Arab literati usually insist.

An additional example of *ishtighāla* can be found in the blog post written by Nael Eltoukhy on 28 December 2007, entitled 'Li-Hadhihi al-Asbab Tallaqtu Layla' ('For These Reasons I Divorced Layla'). In this post Nael opens up his private life to an eager audience, and reveals to them the reasons that led him to divorce from his wife, Layla (Laylā). From the outset, the narrator approaches the readers with an intimate and confidential tone: 'Dear friends', 'let's discuss again our moments of joy and sorrow', 'since I decided to share my life with you', 'I believe that being sincere (*ṣarīḥ*) with you is the only way to face the situation', and he concludes this personal account with '*al-mukhliṣ likū dāʾiman, Nāʾil*' ('Always sincerely yours, Nael'). The account is rendered more realistic by the fact that Nael had already started the narration of this story in the form of Facebook status updates, and this post is meant as a clarification of the entire story of the end of his marriage to Layla. Also, Nael reminds the readers that he had dedicated the title of his novel *Layla Antun*, published in 2005, to his wife. Nael confesses to his readers that the reason for their eventual break-up was an argument, conducted in front of their daughter Yara (Yārā), about moving a sofa from the sitting room into Nael's studio. This argument descended into domestic violence, and after being beaten, Layla moved temporarily to her father's house. Later she returned, but refused to honour her marital obligations. While exaggerating his wife's reaction, the narrator minimises his own actions: 'maybe I struck her, I don't remember exactly' ('*rubbamā akūn maddadtu īdī ᶜalayha, lā adhkuru bil-ẓabṭ*'), and indulges in very masculine assertions. He justifies his actions as a way of instructing his daughter:

> I granted her [Layla] the possibility of discussion, Yara has to learn that a man is man and a woman is a woman, that a man has to be obeyed, her father is what made this house and her birth possible …
> masculinity is the strength of the word, its jewel, my masculinity means my penis, the penis that granted the pleasure, the children and the pain at the same time. From this lesson, I learnt that the function of woman is only to accomplish sexual desires and until now I can't find any other function.[14]

From close reading of the text, we can see that this post is an ironically sarcastic account about masculinity in Egyptian society. The irony and sarcasm are rendered through the hyperbolic description of Layla's reaction and the understatement or minimisation of the narrator's action. The irony also deals with the writing about his personal life and the voyeurism of the readers. The author is playing on the fact that many readers will take this story at face value and attribute it to his personal life – and this is precisely what happens. By examining the readers' comments, we can see that the audience is divided between those who understand his sorrow and support his opinion, and those who think he is 'a psychopath' and suggest he should visit a doctor, and others again who read the post as part of an interactive narrative. The following comment shows the confusion of one of the readers regarding the verisimilitude of the story:

> Anonymous said …
> Either you are a psychologically sick person who needs urgent treatment
> 'Cause you are a danger to your daughter and society
> Nobody in his right mind would do that
> To write the name of his wife and the mother of his daughter like that
> Which manhood are you talking about?

Maybe you don't know [how to do it] and this is causing you a psychological complex that you are venting on your poor wife
The one I really feel sorry for in this issue is your daughter because she will grow up with a psychopathic father like you
Have mercy on the girl and her future and leave her to your wife to raise her
Otherwise your daughter will hate you and herself in the end.
Or you are a great narrator
And your narration this time achieved brilliant success!

Anonymous said …
انت حاجه من اتنين
اما انك شخصيه مريضه نفسيا ومحتاجه العلاج فورا
لان حالتك خطر علي بنتك والمجتمع
مفيش انسان بكامل قواه يعمل كده او
يكتب اسم زوجته وام بنته كده
رجوله ايه اللي بتتكلم عنها
تلاقيك مش عارف وده مسبب لك عقده نفسيه وبتطلعها علي المسكينه مراتك
اللي صعبان عليا في الموضوع بنتك لانها هتتربي مع اب معقد نفسيا زيك
ارحم البنت ومستقبلها وسيبها لامها تربيها
والا البنت هتكرهك وتكره نفسها في الاخر
اما انك فعلا روائي عظيم
وروايتك المره دي نجحت نجاح باهر

The narrative strategies described (pseudonyms, self-conscious narrator, hoaxes) so far show that the bloggers permeate their writing with their personal subjectivity but they blur their identity in order to involve the readers in an active game of interpretation. In addition, we must notice that blogs change the way literature/*adab* is written and read, because of their multimedial nature and un-linear, open-ended structure. Therefore, they demand the reader to choose his/her own way of reading and making sense of the text.

Multimedial Open Texts

In the autofictional blog, as in other forms of electronic literature, writers combine written texts with elements drawn from other media, such as visual and audio.

Often writers insert personal pictures in the narration. They help to assure not only the readers, but also the writers of the reality of their existence. It must be kept in mind, though, that these pictures could easily be fabricated. Apart from personal pictures, blog entries may also include drawings, pictures of contemporary art, and other sorts of pictures. Pictures are used to shed light on the concept of the text, or to set the mood for the story. For example, the blogger Mona Seif started to experiment with drawings as she started blogging, in order to make her blog more personal and original. As such, many of her blog posts combine text with very simple drawings.

Authors also combine texts with audio or video elements. Entries on the blog *ᶜArabiyyat al-Ful*, for example, always include a song. The author explains that the song is usually one that he was listening to while writing the associated post. It is meant to reproduce the writer's mood during the post's composition, and to put the readers in the same atmosphere.

The combination of these media transforms reading into a multi-sensorial experience. Also, it requires the reader to make an effort to interpret the text: he or she has to make sense of different semiotic resources. The meaning of the text stems from the combination of audio, video and visual elements (Serfaty 2004: 27). However, readers may also have a say in the visual aspect of the blog. In *The Red Sofa*, some commentators complain about the colour of the font chosen by Bilal and advise him to choose a different colour: 'Really, Prof. Sofa, your writing style is nice (*ẓarīf*) and strange, but if it is not a hassle, could you increase the font size and make the background (*al-bāg grāwnd*) lighter?' (3 July 2007).[15]

This hybridisation between different media prevents the construction of a unified linear account while creating new meaning and opening up new spaces for interpretation (Serfaty 2004: 29). The disruption of the linearity is also obtained via the juxtaposition of links into the narrative, which I will analyse in the next section.

Links

While print literary texts are usually enclosed between the covers of a book, online narratives are structured as a database, described by Poster as 'an engine for producing retrievable identities' (1995: 89). In this way, the database produces identities that can be dispersed across numerous sites, but pulled together through the particular filter or search function in operation at the time.

Even though there is a certain unity through the appearance of the bits of information together on a website, the narrative is expanded through links. For example, in the blogroll, we find a list of links to blogs or websites the authors read more frequently. The blogs that have been selected for this study are often interlinked to each other. This contributes to create a sense of community among bloggers. The list of links is an important part of the blogger's self-representation because it conveys a picture of the bloggers' cultural, aesthetic and social affinities, and thus their identity. Links also add to the reader's sense of the blog's 'authenticity' because the narrative is anchored in 'actual' real places and features people whom members of the audience may also recognise, making them feel part of the narrative (McNeill 2003: 33).

Links are also inserted into the main text and expand the narration outside the blog space. A common practice that I found in Egyptian blogs is to insert a link to another blogger's online diary, whenever he or she is mentioned in the narration. In this way, the author gives the reader the chance to gain a greater understanding of the characters through their blogs. Bloggers may also repost links leading to previous blog entries. I have found several examples of this in Amr Ezzat's and Mona Seif's blogs. In this way, bloggers reflect about the changing of their personality over time. They also provide the reader with a long-term vision and a sense of perspective (Serfaty 2004: 31).

This space distribution opens up for a random exploration and not for one specific way of reading, thus the reader has to find his way through the different paths to which hyperlinks lead. Himmer (2004) says that the definition of 'ergodic literature', coined by Aarseth in his famous book *Cybertexts: Perspectives on Ergodic Literature* (1997), may be well applied to blogs. Ergodic literature – Aarseth derives the term from the Greek words for 'work' and 'path' (*ergon* and *hodos*, respectively) – is a type of literature that requires significant, engaged effort on the part of the reader in the construction of the text.[16] In other words, the reader can open and begin reading the weblog at any point along the process of its production from the earliest post to the most current. A reader can use an internal search mechanism (common on many weblogs) to seek particular topics or terms, browse by category, month or day, all offering myriad paths through the narrative 'space' of the weblog, or to other weblogs, articles or general websites (Himmer 2004). In this sense, the reader's pleasure is equivalent to that of exploring a labyrinth, a game or an imaginary world in which he can get lost, discover secret paths, and play around.

Ongoing Narrations

The spatial distribution of the narrative runs parallel with its temporal distribution. A defining quality of a blog is its dynamic updating within a dated entry format. Blogs are not merely a way of writing the self, they are 'a continuous way of writing oneself' (Walker and Mortensen 2002: 258), they are 'published bit by bit; they are always in progress, always becoming' (ibid.: 267). Thus, the author/main character identity is also never fixed; rather, it is a dynamic identity, which changes over time.

This refusal of closure, this interruption, deferral and waiting produces the desire that makes readers return to the blog site and therefore brings it close to earlier narrative forms such as the picaresque and the epistolary novel, but also the soap opera (Fitzpatrick 2007: 174). In fact, the novel reader's or soap opera watcher's desire to reach the end may be compared to the blog reader's waiting for the upcoming blog entry. Sometimes the blogger also inserts cliffhangers to make the narration more compelling.[17] However, while novelistic forms and the soap opera do have ends, most diaries do not. In my research sample, some bloggers have stopped blogging, but without giving a definite end to the narrative. They have simply stopped writing. They might come back at any time, and the simple fact that the blog is still online gives the reader hope that they will.

Fitzpatrick argues that like any work of literature the blog has a plot. However, this plot is not pre-planned but it is constituted by the accumulation of the posts published regularly on the blog (2007: 168). Each post makes sense in itself, but combined together, the several entries compose a larger story.

We can see, for example, how the plot unfolds in Amr Ezzat's blog from the first blog post published in 2005 to 2011. In the first entry, he introduces himself as a twenty-five-year-old engineer who has a passion for writing and an interest in philosophy. He also informs us that he is in love with Radwa, the daughter of an established journalist and poet. Gradually we learn about Amr's political engagement with the *Kifaya* movement and the Engineer syndicate, and his acquaintance with other Egyptian bloggers. We follow his anxiety and excitement towards political developments in Egypt, the results of which see several of his friends imprisoned. We also follow the evolution of his love affair with Radwa, their search for a flat, their engagement, their wedding ceremony and the beginning of their life together. As already noticed by Walker, we follow the blogger's story on his blog, but we also come across his name elsewhere (2004: 9). Other bloggers, for example, recount Amr and Radwa's wedding ceremony on their blogs. The story splits, spreads, and continues across multiple sites. Later, we perceive Amr's gradual political disillusion, his gradual loss of hope in the country and the breakdown of his relationship with Radwa. Amr writes about his despair and his struggle to restart a new life as a single man. He leaves his job as an engineer and decides to follow his aspirations by working as a journalist in a leftist independent newspaper. Finally, we read about his participation in the 25 January uprising, his enthusiasm for the revolution, and his celebration of the new country. After 2011, new entries have been added and the plot continues to evolve.

However, in addition, on the blog the plot is not exclusively driven by the author. Readers can also contribute to the plot's development. This is evidenced in the blog *al-Kanaba al-Hamra*, in which the blogger tells the story of his daily life on the sofa that he has inherited from his mother, who had died shortly before. At the beginning the account is focused on the present: Bilal describes his present staying on the red sofa in a poor flat in Alexandria. Through the description of the sofa we are introduced to the characters who usually sit on it: his flatmate and best friend Bahz; the nosy doorman Uncle Saad; the Spanish flatmate converted to Islam; his girlfriend Amirah; Matthew, the Scottish flatmate; and of course, his mother, to whom the sofa originally belonged. Then, on 25 September 2007, Bilal announces that an anonymous reader has suggested in a comment that he should auction the sofa.

> In the name of God let's open the auction
> I am a real estate agent from Jeddah
> And I am serious
> And my words are right

I pay 5000 Egyptian pounds for the Red Sofa
And if the owner agrees tomorrow he will get the payment from an agent in Cairo that will pass by, pay and receive the item
Waiting for a confirmation if nobody wants to raise the price
Best

('al-Ayyam al-Akthar Ithara fi Hayat Amrika ᶜala al-Kanaba al-Hamra' ('The Most Exciting Days in America's Life on the Red Sofa'), 3 July 2007)

بسم الله نفتح المزاد
انا تاجر عقار من جدة
وأنا جاد[18]
وكلامي صحيح
انا بدفع في الكنبةالحمراء 5000 جنيه مصري
واذا وافق صاحبها بكره يكون الدفع والمشترى عن طريق وكيل اعمال بالقاهرة يمر يدفع ويستلم
بانتظار الرد بالقبول اذا ما احد زاد على المبلغ
والسلام

This comment leads to an unexpected change in his narration of events. It encourages him to go back to his past and recount to the readers the entire story of his past journey with the sofa, a journey that has taken him to his present flat. Once again, he points out the mixing of factual and fictional events in his narration.

This is the offer that someone sent in the comment section in one of my last entries
And no matter if it is serious or just a joke, he opened the auction
The auction of the sofa
Then these are the chapters that compose the life history of the sofa
Despite the authenticity of the events, in these following chapters the narration is not free from fabrication as implied in the chronicling of the life of a sofa, which in the end is merely a sofa.

('al-Mazad (1) al-Buqᶜa al-Baydaᵓ ᶜala al-Kanaba, Kaᵓinat Hayya' ('The Auction (1) The White Spot on the Sofa, Alive Creatures'), 2 October 2007)

ده العرض ال بعته حد على كومنت فى احد البوستات مؤخرا وال مهما كان جاد
او مجرد لعبه فهوه فتح المزاد
مزاد الكنبه
الاتى فصول قصه حياة كنبه
لا تخلو فصول السرد التاليه من الافتعال وتأرخة كنبه هى مجرد كنبه حتى برغم
مصداقيه الاحداث

The journey on the sofa has an itinerary that starts from death and goes towards a new life: it takes him from his mother's flat to one situated in the basement of an old building that resembles a tomb, where an old beggar had recently died; then to a flat where he spends his days tinkering on a bicycle; then onward to another flat which he shares with a lazy teenager; until finally he settles down with his peer Bahz. The disclosure of memories of his past runs parallel with a description of more intimate and embarrassing details about the present, including verbal depictions of the blogger's fat, nude body. This goes on for several months until Bilal starts confessing his gradual frustration with blogging, his need for separation from Bahz, and his desire to dispose of the sofa. Indeed, the result of this 'revelation' is a feeling of breakdown, both existential and professional, as 'this feeling of failure comes from inside' (31 December 2007). Bilal loses his desire for confession in an open space as he feels his complete disclosure on the blog has only opened him to a 'big social whipping', both in the blogosphere and in offline reality (as he blogs with his real name). Also, he feels that the blog has led him to a dead end where he rotates around the same fictional characters that he has created (13 August 2008). The end of the blog is foreshadowed but not properly announced, leaving the readers with the choice of creating their own conclusion, or waiting for the blogger to return and pick up the narrative.

Readers may also contribute by directing the author towards a certain style. Ghada Abdel Aal, for example, claimed in the interview I conducted with her that initially she did not write her blog with a humorous purpose in mind. However, the audience appreciated her sarcastic attitude and persuaded her to bring her humour to the fore.[19] Readers may also contribute by adding personal anecdotes, jokes, or by describing the feelings evoked by the text. They might insert hyperlinks and directions of their own into the original post (or an easily accessible addendum), again creating additional possibilities and paths through the labyrinth of the weblog.

Readers as Gatekeepers

An aspect related to the interactivity of blogs is the fact that, in the absence of gatekeepers who regulate what should be published or not, readers may themselves take charge of this task. In academic studies on online journalism, this phenomenon is defined as 'audience gatekeeping' (Shoemaker and Vos 2009) and refers to the process in which readers regulate the flow of information by sharing or commenting on certain news articles. In the Egyptian blogosphere, this concept may be applied to the fact that often readers want to have a say on what can be shared publicly in the blogosphere, and how. This is true especially in cases in which bloggers address issues that are considered taboo in Egyptian society. The issue may escalate into a heated debate between the audience and the blogger, who wants to remain as the only administrator of a personal page who decides on its content and style.

For example, one day Bilal writes a post saying that he and his flatmate Bahz are considering taking a prostitute back to their flat. Some readers react angrily, as evidenced by this comment:

> Anonymous:
> Don't talk about Egyptians and Egyptian morality because you are the worst example for an Egyptian
> You represent the Egyptian that inhales glue and smokes marijuana and rubs himself against women on buses and harasses girls in downtown
> The example of the young failed street guy that has no religion nor morality nor shame
> ...
> If you are a pervert [*shādh*] and you do massages to your friends I don't care
> If you bring a dirty disgusting prostitute from the street you are free to go to hell [*fi dāhiya*] with the diseases that you and her have
> But you write these words openly in public, and thus make our general image as a people dirty and rubbish when it is already bad as it is[20]
> You [bloggers] have become a mafia [*tanẓīm*]

May God take you all so the country becomes cleaner.
Bahẓ:
I don't understand why you are annoyed … for us the blog is a space where we can reveal ourselves freely, talk and swear, and nobody has the right to say anything to us … I am asking you seriously to reply politely and tell us what you are doing for your country and your religion.
And next time I will tell you what we are trying to do.

Anonymous:
بلاش انت تتكلم عن المصري واخلاق المصري لأنك اسوأ نموذج للمصري
نموذج للمصري اللي بيشم كلة ويضرب بانجو ويتلزق في النسوان في الاوتوبيسات
ويتحرش ببنات وسط البلد
نموذج للشاب الفاشل الصايع اللي لا عندة دين ولا اخلاق ولا حياء
…
كونك شاذ وبتعمل مساج لاصحابك مايهمناش
كونك بتجيب بروستيتيوت من الشارع وسخة ومقرفة انت حر في داهية بالامراض
اللي فيك وفيها
انما كونك تكتب الكلام دة عالملأ وتخللي الصور العامه عننا كشعب انة وسخ وزبالة
وهيهه اصلا مش ناقصة
دة انتوا بقيتوا تنظيم
ربنا ياخدكم بقى خللي البلد تنضف

Bahz Baih:
نا مش فاهم انت أيه اللى مضايقك ... البلوج بالنسبالنا حته كده على راحتنا
نفضفض فيها و نتكلم و نشتم و ماحدش ليه عندنا حاجه ...انا بقى بطالبك بجد
ترد من غير قله أدب و تقوللى انت
عملت أيه لبلدك و دينك
و المره الجايه أ قولك أحنا بنحاول نعمل أيه

Similarly, in the entry 'Daqqat al-Hatif' ('Phone Beatings', 17 November 2009) al-Baraa Ashraf describes the practice of phone sex widespread among Egyptian youth, using a first-person narrative. A while later he writes that he has received many comments through his blog, private emails and text-messages advising him to delete the entry. Al-Baraa replies by saying:

Since I write for myself, considering the blog an alternative to the brown agenda that my mum gave to me as a gift, suggesting I should keep a diary,

> and since my handwriting is bad enough, I learnt to type on the keyboard, and because I am afraid of losing the pages I've written, I publish them on this blog, and I thought it was useful (for me) that your excellencies share in these ideas that belong to me alone and that I alone am responsible for. ('Bi-Khussus al-Kalam al-Balbus', 19 November 2009)
>
> حيث أني أكتب لنفسي، معتبراً المدونة بديلاً عن أجندة بنية أهدتها لي أمي ونصحتني بكتابة يومياتي، ولأن خطي سيئ بما يكفي، فقد تعلمت النقر على لوحة المفاتيح، ولأني أخشى أن تضيع الصفحات التي كتبتها، فقد نشرتها على هذه المدونة، ورأيت أنه سيكون من المفيد (لي)، مشاركة حضراتكم هذه الأفكار التي تخصني وحدي، وأنا فقط مسؤل عنها.

Both examples highlight the fact that the bloggers conceive the blog as a place of their own, in which they can feel free to talk about anything. In response, the readers argue that since they are publishing in a public space, then they are speaking in the name of Egyptian society in general.

Readers also regulate blog-posting as they often ask the blogger to clarify whether the story narrated is fictional or non-fictional. An example of this can be seen in Abeer Soliman's post recounting a story of sexual harassment (see Chapter 5) in first person:

> 77 math: My only comment is to encourage the character of the story for what she did in the end. Is this a story or did it happen to you?
> Abeer: Would it make a difference for you?
> TAFATEFO: But 77math is right in her question, in this post at least. If I narrated a hurtful experience that happened to me, I would have taken at least half of the story to describe its impact on me and on my feelings at the time. You summed up your feelings in one line and its impact upon you in two. There is a certain difference in your treatment (or rather my reception of it) between this post and your post on your rascally friend in Ramses train station and the Peugeot driver. The latter, when I read it, I felt it really happened to you and it was not made up. I had this feeling because I felt the entire experience, your feelings throughout it and its impact upon you were transmitted to me, and I was almost moved by it.
> River Nael: French Philosopher and literary critic Roland Barthes argued that writing is the destruction of every voice, of every point of origin.

> His 'death of the author' theory is premised on the idea that when writing begins, the author enters into his own death, and the reader is born. In short, the literary text is what matters. So, indeed, mesh 7atefre2 [my translation; it does not make any difference] whether this story is based on a personal experience or not.[21]

> Math77 قول...: ليس لدي تعليق سوى تشجيع بطلة القصة على ما فعلته في النهاية. هل هي قصة أم أنكِ تحكين عن نفسك؟
> Abeer Soliman يقول...: هاتفرق فى حاجة؟
> TAFATEFO يقول...: بس 77 ماث محقة في السؤال دا البوست دا على الأقل أنا لو حكيت عن تجربه مؤلمه حصلتلي هحكي عن وقعها علي ومشاعري وقت حدوثها نص الكلام .. وحضرتك أجملتي مشاعرك وقت حدوثها في سطر ووقعها عليكي في سطرين
> في فرق (ما) بين تناولك (أو الأصح إحساسي) في البوست ده وبوست صديقك الندل بتاع محطة مصر وسائق سيارة البيجو .. الثانيه لما قريتها حسيت انها حصلتلك مش مفتعلة .. إحساسي ده كان من اني حسيت ان التجربه كلها ومشاعرك فيها ووقعها عليكي اتنقلي وأكاد أكون انفعلت معاه

In this last example one can see that a debate arises among the readers, who inquire about Abeer's style and the verisimilitude of her texts. The readers express a voyeuristic attitude. Abeer, in response, does not define the fictional or factual nature of the story, rather she invites her readers to focus on its content and style.

Other readers point out that even if the narrative is fictional it has to be 'proper, polite'. In this sense, the readers refer to the double meaning of *adab* as both 'literature' and 'politeness', therefore they expect a work of literature to be decent. For example, when Bilal confesses to his readers the fact that he has taken a peek at the private mails of a young girl in an Internet café, one of the readers writes:

> Although your writing style is very strong and your way in transmitting feelings is magnificent, I find in this writing of yours a kind of privacy violation …
>
> I know that you find it to be a sheer literary work but what about the feelings of these two girls and their surrounding environment if they knew the truth? That's the question zzz ('Daffayni' ('Two Tambourines'), 3 August 2007)

مع إن إسلوب كتابتك جامد جداً و طريقتك في توصيل الإحساس رائعة إلا إني أجد في كتابتك دي نوع من إنتهاك الخصوصية...
أعلم أنك تجده أنه عمل أدبي بحت ولكن ما شعور هاتين الفتاتين و البيئة المحيطة بهما إذا ما علموا الحقيقة هذا هو السؤال زززز

On the blog written by Emraamethlya, it is also possible to see the reaction of 'online haters', that is, users that express their dislike of the blogger's opinion using unpleasant words and expressing hate and contempt (Reagle 2015: 9). Many accuse her of being a 'prostitute'; intimidate her with dirty sexual insults; accuse her of being fake, as there is no such thing as Arab lesbians, and it is not possible that people like her exist.[22] Instead of replying to these insults and accusations, the blogger requests her readers to maintain a mild tone of discussion. She stops writing for a while, and then returns to provide more personal life stories with the ability to dismantle the readers' prejudices and justify her life decision.

> I am not responsible for the comments of others. Everybody can write what they like but, please, we should respect each other and learn the manners of dialogue without degradation of others. I thank the ones who wrote respectful comments even if they disagree with me. I stopped writing for a while for personal reasons and because I was frightened a bit but, God willing, I will come back. By the way for the people who are still adamant that I am sick, I am not sick by God. I excuse you because of your ignorance. I may narrate the details of me going to a psychologist a long time ago, when I was forced, put under pressure and threatened by those I thought understood and loved me. ('Marrah Tānya' ('One More Time'), 6 August 2006)

ليس لي ذنب في تعليقات الآخرين كل واحد يكتب ما بدا له بس نحترم بعض لوسمحتم ونتعلم ادب الحوار دون تطاول بشكر اصحاب التعليقات المحترمة وان اختلفوا معي وتوقفت عن الكتابة شوية لظروف خاصة ولاحساسي بالخوف شوية بس راجعة انشاء الله بالمنسبة الناس الي لسه مصممة اني عيانه انا مش عيانة والله وبعذركم لجهلكم قد اسرد هنا تفاصيل ذهابي لطبيب نفسي منذ فترة بعيدة مجبرة تحت تتهديد وضغط من ظنتهم يفهموني و يحبوني

I haven't been writing for a while. I was scared. Well what can I do, I have to confess I was scared. I am convinced about my choice and about what I

> am doing but I am scared because I live in a society that does not accept me as a homosexual woman. When I think about the reasons for which society does not accept me and even punishes me, it could be religious, since it is commonly known among people that homosexuality is considered *ḥarām* and an abomination, therefore homosexuals deserve punishment, and this punishment is determined by our society. ('Kunt Khayfa' ('I Was Scared'), 19 May 2007)
>
> منذ فترة لم أكتب كنت خايفة طيب أعمل إيه لازم أعترف إني خايفة أنا مقتنعة بإختياري و باللي بعمله لكن خايفة عشان أنا في مجتمع مش حيقبلني كإمرأة مثلية لما بفكر في الأسباب ليه المجتمع مش حيقبلني بل و كمان حيعاقبني ممكن يكون السبب ديني يعني الناس متعارف بينهم أن المثلية حرام و فاحشة و طبعا لازم المثليات يكون لهم عقاب و العقاب ده بيحددوا المجتمع

Gradually, the comments become milder. While many still urge her to visit a psychologist or to revise her reading of the Quran, more and more readers praise her courage and advise her to ignore the negative reactions and follow her feelings. But what is more striking is that over time, more and more male and female homosexuals access her blog and, encouraged by her example, tell their own stories in the comment section and express their desire to contact her in private email conversations. Over time, the blog turns from a personal autobiographical page to a polyphonic narration of Arab Egyptian homosexual life experiences, involving homosexuals and more open-minded heterosexual readers.

Finally, in the absence of language checkers and proofreaders, the audience might also point out linguistic and typographical errors within the text. This case is retrieved from Naji's blog, and it shows how the reader reproaches the author for his language mistakes:

> I would just like you to put the *manṣūb* endings on direct objects, the subject after *inna* and the predicate after *kāna*; if that happened you will be a great writer.
>
> نفسي بس لو تنصب المفعول واسم إن وخبر كان، لو ده حصل هتبقى كاتب عظيم
>
> Take care a bit of the language you are writing in, you 'father of the devils', because you have made more than 25 grammatical and linguistic mistakes,

> and this is a shame for a pretty good writer like your excellency … By the way, I am talking seriously … you are a very good writer … do yourself a favor and show more concern for the language since it is the language you are writing in, not just because it is the Arabic language. A writer has to take care of the language he writes in, whatever this language may be … despite this you are a fine writer. (23 October 2005)
>
> اهتم شوية باللغه اللى بتكتب بيها ياابو الابالسة لان عندك اكثر من خمسة وعشرين خطأ نحوى ولغوى وده عيب بالنسبة لكاتب حلو زى حضرتك ..على فكرة انا باتكلم جد .. انت كاتب كويس جدا .. كمل جميلك واهتم باللغه طالما هى اللغة التى تكتب بها وليس لمجرد انها اللغة العربية على الكاتب ان يهتم باللغة التى يكتب بها مهما كانت او ايا كانت هذة اللغة .. رغم هذا انت كاتب جميل

The reader's comments point to an understanding of *adab* as a literature written in correct Modern Standard Arabic, which bloggers contest. This again serves as an example of how the readers challenge the authority of the writer. The writer is not seen as the master of the text whose form cannot be questioned, but as the author of a text that can be constantly changed thanks to the collaboration of the readers and writer. The informal tone of these comments suggests that in the blogosphere the author and the reader enjoy an equal status. It is from this interaction that new communities of authors and readers emerge. Within these communities, new values, stories and subjectivities are being played out, discussed and validated.

Notes

1 In Dubrovsky's novel, even the title, *Fils* (*Threads/Son*), is left to the readers' interpretation. In 2007, the writer Marie Darrieussecq spoke of a pact of 'assured no confidence' saying: 'Reader, do not believe me. Do not be naïve enough to adhere to the narrative, do not be fooled. Writing is not real life' (Darrieussecq 2007: 8).

2 *Adab* is a multilayered, ancient term, initially meaning 'Sunna' (Muslim customs and practices). Then, after the spread of Islam, it was used to indicate the entire body of non-religious knowledge, whose function was to 'discipline, educate the mind' (F. Gabrieli's *Encyclopedia of Islam*, 2012). With the rise of court culture in the Abbasid period (second Hijri/eighth century CE), it came to identify works intended to educate and entertain members of court, includ-

ing manuals of behaviour and conduct, as well as genres such as biography, history and travel accounts. During the Nahda the term absorbed the English meaning of 'literature'. See Michael Allan (2012), 'How Adab Became Literary: Formalism, Orientalism and the Institutions of World Literature' and Stephan Guth (2010), 'Politeness, Höflichkeit, ᵓAdab: A Comparative Conceptual-Cultural Perspective'.

3 For a discussion of interactive literature in Arabic, see al-Sahrawi (2007), 'Al-Adab al-Tafaᶜuli fi Dawᵓ al-Talaqqi' (Interactive literature in the light of reception). This attention to the reader had already been advocated earlier in Arabic literature, by critics like the theoretician of 'national literature' (*adab qawmī*) ᶜĪsa ᶜUbayd, in the introduction (*muqaddima*) to his collection of short stories, *Ihsan Hanim* (1921). In this introduction, ᶜUbayd rejected earlier traditionalism and neo-classicism as dated and elitist as well as Manfalutian 'romanticism', too idealistic and 'passive' and called for a non-elitist, functional style (Guth 2013). A previous attempt at mobilising the recipient was also made by the authors of the 1960s generation, the writers of the '*ḥassāsiyya jadīda*' (new sensibility) in the 1960s, such as ᶜAbdu Gubayr and others, who tried to create an '*adab al-talaqqī*' (recipient literature). Here, the authors were eager to refrain from acting as authoritarian institutions or despots who would use beautiful language and prescribe the meanings of a text. In order to create conscious citizenship in the readers, they had to find the meaning themselves. More recently, the young Egyptian writer Ahmad Alaidy has used techno-writing as a fictional device in his novel *An Takun ᶜAbbas al-ᶜAbd* (*Being Abbas el Abd*, 2003), in order to shake the readers and stimulate their intervention (el-Ariss 2010).

4 See Para. 4, 'Ignorance, not links' in Hans K. Rustad (2009), 'A Four-Sided Model for Reading Hypertext Fiction'.

5 Ibid. Para. 2, 'Subvertion and absorption'.

6 The root in Modern Standard Arabic is *sha-gha-la*, and according to the *Dictionary of Egyptian Arabic* written by El-Said Badawi and Martin Hinds, '*ishtaghala ᶜalā ḥadd*' means 'trying to deceive, to kid somebody'. It is 'a lie' but it involves the meaning of 'playing a trick on, or fooling someone'.

7 Interview, January 2012.

8 (لسيئي النية ملحوظة)
البوست ليس له اي علاقة شخصية بصاحب المدونة ، وليس له علاقة من قريب او
بعيد بحياته الشخصية ،
تحياتي

9 Jill Walker points out that the first 'hoax' was performed in 1938 by the American Orson Welles on the radio. At that time the generic conventions of radio programmes, just as personal blogs today, were not yet established. In his radio-production entitled 'War of the Worlds', Welles proclaimed that Martians had attacked the planet Earth and destroyed much of the United States. Hearing the news, many listeners left their homes in panic, and did not hear the following ad that confirmed that the story was fictional. There are many other cases of 'blog hoaxes' or 'fictional blogs' that Walker presents in her book *Blogging* (see chapter 'Fictions or hoaxes?', 2008: 121–6).

10 Lilith 12/24 10:39 –

إن شاء الله لن يطول الأمر عليك ... ابقي طمنا الدكتور قال ايه بعد ما ترجع
اجمد يا باشا ...

Zaytuna Sha 12/24 00:46 –

ابليس ارجوك وضح ، انا فى صدمة من امبارح ؟ و مش عارفة اكتب ايه

11 ماشوفتش الراجل بتاع كفكا اللي صحى لقى نفسه صرصار؟ على الأقل أنت أهلك لسه حواليك ، التاني سابوه يعفن

12 طيب ابقى سيب تنويه يا أخي انه خيال .. فرضاً دخل واحد زيي عنده عطب في جهاز التفريق بين الحدث المتخيل و الحدث
الحقيقي

13 خللتني أحس اني عبيطه. كالعاده

14 فالذكورة هي مجد العالم، هي جوهرته، و ذكورتي لا تعني إلا قضيبي، وقضيبي يعني أني قادر على منح المتعة ومنح
الأطفال والإيلام في نفس اللحظة

15 والله يا أستاذ كنبة أسلوبك فى الكتابة زريف وغريب بس ياريت لو مافيهاش رزالة تكبر الفونت وتخلى الباج جراوند أفتح

16 Aarseth positions in this category both print and digital literature, so not only hypertexts but also classic texts, such as the *I Ching* (late ninth century BC) and Raymond Queneau's *One Hundred Thousand Billion Poems* (1961).

17 An example of that can be found in the blog *al-Kanaba al-Hamra* by Bilal Husni. He concludes one of his posts (6 January 2007) writing:

> Follow me, the red sofa beside the orange mattress / the lazy guys [lit. who sleep in supine position].
>
> تابعونى الكنبه الحمرا جنب المرتبه الاورنج/ الولاد بتنام على ضهرهم

18 Pun on words Jeddah (city in Saudi Arabia) and *jād* (serious).

19 Interview, June 2010.

20 Idiom. Literal translation: 'it does not lack this to be bad'.

21 The comment is originally written in English.

22 It is quite problematic to quote these kinds of comments here because they include indecent and very offensive insults and are very often disturbing to read.

5

Bytes of Freedom: Fictionalised Bodies in the Egyptian Blogosphere

The Quest for Truth and Imagination

Autofiction has been linked to post-structural theories that assert the fragmentation and disjointedness of the self and the impossibility of writing to achieve self-unity and originality. This sense of fragmentation is anticipated by some of the titles bloggers assign to their work. In Chapter 2 I have pointed out that Mona Seif defines her blog as '*tanatīf*', scattered pieces of her life. Likewise, the blogger ᶜAzza Mughazi (ᶜAzza Mughāzī) titles her blog *Nithar* (*Scatters*), reflecting that in the blogosphere, sense of identity is constituted by fragments and segments, each of which is separately meaningful and equally significant. AZ similarly titles her blog *A7lami al-Mob3athara* (that is, *Ahlami al-mubaᶜthara*, *My Scattered Dreams*) and explains it thus:

> Sometimes I stand in front of myself, maybe so that I can figure out why I chose this name for my personal blog. I see myself confused … disoriented … torn apart … and my thoughts are scattered everywhere … I don't find anybody to gather them or to gather me … I look more into myself and my confusion increases, to the point that I don't know what is more scattered, me or my thoughts.
>
> And here is the rest of it. (*Ahlami al-Mubaᶜthara* (*My Scattered Dreams*), 15 May 2005)
>
> أتوقف امام نفسى للحظات على اعلم سبب اختيارى لهذا الاسم للبلوج الخاص بى ارانى مشوشه.. مشتته...... ممزقه....... وافكارى فى غايه البعثره....... ولا اجد من يلملمها او يلملمنى.....انظر الى داخلى اكثر فأزداد شتاتا حتى انى لم اعد اعلم اينا اكثر بعثره ... انا ام افكارى
>
> And here is the rest of it.

Here the fragmentation of the mind is echoed in the mixture of languages. In this passage, as in many other entries of her blog, Arabic is mixed with English, as if the blogger has to rely on both languages in her vain attempt to collect the scattered pieces of her identity. Despite this fragmentation, the bloggers analysed in this study seem interested in using the blog form to locate or build, for themselves and for others, an identity that they can understand as unitary, as 'real'. Several bloggers seem to express the idea that the form is used as a counter-movement to postmodern destabilisation, as a 'healing', a repair kit for their fragmented personality, or as Miller and Shepherd write with reference to blogging in general, 'a generic effort of reflexivity within the subject that creates an eddy of relative stability' (Miller and Shepherd 2004).

The quest for truth or authenticity, or showing oneself in one's true nature, is at the heart of the autofictional project. This truth, however, does not necessarily lie in factual accuracy, because writing sometimes requires a concentration of facts, so as not to be repetitive, and also because memory is not accurate. The truth pursued by the autofictional writer is the 'intimate truth'. In the context of autofiction, Catherine Cusset (2012) calls truth the

> capacity to go back inside an emotion, to erase anything anecdotic that wouldn't be part of that emotion and would water it down, in order to offer it to the reader in a bare form, devoid of anything too idiosyncratic, so that he/she can claim it as his own.[1]

Autofiction is dominated by a quest for truth but at the same time it is considered a loosely referential literary genre. Doubrovsky insists on the referentiality of the narrator but still allows a form of poetic license, since to picture the self is inexorably to let the imagination, more than facts, play a central role in the narrative. The reference to psychoanalysis frees the narrative from the burden of factual accuracy. The focus of the narrative is not on the author's life but rather on the author's mind. Imagination supplies the flaws of memory but also allows the writer to escape from their limited empirical experience (Schmitt 2010: 129).

This double tendency of revealing one's true self, while inventing different versions of oneself, is actualised in the way Egyptian bloggers write about themselves on the blog. The metaphor of the screen as both a 'mirror' and a 'veil', elaborated by Serfaty (2004) in regard to American blogs, may be well applied to the Egyptian ones analysed in this study. Serfaty argues that the computer screen functions as a mirror, because it allows the diarists to create a reflection of themselves through the blog. At the same time, the screen is a veil, which allows them to reveal only certain aspects of their personality, while concealing others (ibid.: 13). Likewise, the desire to express and share confessions is the major force that has driven many Egyptian bloggers.[2] From the presentation of the case studies and the motivations that drive young people to blog laid out in Chapter 2, we have seen how several blog authors make it clear that to express their true self they need to speak out, to confess, to express their emotions openly without fear or hesitation. At the same time, we can see that besides revealing their innermost feelings and emotions, Egyptian bloggers also use the blog to express 'who they want to be', to imagine different versions of their bodies, to perform different aspects of themselves or to stress certain aspects of their personality, to '*se projeter dans sa propre vie*' ('to anticipate events that may or may not happen', Hugueny-Leger 2011). Bloggers use the blog as a means of reaching beyond the confines of quotidian life, beyond the people with whom one has daily contact, perhaps to discover and perform a different version of oneself. The online diary enacts a certain escape from the everyday, even as it takes the everyday as its topic (Sorapure 2003: 13).

In this chapter, I will show how bloggers actualise this double quest for truth and imagination in the way they write about their body on the blog. The body, in fact, constitutes the main element of their identity on the blog.[3] The body is actualised in two main ways. The first is through the description of emotions and feelings. Emotions are strictly linked to the body. Deborah Lupton (1998) writes that emotions can be described as embodied simply because they are experienced by humans who are, themselves, inevitably embodied. As we can only experience the world through our own corporeal senses, the body becomes our medium for the world. Therefore, as our emotions are formed through our reactions to the world, they are inherently linked to our bodies. One perceives the world and constructs notions of reality through the body and its senses. Being in the world involves not only thought and bodily actions but also emotionality. All of these are related in ways that cannot easily be separated from each other, because they are part of the same phenomenon of lived experience (Lupton 1998: 32).[4] On the other hand, blog-writing allows bloggers to explore and depict different versions of their bodies, as a means of dealing with and liberating themselves from the constraints imposed by society, religion and tradition: in effect, the outside world. In this sense, it allows the blogger to invent different body shapes, or to show only certain parts of it.

The presence of corporeal description in bloggers' autobiographical writing must be understood as a changed attitude towards corporeality and sexuality that has taken place in Arabic literature in the last two decades, especially in women's writing (Anishchenkova 2014: 77).[5] However, as we will see in what follows, the practice of writing the body is not only a prerogative of female bloggers, as it involves male bloggers as well. The chapter shows how a focus on the body allows us to see how the bloggers negotiate their identity between the private and public, personal and political, gender, individuality and community; and how in fact, the body, just like the blog, stands at the intersection of these various binaries.

Sexual Harassment

For a number of female bloggers, writing the body entails bringing to light the issue of sexual harassment that is often silenced in society. As autofiction focuses on the truth of emotions, women bloggers abstain from writing detailed accounts of their experience of sexual harassment, but rather focus on the feeling of fear that derives from it. Mona Seif was among the first women bloggers to tackle this issue from a personal perspective. After the big episode of sexual harassment that took place in Cairo in Ramadan 2006, Mona/Maat, as a self-styled goddess of Truth, felt impelled to write the blog post 'Kasr Jidar as-Samt: ᶜan at-Taharrush al-Jinsi' ('Breaking the Walls of Silence: On Sexual Harassment in Egypt', 29 October 2006). While the mainstream media have tried to deny the evidence of the pictures, videos and testimonial accounts, she declared that

> we have to break the walls of silence that we have built, and talk about what really happens to us, how we bear the burden of every day we go out onto the street or we use public transportation. Perhaps, if people can see through our eyes the ugliness of what we go through, they will have no choice but to believe us.

> It is hard (for a girl) to tell these things, at least for me it is very difficult, because I feel so humiliated and helpless that I would prefer to deny these things happened, to put them all together in a box in my mind called 'it did not happen'. But I will tell …
>
> لازم نكسر جدار الصمت اللى حطيناه ، و نحكى عن اللى بيحصلنا فعلا،عن ازاى
> بنشيل هم كل يوم نمشيه فى الشارع،أو نركب مواصلة عامة.
> جايز لما الناس يشوفوا بعينينا قبح اللى بيحصلنا ، يبقى ما فيش قدامهم حل غير انهم
> يصدقوا.
> صعب الواحدة تحكى الحاجات دى ؛ على الاقل بالنسبة لى صعب اوى ، لأنه من
> كترالاهانة و الضعف اللى باحسه فى المواقف ديه ، بابقى عايزة انا نفسى انكر
> حدوثهم ، احطهم كلهم فى صندوق جوه دماغى اسميه "ماحصلش"
> بس هاحكى

Using the anonymity granted by the blog medium, Mona/Maat recounts episodes in her life in which she was the victim of sexual harassment in the street, on public transport and even in her residence, from the age of nine years. As a result, she experiences shame and a sense of uneasiness about her body, as she comments in her blog. Her account, written in very plain Egyptian dialect and with a very direct communicative style, also encourages other women to contribute with their own personal stories in the comment section. (Note the use of *lāzim*, '(we) have to' and the plural first person used as a way to exhort the readers to do the same.) Curiously, her brother Alaa Abdel Fattah comments on her blog post without knowing that Maat is his sister, saying: 'I hail you for your courage.' Maat replies, 'You can't imagine how your comment encourages me.'[6] Due to the nature of Internet publishing, she is also able to link her account to those of other female bloggers; consequently, we find hyperlinks leading to other posts from women who have broken the walls of silence just like her.

In fact, the description of this issue is picked up by other women bloggers immediately after. For example, in the blog post 'Shayʾ min al-Khawf' ('A bit of fear', 30 October 2006), based on her own personal experience, Zubayda describes the fear related to sexual harassment as something that grows and develops from early childhood, and becomes so strong that it prevents women from caring for more important issues. Zubayda links this fear to social isolation, because it isolates women more and more from society.[7]

The denouncement of sexual harassment is not only restricted to this particular event taking place in 2006, but recurs throughout the years, as the problem does not cease to exist. On 3 April 2007, Mona Seif again describes her first experience of sexual harassment as the moment in which she lost her virginity, which metaphorically stands for the loss of innocence. In her words:

> I lost my virginity the first time a male stranger grabbed me when I was little and kept caressing my body. He touched my breasts that were just about to grow, turning me slowly from a child into a girl. When he passed his hand over me, I felt fear, and something contracted inside me. I have never understood that fear. How can so many girls be exposed to these acts and freeze down in their places, how can they be scared of running away from a thing that is the source of their fear? I lost my virginity when he – a man, my father's age – created in a moment, besides the little child, another girl, conscious of her body and hating it; [a girl] who [now] saw her curves and wanted an eraser to wipe them clean, to turn again into a stick with two hands and two legs, a round head with untidy hair and a laughing mouth. ('An Tuslab ʿUdhr(iyy)atuki' ('To Have Your Virginity Stolen'), 3 April 2007)
>
> انا فقدت عذريتى عند اول راجل غريب مسكنى و انا صغيرة و قعد يحسس على جسمى
> لمس صدرى و هو لسة يا دوبك بيكبر و بينقلنى بالراحة من طفلة لبنت
> لما مشى ايده عليا و حسيت بانقباضة جوايا و خوف
> خوف عمرى ما فهمته. ازاى بنات كتير فينا بيتعرضوا لحاجات كدة و يتسمروا فى مكانهم, ازاى بيخافوا يجروا من الحاجة اللى اصلا مخوفاهم؟
> انا فقدت عذريتى لما هو -راجل قد ابويا- فى لحظة خلق جوايا جنب العيلة الصغيرة,
> بنت تانية حاسة بجسمها و كارهاه, شايفة منحنياته و عايزة استيكة تمسحها و
> ترجع بس عصاية بايدتين و رجلتين, راس مدورة شايلة شعر منعكش , و بق بيضحك

The text is accompanied by a drawing she made herself. The first sketch (see Figure 11) depicts the hands that try to reach her breasts and her genitals (drawn in the shape of a heart). In the second sketch (see Figure 12), Mona depicts herself just as described, as 'a stick with two hands and two feet, a round head with untidy hair and a smiling mouth'. This portrays her fear of growing up, her uneasiness with her body, and thus her refuge in childhood as an escape from the society in which she lives.

Figure 11 On Losing Your Virginity 1, by Mona Seif. Source: http://ma3t.blogspot.no.

Figure 12 On Losing Your Virginity 2, by Mona Seif. Source: http://ma3t.blogspot.no.

Mona's fictional refuge in childhood is a means of resistance against the societal view of the female body. If her body attracts continuous attention, then she finds relief by imaging her body as a stick figure, a body that has no sexual connotations. Additionally, childhood is frequently and paradoxically represented as a period of human development characterised by such universal and changeless values as spontaneity and innocence (Jo-Ann Wallace 1992: 65). Thus, taking refuge in an imaginary childhood is a means of ignoring, or forgetting, the cruelty of a reality composed of police brutality, and the violence of the political regime.[8] These sketches recur very often in Mona's blog combined with a brief text, sometimes only one sentence, and are collected under the tag '*inshikāḥ*' ('enrapture'). In these drawings, she depicts herself as the child mentioned before, namely a stick figure with hands and legs emitting butterflies, flowers, balloons, hearts and music notes (see Figures 13 and 14). The text in Figure 13 says, 'Things that I have to do: Get ID; bank account; define my study specialization; repair house phone; renew my passport; obtain a temporary certificate'. Conversely, the text underlying Figure 14 says: 'Things I have to do: Have a bath, buy Mickey, Sleep a lot, Brush my teeth'.

Figure 13 Things I have to do (as an adult), by Mona Seif. Source: http://ma3t.blogspot.no.

Figure 14 Things I have to do (as a child), by Mona Seif. Source: http://ma3t.blogspot.no.

In other entries, Mona/Maat describes herself as a brave girl, escaping with her lover from the reality in which she lives. She assures her readers that this is just 'a piece of my imagination' (*tantūfa min khayālī*), or a 'girl that is supposed to be me, if I had enough courage' (21 February 2007). The place that is most often mentioned as a refuge is the sea, the beach, in effect the exact opposite of the noise (*dawsha*) and hot weather in Cairo. For example, in 'Yalla Nihrab' ('Let's Escape', 30 November 2008), she imagines taking her beloved to the sea, so that she can finally enjoy his company.

This longing for a more courageous self is also realised through drawing. If, in most of the '*inshikāḥ*' entries, Mona draws herself with untidy hair collected in a ponytail above her head, in others she displays her hair as long, curly and loose (see Figure 15). Here the hair emphasises the feminine and rebellious side of her personality, the longing for freedom instead of imprisonment and the unfolding of her femininity.[9]

Figure 15 Self-portrait by Mona Seif. Source: http://ma3t.blogspot.no.

These flights of imagination alternate with outbursts of anger and fear. On 29 January 2007, she simply writes 'Cairo is slowly killing me', in a large font. For her readers, who are familiar with the Internet language code, it is clear that the size of the font transforms the sentence into an exhausted, exasperated scream. In the post 'Law Samaht, Sībnī A^{c}īsh' ('Please Let Me Live', 21 June 2007), Mona/Maat explains how discrimination towards women and the continuous comments that she receives regarding her body while walking in the streets creates in her a feeling of tiredness, depression and insecurity with her body.

In a similar vein, Abeer Soliman deals with these same feelings of fear and insecurity related to the risk of sexual harassment in her blog *Yawmiyyat ^{c}Anis*. In a blog post entitled 'al-Tuhmah … Untha!' ('The Charge: [Being a] Woman', 1 May 2009) Abeer describes the challenge of living as a single woman in Cairo. She recounts that she has been sexually harassed by a young boy in the lift in her building. She tried to call for her neighbours, but nobody came; she managed to defend herself and scare the boy away. While telling the story, the author invites her readers to reflect on sexual harassment in Egypt: women now feel in danger – even in their homes – as nobody is willing to help. The female body has become a crime for which society punishes you. Unlike Mona Seif, Abeer courageously writes the story in the first person and signs it with her name. As a result, many readers inquire whether the first-person-narrator corresponds to Abeer herself (see Chapter 4). The fact that readers tend to attribute these stories to her own life is perhaps the reason why, in a later entry, the topic is presented as a short story (*qiṣṣa qaṣīra*) written in the third person, entitled 'ᵓAhu Da Illi Sar' ('This is What Happened', 18 February 2009). Despite the story being presented by the author as fictional, one might assume that it includes autobiographic details, as the main character is a young journalist, Salma (Salmā). The story denounces the hypocrisy and immorality lying at the basis of the Cairene intellectual-artistic milieu in which Abeer most probably moves. In this story, Salma encounters Khalid (Khālid), a famous film director, at the premiere of his movie, and she accepts Khalid's suggestion to skip the party and to go to his place located in New Cairo, a residential neighbourhood located one hour away from Downtown Cairo. Khalid's high class status is indicated by the detailed description of his house (he lies on a La-Z-Boy, has a huge TV screen and serves Spanish wine in crystal glasses) and his mixing of Arabic with English vocabulary ('interview', 'living room', 'cheers'). Salma feels estranged from this kind of social setting, but she still decides to be herself. Indeed, when Khalid asks her to interview him about the movie, Salma admits that she does not consider it worth writing about. Shocked by her reaction, Khalid screams at her, insults her and threatens to beat her. Finding herself alone with him and in such a remote place, Salma has no other option than to wait for him to calm down and beg him to take her back to her car, which she had left downtown. When she is finally safe in her car but still shivering from fear, she says to herself: 'This is what happened and this is what it was ... you have no right ... you have no right to blame me.'[10]

Love and Sexuality

For several women bloggers, the expression of love and sexual desires is considered as an essential requirement to explore one's own individuality. Since they are prevented from doing so in offline society, they use the autofictional nature of the blog to express these feelings.

For example, in Abeer's blog, love is described as a basic requirement for self-realisation, to become a free individual. She prioritises love over the urgency to get married. This theme is elaborated in the text 'Itnayn fi 'l-Hawa' ('Two in the Air', 9 September 2009). The main character and narrator, Abeer, is travelling on a plane and cannot prevent herself from watching a couple of young lovers exchanging kisses and cuddles. At the same time she is reading the book *The Power of Now*, a best-seller (1999) by the German-Canadian Eckart Tolle that gives instructions on how to leave behind a self created by the outside world and our own egos to reach our inner being. Inspired by Tolle, Abeer decides 'to focus on the present, to put aside the memories from the past and the worries for the future, to free herself from the surrounding elements' (ibid.). However, her mind keeps going back to the two lovers and she asks herself (and her readers) why she is prevented from achieving both love and self-realisation. The great number of questions adds a feeling of anxiety and preoccupation. It also indicates that the blogger is asking for answers and support from the readers.

Likewise, Emraamethlya considers her love for a woman as a basic human need and a consistent aspect of her identity. She affirms that being lesbian does not mean having sex with another woman, rather to be able to love another woman. In many diary pages, she expresses her love for her woman with poetic, tender descriptions. An example of this can be seen in the following extract from 'Itsaliht Ma^{c}a Nafsi' ('I Was Reconciled with Myself', 30 January 2006):

> The most beautiful moment is when we are sitting together. Even if we are surrounded by thousands of voices we don't feel anything, we become forgetful that there are people around us, and we keep talking and talking, neither the words end nor do we stop talking, we talk about everything in life, philosophy, literature, religion, we love books and we read together. Hours pass by quickly and we wish the time would stand still and give us a chance. Every time we discover something new in the other that we had never seen, we dance and sing and tell jokes and laugh, we run together and we enjoy walking in the street holding each other's hand, since it is

> normal, and what is funny is that while we walk we are both flirted with in the street.
>
> أحلى لحظة لما بنكون قاعدين مع بعض ولو في ألف صوت جنبنا مش بنكون حسين بأي حاجة بنكون ناسيين أن في حد حولينا و بنقعد نتكلم نتكلم لا الكلام بيخلص و لا إحنا بنبطل كلام كلامنا بيكون في كل حاجه في الدنيا في الفلسفه الأدب الدين بنحب الكتب و بنقرا سوى ,الساعات بتعدي بسرعه و بنكون عايزين الساعه تقف و الوقت يدينا فرصه تانيه كل يوم بنكتشف في بعض حجات مشفنهاش ,بنرقص و نغني و ننكت و نضحك و نجري سوا و بنستمتع اوي لما نمشي في الشارع ماسكين إيد بعض بما إن ده عادي و اللي يضحك إننا لما بنمشي في الشارع بنتعاكس إحنا الإتنين

In this passage, the author recounts romantic moments with her lover and emphasises the sentimental (laughing, holding each other's hand) and the intellectual (books, religion, philosophy) affinity between herself and her lover.

Emraamethlya also expresses her maternal desire and the impossibility to realise it, at least not in Egypt. The post 'Kalam Bayni wa-Baynik' ('Words Between Me and You', 31 December 2006) reports a dialogue between her and her lover concerning the possibility of IVF (in vitro fertilisation). Her lover dismisses her poetic expression of love and maternal desire with a simple '*Mayinfa*^{c}*sh*' (It won't work). In 'Ihsas Akhar' ('A Different Feeling', 7 December 2008), she describes her ambivalent feelings toward a woman breastfeeding in public, that oscillates between sexual attraction and female solidarity. The description of maternal feelings as expressed by a Muslim homosexual woman is highly subversive, as it sabotages traditional family models and advocates for homosexual reproductive rights. The blogger does not prevent herself from writing provocative stories that complicate the relation between religion and sexuality, such as 'Min Wara$^{\circ}$ al-Khimar' ('From Behind the Veil', 7 February 2010), which details the love story between two girls, who meet each other in the university mosque and share their bed in a university student house. The fact that they are wearing a *khimār*, that is a veil that covers the head and shoulders leaving the face uncovered, indicates that they are both devoutly religious. The story explores the feeling of tenderness and love between the two women:

> They sat sticking to each other in the women's car of the metro; she leaned her head on her shoulder, she gave her a tender look, she sighed and stretched

> her hand searching for the other's hand, seeking warmth in it … caressing it, drawing warm hearts and music scales on it with her fingers. She comes closer to her ear, nothing separating them except for their *khimār* … she whispers from behind the *khimār* 'I love you'. A smile draws on her lips and their eyelids get heavier; as if they were drunk from alcohol, they close their eyes for a while. She replies: 'I love you too, very much.' There are lots of people around them and thousands of eyes but they only see each other.
>
> و في عربية السيدات بالمترو جلستا متلاصقتان و اسندت رأسها على كتفها نظرت لها نظرة حانية و تنهدت و مدت يدها تبحث عن يدها تتلمس الدفء فيها ... تتحسها ترسم عليها بأصابعها قلوبا دافئة و سلما موسيقيا تقترب من أذنها لا يفصلهما إلا خمارهما ... تهمس من وراء الخمار «بحبك» فترتسم إبتسامة على شفتيها و تتثاقل جفونها كانها الخمر قد أسكرتهما فيغمضا لبرهة و ترد "بحبك أوي"... و الدنيا مليانة ناس و ألف عين لكنهما لا تران إلا بعضهما

The story ends with a juxtaposition of the words *khamr* (alcohol) and *khimār* (veil), to indicate that the love lived from behind the veil is equated to a feeling of drunkenness. Many readers point out that they are particularly offended by the expression 'I love you for God's sake', pronounced by two lesbian women, but the blogger replies with the assertion that the post is based on a true story, demonstrating that being lesbian and Muslim is neither contradictory nor hypocritical.

Love is essential to Egyptian youth's lives just as much as satisfying sexual desires. Sexual relationships are described as an expression of amorousness, as well as a basic need that the body must satisfy. In a provocative text entitled 'Al-Ju[c] Kafir' ('Hunger is Faithless', 4 March 2008), Abeer argues that 'feeding the body', that is, satisfying a sexual desire, is equal to other basic human rights:

> I have the right to dream … I have the right to eat … I have the right to have goals that I seek to achieve in life … I have the right to drink … I have the right to love … I have the right to work … I have the right to dream of becoming a mother … I have the right to live … I have the right to marry … I have the right to write … I have the right to satisfy my body … (4 March 2008)
>
> من حقى أن أحلم.. من حقى أن أأكل.. من حقى أن تكون لى أهداف فى الحياة أسعى إلى تحقيقها.. من حقى أن أشرب.. من حقى أن أحب.. من حقى أن أعمل..

من حقى أن أحلم بالأمومة.. من حقى ان أعيش.. من حقى أن أتزوج.. من حقى أن أكتب.. من حقى أن أُشبع جسدى..

Abeer warns her readers to stop reading if they are close-minded, and then goes on to state explicitly: 'Today I want to talk about sex.' She poses the question of how the 30 per cent of unmarried women living in Egypt can survive if their bodies are angry, and if the hunger of the body is considered 'a rejection of religious faith' in their society. 'Sex in this geographic area is considered a privilege for the man and prostitution for a woman', and then – in a very large font size – 'how am I going to live as a free human being in this society?' From her individual case she expands the question to the other Egyptian 'spinsters': 'How do the 9% of spinsters live in Egyptian society? How are hungry bodies productive in a work environment? How do we escape the torture of society and religion, if we've decided to set ourselves free?' These words are highly provocative and courageous. By linking her own experience to that of other 'spinsters', Abeer asserts an important concept: individual freedom cannot be achieved without the freedom of the body. Conservative religion prevents women from satisfying their bodies, thus it prevents women from exercising a basic human right. In order to become free individuals, women must free themselves of social and religious constraints.

The posts written by Abeer and other female bloggers differ from the ones written by male bloggers. While Abeer Soliman advocates sexual freedom and the right to satisfy the body, Bilal and other male bloggers instead write more obscene descriptions of sexual intercourse. In *The Red Sofa*, Bilal gives very intimate details about his sexuality. In 'Brustityut' ('Prostitute', 28 January 2007) he writes humorously about his desire to take a prostitute home to his flat, as a way to provoke the doorman of his building. However, in the last line, he concedes that the experience pales in comparison to sleeping with a loved one. In 'Daffayn' ('Two Tambourines', 3 August 2007), he confesses that as a teenager, he peeked at a small child's vagina, the daughter of a friend of his mother's and he maliciously laughs at the idea of having destroyed her life for ever. Likewise, in the same passage, he confesses to peeping at his flatmates having sex from behind the door of his room, and to even trying to catch their eye to signal his presence ('Bi-Tafsil al-Malal' ('In Boring Detail'), 16 September 2007). These passages suggest a level of perversion and maleficence in the narrator/main character. In the same post, he also describes his masturbation towards the sky as a reaction to his mother's illness the night before her death; his prayer without ablution at his mother's funeral. This act of masturbation, which recalls his reference to 'the small stains of sperm' on the sofa, expresses feelings of helplessness: it echoes the blogger's wish to live, to overcome illness and death, which is hindered by outside circumstances.

In 'Ashyaᵓ Tastahaqq al-Ihtimam' ('Things Worthy of Attention', 22 October 2008), Al-Baraa Ashraf describes the sexual intercourse he has had the night before and argues that sex is a means of understanding oneself and the surrounding world. The asterisk besides the first pronoun 'I' leads to a footnote saying: 'there is no relationship between the author of the blog and the events narrated',[11] discouraging the reader from attributing the events narrated to his personal experience. In another entry, he dedicates a comic description to the practices of phone sex, and gives his readers precise tips on how to do it ('Daqqat al-Hatif' ('Phone Rings'), 17 November 2009). Similarly, Jimmy Halim, in the post 'Malal' ('Boredom', 3 October 2011) describes online sex as a cure for boredom; although boredom also becomes a consequence of his experience, as the woman on the other side of the screen refuses to take her clothes off. Here is an extract from the post:

> Three o'clock in the morning.
> I wake up from a short nap in front of the computer screen; the hot girl [*mozza*] on the other side of the screen says that she will not take her clothes off unless I give her the code of the mobile top up card. I suggest that we start together and then I give her the code before I climax. I open the zip of my trousers and she wriggles in front of the camera while hissing intermittently like a snake. I turn down the speakers' volume to its lowest degree in order to shut her up and I carry on with what I was doing. (3 October 2011)

الثالثة صباحًا
أستيقظ من غفوة قصيرة أمام شاشة الكمبيوتر ، المُزّة على الطرف الآخر تقول أنها لن تبدأ بخلع ملابسها إلا بعد أن أعطيها كود كارت الشحن . أقترح أن نبدأ سوياً ثم أمليها الكود قبل أن أصل للذروة . أفتح سوستة البنطلون و تتلوى هي أمام الكاميرا

و هي تطلق فحيحاً متقطعاً كالأفعى ، أدير مؤشر صوت السماعات إلى ادنى درجة
لكي أخرسها و أعود لأتابع ما كنت أفعله

The expression of sexual desires and the description of more obscene sexual practices in a public space such as a blog are highly provocative, particularly if we consider that Muslim societies forbid the act of sexual intercourse between men and women outside marriage. The function of these pieces is to normalise sexual desires. In line with classical Islamic jurists, these bloggers highlight that having sex is a human need, but in contrast to them, they are convinced that it cannot be prohibited by social or religious rules. They seem to support the idea that the limits imposed by religion and society do not just fail to suppress bodily desires, but actually act to provoke even more perverse thoughts. Additionally, the blog posts suggest that even if religion and society try to set rules for it, people will always find ways to circumvent them. It is the body that matters, and its carnal existence is much more real than the moralistic theories postulated by the religious establishment.

Body Ailments

As well as speaking out about their inner feelings, bloggers also anchor the body itself in the online environment. The blog is a place where they often register and discuss their bodily ailments and disorders.

In 'Al-Banadul la Yahtaj Musaᶜada' ('Panadol Does Not Need Help', 2 December 2008), Amr dedicates an entire post to his headache. He describes in detail how the pain affects his entire body, how the body responds to medicine, and only in the end does he mention that the pain might be due to a difficult decision he took the night before. In 'Liᵓanni Lan Ataᶜallam Abadan' ('Because I Shall Never Learn', 6 May 2010), Amr briefly mentions his separation from his wife, but dedicates most of the narration to his body's reaction to the event: he has lost weight, he feels weak, he almost faints while playing football with his friends, and he bursts into tears during conversation. In a similar vein, in a piece entitled 'Fi Ritha' Akhir Buqᵓa Naᶜima' ('In Lamentation of the Last Soft Spot', 8 November 2006), Zubayda describes her rough skin and her vain attempts at making it softer. She cannot even remember how her body turned into 'palm fibre',[12] and she compares herself to a doll made of straw.

In these two narratives, the body seems to be the only possible transmitter of a message. It seems that both Amr and Zubayda are in a situation in which bodily ailments cannot be explained, but only described as they are. The description of these symptoms may also have a metaphorical meaning. In the case of Amr, describing his illness may be a way to depict his crisis with his wife, especially at the time of his divorce, without explicitly referring to it. In the case of Zubayda, the roughness of her skin might be a metaphor for her psychological situation. It might hint of an existential crisis for which she and the people around her cannot find any remedy. According to Serfaty, the bloggers' strategy in writing about their bodily ailments is twofold:

> it is illocutionary, i.e. narrating the disorder is an action unto itself which may be interpreted in a variety of ways by the readers, but it also is a 're-enactment through language', and as such it creates the discursive space necessary to distance the narrator from his own experience. The online diary functions as a writing space in which these physical traces can be both acknowledged and got rid of. This is necessary because pain turns the body into the Other, unpredictable and threatening, which puts the self in danger. Writing about the pain is a means of controlling the body and taking distance from it. (Serfaty 2004: 113)[13]

The ailments that we find in these two blogs pertain to the factual, as they describe how the body is affected by the world. However, they may also be interpreted as a metonymy of a deeper existential crisis.

Animal Bodies

In some entries, bloggers imagine themselves as inhabiting animal bodies. Animals like birds, cats and cattle were worshipped in Ancient Egypt. Animal figures also abound in the Quran, as do birds, dogs, sheep, snakes, and more. Animal bodies often carry cultural significances (Hamilton 1992: 77). To imagine oneself as an animal might also have some psychological explanations.

Following her imagination and her professional scientific interests,[14] Mona dreams of turning into a sea animal ('al-Kawkab al-Azraq', 27 May 2007) or of having been a sea animal before. By imagining herself as a fish, Mona emphasises her will to wander free in a multicoloured, unlimited space, inhabited by a wide diversity of flora and fauna, the opposite of the claustrophobic reality she lives in. The fish's gasping also recalls her attempt at surviving in a reality that is 'killing her'. The beach is also the only place where she can undress herself, as far as she can, in opposition to the strict dress code that is required in Cairo, because of the risk of sexual harassment.

Ahmed Naji also longs for an underwater environment, but he imagines himself as a whale. The whale is a recurrent visual theme in his work: so much that it appears on the cover of his novel *Rogers* (2007), and uploaded onto the banner of his blog. In a post entitled 'Ana Hut Yaltahim al-ᶜAlam' ('I am a Whale Swallowing the World', 23 October 2005), he expresses his desire to turn into an enormous white killer whale, one that nobody can ride (*anā lā aḥad yarkabny*, the expression in Arabic is ambiguous; it also means 'nobody can impose their will on me'). He imagines himself as 'a huge whale that moves slowly into the ocean as a Buddhist guru', a whale that 'emits a huge water fountain, that closes its eyes to dive into the ocean and opens its jaws to swallow the entire world'. His self-description as a whale matches with his self-description as a devil (*Iblīs*), and reinforces his violent, subversive nature.

Abeer often imagines herself as a bird. The metaphor of flying recurs often in her writing; it is used to indicate the wish for personal freedom. Her description in her 'About me' page includes a quotation from the famous Egyptian poet Salah Jahin: 'I am a silly sparrow … a silly sparrow I am',[15] which may refer to her state of independence and freedom as an unmarried woman ('sparrow'), but also to her incapacity to see and accept the social constraints which Egyptian women usually undergo (and therefore she describes herself ironically as 'silly'). In another entry she writes: 'As for me, I will keep flying in freedom, looking for a nest, not for a cage.' The nest here indicates that despite her disillusion about men's behaviour, she is still looking for real love.

These recurrent imaginings of the body in animal forms (fishes, whales, birds) share a common element: both birds and marine life are animal species that do not live on land and are not subject quite so definitely to the laws of gravity. This suggests that these bloggers all share a strong desire for freedom in their imaginative descriptions.

Animated Objects

Self-representation may also take the shape of animated objects. Deborah Lupton argues that, as an outcome of appropriation, the object may serve as an extension of the self, outwards in space, becoming a territory of the self that surrounds the body (1998). These objects become 'prosthetics' of the self, in the sense that they become autobiographical as they bear the mark of the individual's use (Gonzalez, quoted in Lupton 1998: 144).

In Bilal Husni's blog, the red sofa is the main character of his blog-narrative. The sofa may be considered his alter ego, or his fictionalised body. In fact, the body of the sofa is huge and heavy, just like the blogger's physical body. Through the narrative, the body of the sofa undergoes a process of transformation that reflects the passing of time and the different stages of life. The disclosure of the history of the sofa runs parallel with Bilal's description of intimate and embarrassing details about his present. Furthermore, the more the blogger talks about the sofa, the more he also describes his fat and nude body. Just like the sofa is old and marked with a spot of sperm, the blogger's body is fat, unfit and inhabited by perverse thoughts. The blogger's self-identification with the sofa is also highlighted by the fact that his gradual frustration at blogging goes together with his desire for getting rid of the sofa. Indeed, he feels the sofa is swallowing him; his fictional alter ego is overshadowing his 'real' personality. Like the sofa, a bicycle is described as a living creature, to the extent that the character has to sleep facing away from it, as he is disturbed by the presence of 'her' body: 'I would sleep in front of the bicycle; but because of my rich imagination, being a writer, I would face away from it, because it was the only other body in the house other than mine' ('al-Mazad 2' ('The Auction 2'), 1 November 2007).[16] Not only are objects considered alive, but they are also assigned an active role in the unfolding of events: by linking the sofa to his mother's death, pretending that he inherited it from her, Bilal turns the sofa into the element that connects his separation from his mother to the start of a new life. Likewise, the bicycle seems to represent the start of a new childhood. For Bilal giving life to objects is a way of asserting life against the cruelty of death. If humans are swept away by death, then Bilal seems to state that the only hope is to emotionally attach oneself to objects.

In a similar vein, the blogger Rihab, in 'A^{c}maq A^{c}māqi' ('The Depths of my Depth'), explores her inner self through objects by describing the contents of her handbag, as noted by Hoda el-Sadda (2010: 316). As she pulls out one item after another, she highlights her interests and her likes and dislikes. Each object represents an aspect of her personality. Writing is a means of exploring the fragments of her identity, just as searching in her own bag. Exploring and pulling out these fragments and objects is a source of fun and pleasure.

Niceness

Peeters (2007) maintains that one of the fictional elements of online self-construction consists of amelioration or self-improvement. Online we tend to display only the better aspects of our personality: the most beautiful pictures, the happiest moments of our lives.

Given the total exposure that the blog form fosters, some bloggers naturally tend to show socially acceptable versions of themselves. This is particularly true if they write with their own name or if they are known to other members of the community. For example, Radwa often writes about her marriage and subsequently about her divorce. As they often link to each other's blog in their account, Radwa and her ex-husband give detailed information about each other's lives. They are also well known in person to other bloggers as they take part in political demonstrations or bloggers' meetings. The community follows their love affair passionately, by providing advice and expressing sorrow. In 'Subhiyyat' ('Mornings', 24 February 2010), Radwa exposes her feelings about her divorce. In the first part, she reflects about her parents' discontent with the fact that she writes about private issues in public. Their discontent may come from the fact that they are from a different generation, which divides more neatly the private and the public sphere. Indeed, her father also keeps a blog, but he mainly uses it to publish his writing and to promote literary events. Her parents are also afraid of the social consequences of this publicity. However, Radwa justifies it in terms of relief: by speaking out publicly about private issues, Radwa is able to achieve personal relief and to receive support from other people. Radwa's writing about the divorce is also driven by a need for self-justification in front of her readership. We need to remember that in Islamic society there is a stigma attached to divorced women. If a woman is divorced by her husband then she must have been the cause. Here Radwa presents their divorce as an 'intellectuals' divorce' (*ṭalāq muthaqqafīn*), made by open-minded, cultured people, who do not carry resentment for each other. She presents herself as a woman in love, a loyal wife, to the point that her friends accused her of 'growing wings', that is, of being too good, almost angelic. Her good-heartedness is also reinforced by the fact that she presents herself as a good Muslim, who believes in and prays to God. In brief, Radwa is exposing her private life in public, but she is showing a socially acceptable version of herself.

This tendency is termed 'niceness' by Serfaty (2004). Being completely transparent to others and being subjected to maximum visibility can lead to a strong internalisation of social conventions that results in writers becoming unable to textualise anything but the most conventional feelings, actions or thoughts (Foucault, quoted in Serfaty 2004: 88). Marie Therèse Abdel-Messih finds the same attitude in the blog-book *Ma^{c}a Nafsi* (*Together with Myself/On My Own*) by Ghada Mahmud (2009). In one entry, Ghada expresses her affiliation to a 'patrimonial legacy' that orders her to restrain her female inclinations. Despite her objections against her overwhelming household responsibilities interfering with her desired feminine image (8 January 2009), she does not blame her husband. Abdel-Messih argues: 'Her private life is a public construction, as she is constantly preoccupied with her sense of inclusion in her social community. In her view, the subjection of women is a given and she neither conceives nor questions the socio-political aspects to that phenomenon' (2009: 516).

Switch On, Log In, Drop Out[17]

So far, we have seen how bloggers write about the self by combining a quest for truth with a quest for imagination. The adoption of these two tendencies is meant to allow the author to explore and express an identity that is perceived as 'true', 'real'. This focus on the body denotes a tendency towards individualism among Egyptian youth, which implies the moral importance of the individual in opposition to traditional social groups and authorities (Bauman 2002).

Several observers have pointed out that computer technology has accelerated a process towards individualisation in Middle Eastern society. The

Iranian scholar Masserat Amir-Ebrahimi (2008) has researched the Iranian blogosphere and she maintains that (1) the structure of the blog, as well as (2) the daily and repeated writings and the existence of an archive and (3) the permanent exposure to others' opinions have given young Iranian bloggers a broader conception of the self. In the Arabic context, Hofheinz asserts that the Internet strengthens more critical or distanced attitudes toward established authorities: individuals are in greater control of what they want to read and look at, are entitled to judge authorised sources of information and have the right to express themselves publicly, to be active participants in the formation of public opinion (Hofheinz 2011: 1427). In what follows, I will discuss how the autofictional blog helps authors to engage in a process of individualisation, that is, a process of emancipation from traditional authority which prescribes in detail how they are meant to behave, and to search for a self that is perceived as true, as authentic. I will focus in particular on the family, the traditional religious authorities and the literary 'family', which I have identified as recurrent themes in the blogosphere.

The Family

The quest for freedom entails, firstly, freedom from the rule of the father, and the family in general. Indeed, we need to keep in mind that in Arab society, the family is based on a patriarchal structure and represents the society in microcosm (Barakat, quoted in Rooke 1997: 240). Family descriptions are recurrent in the bloggers' self-descriptions. The father appears more often than the mother as a target of the blogger's criticism, particularly in blogs written by male writers. Rebellion against the father is a recurrent topic in the conventional autobiographical writing in modern Arabic literature (Anishchenkova 2014: 88). In his study of Arabic autobiography of childhood, Rooke asserts that the child's rebellion towards his father may also be understood as the child's rebellion against the established order in society. In both traditional and modernised societies, the father is the highest authority, who exerts his power on his wife and children. It is not by chance that many Arab rulers refer to themselves as 'the fathers' of their nations, addressing their citizens as their sons.[18] In addition, together with the religious sect, the family constitutes the source of material and emotional security for the average Arab citizen. For this reason, revolt against the family and their values involves taking a personal risk, both socially and economically. Furthermore, patriarchal obedience is a duty placed on the believer by God, both in Islam and Christianity, so attacking the father also means going against the religious order (Rooke 1997: 238).[19]

The family descriptions suggest that bloggers lament the fact that they cannot recognise themselves in the values established by their parents. Even if these accounts differ from each other, they all dramatise a conflict between a growing, developing, exploring and curious youth and an immobile, constraining family environment. In the post 'al-Akharuna Da'iman' ('The Others Always', 28 February 2006), Amr resorts to an unknown online audience to explain that he does not feel at ease with his family, that is 'people with whom you lived for a period of time, your entire life', as they are unable to understand him. His room becomes his space of refuge, and he makes sure that the door is well locked. The juxtaposition of the text with Van Gogh's painting 'Bedroom in Arles' (1888) indicates that the blogger perceives the online page as a space of his own, where he can establish his true self away from family bonds. As a result of this interactive element, Amr discovered that the other members of the community were affected by the same sense of alienation from society and dissatisfaction with the political regime.

One of his readers in fact comments on the above-mentioned post:

> I think this is a general situation, I mean for the youth, I also suffer from this problem somehow.
> May God help, the best thing is to put oneself afire, to be relieved and to relieve the others! :D
>
> أظن أنها حالة عامة إلى حد ما، أقصد بالنسبة للشباب، أنا ايضا أعاني من هذه المشكلة بشكل او بآخر
> كان الله في العون
> احسن حاجة الواحد يولع في نفسه عشان يرتاح ويريح :-D

Blog narratives evince that families are perceived as authoritarian and overprotective. As the parents developed in a time in which education and hard labour were the only means to improve their life, they insist that their sons and daughters achieve a high standard of education and pursue specific vocations, such as medicine or engineering. They encourage their children to make material profits, rather than follow their aspirations. This is exemplified in the post 'Kamal al-Tukhi' ('Kamal al-Tukhi', 29 February 2008) in Nael Eltoukhy's blog. The narrator ironically describes his father's disapproval of his choice to study Hebrew by saying: 'There is no use! Israel will be a dead civilization in fifty years!' hinting at the possibility that his father is still influenced by Nasser's optimism about the defeat of Israel. The critique of his father is tempered by a kind humour, which makes the text funny and serious at the same time.

Another distinction is the fact that some families have a conservative approach to religion. This is due either to the fact that they have been influenced by the Gulf nations' religious attitudes during their years of migration, or that they lived in an age where religious preachers were given more importance and credit than public intellectuals. As an example, in Al-Baraa Ashraf's post 'ᵓAbi Yuhibb Ummi, Qissa Ghayr Haqiqiyya' ('My Father Loves My Mother, Untrue Story', 24 October 2007),[20] the narrator recounts the divorce between his mother, a schoolteacher, and her husband, a member of the Muslim Brotherhood. The narrator criticises his father's religious conservatism that admonished his mother's beauty and intellectual disposition by forcing her to wear a *niqāb* and to stay at home; he also laments the fact that his father impeded his children's creative spirit by preventing them from watching TV or listening to music, activities that are considered *ḥarām* in conservative religious circles. His personal revolution starts from the moment he decides to leave his father's house and move to Qena, Upper Egypt, where he is finally free to listen to music and watch TV in his own house.

For Arab young women, the rebellion against the father may be even more tragic, as it implies that the woman needs to achieve economic independence in order to live on her own, and this might not be easy for a single young woman. This dilemma is narrated as the entry to the blog 'Dahiyyat Harb' ('Victim of a War', 5 March 2008) by Abeer Soliman. Here, Abeer describes herself as a 'victim of a war against the family, the society, the man, and the religious views about women'. To clarify her point, Abeer presents her readers with a story (*qiṣṣa*). The story, narrated in first person, tells of Abeer's decision to liberate herself from the shackles of 'an ill-tempered father who sought to secure the future of his children, but who forgot in the midst of his journey that we also need emotional security against the vagaries and crises of life'. This implies that her youth was marked by economic difficulties, constant struggles at work and plenty of lies, to hide that she had left her father's house to go and live on her own. The character is described as a victim because she is left with a feeling of duty towards the others, where she always has to prove worthiness (*jadārtī*). Nonetheless, her writing is permeated with nostalgia for her origins. In 'Rahil Habibati' ('My Beloved's Departure', 21 July 2008), for example, she describes a visit to her family in the village on the occasion of her grandmother's death. Here Abeer is divided between a melancholy towards her place of birth and alienation from the habits and customs of her family and the village in general. Once in the house, she sits alone in the corner, as she feels she no longer belongs there. One of her aunts addresses her as 'stranger' (*gharība*).

Likewise, 'al-Jahim' ('The Hell', 26 May 2009) by Emraamethlya offers a further reflection on women's struggle to escape patriarchal authority in order to achieve their own independence as a woman. She tells that, forced to accomplish the social and familial expectations of marriage and reproduction, she married a man and tried to adapt to a heterosexual marital life. This effort was to prove a failure, as they divorced shortly after. She justifies this 'failed attempt' as a test for herself that has made her even more aware of her sexual identity, and that deceiving a man is more sinful than loving another woman. Nonetheless, she admits to her readers that the status of divorced woman has given her the opportunity to work, to earn her own money and live on her own without being dependent on her family.

Unlike paternal descriptions, the portraits of the mother are permeated with warmer feelings. Again this is a recurrent pattern in Arabic autobiography, where the mother is an idealised figure of high morals, purity and self-sacrifice (Anishchenkova 2014: 89). However, even though mothers are described in a more positive light, bloggers' family descriptions nonetheless subvert established family patterns. In *The Red Sofa*, Bilal evokes his mother in almost every entry, as a means of healing himself through writing from the shock of her death. The mother is described in the phase of her illness, therefore in her most absolute weakness. In the post 'Kaᶜb Mama' ('My Mum's Ankles', 12 January 2007), Bilal endows his filial love almost with a hint of Oedipal love.

Her influence on me after her death embraces me
And up till now she is still haunting me, in my dreams it appears to me
that I could have done something better for her
that I had not done.
Many sad and scary wrinkles appear (on her face)
...
The steady factor is that I was infatuated with my mom but hated her to a harmful extent
To the point that I imagined that her illness would purify her
To the point that her eyes laughed at me in a dream
that she will recover from the illness after her death
This poem is about her
About her warm ankles
Seriously, her death was not dramatic, it was a death of my brown color
My skin color
Oh

تأثيرها بعد موتها احتوانى
وفضلت لحد دلوقت تطاردنى ف تظهر لى فاحلامى انى كنت ممكن اعمل حاجه
احسن ليها ومعملتهاش
بتظهربتجاعيد كتيرة ومخيفه وحزينه
...
الثابت انى كنت متيم بماما وبكرها لحد مؤذى
لدرجه خلتنى اتخيل مرضها هيطهرها
لحد ما عنيها تضحك لى ف حلم
هتخلص من مرضها حتى بعد موتها
القصيده الفوق دى عنها
عن كعوبها الدافيه
بجد مش دراما موتها كان موت للونى البنى
لون جلدى
اوه

The thought of her death obsesses him, possibly to the point of paranoia. His filial love is embedded with a feeling of guilt. The last parallel between her death and his skin points out that her presence becomes ingrained into his body.

An unconventional description of the mother figure can also be found in Mona Seif's blog. In the entry 'Aqaddim-Luku Mama' ('I Introduce to You my Mother', 17 November 2007), Mona describes a day in which she lost sight of her mom during a demonstration, to only find out hours later that she had been taken by the police and released after interrogation. The story is coupled with a picture of her mom shouting at a row of policemen. This subverts the usual descriptions of the mother figure as the caring mother who takes care of the household. The description of her mother sits alongside other posts in which Mona writes about her family members and the people who are close to her or, as she writes, 'who makes a difference for me', such as her brothers and sister, her grandmother, her father, and so on. In those portraits, Mona's family relations are given fictional names: her grandmother is simply named Hiya (She), until 2011 her brother Alaa is named 'At-Tinnin al-Bambi' ('The Pink Dragon', 18 November 2006) and his wife Manal 'Sayyidat al-ᶜUmraniyya al-ᵓUla' ('The First Lady of Omraneya', 7 April 2007). The choice of these fictional names is perhaps aimed at retaining their anonymity online, due to their continual exposure to prison and police brutality. At the same time, Maat is aware that her family members are already known to many members of the blogging community, especially the ones who are actively engaged in political dissent; however, by writing about them, she proudly claims her family ties and she offers her personal perspective of them. In addition, she intends to shed light on the extent that her family has contributed to the formation of her identity.

It often occurs that bloggers present family stories as imaginary ones. During their interviews, several bloggers claimed that in their blogs they try to avoid writing about their close relatives, because despite their lack of concern over their own privacy, they still want to protect their family's social respectability. As Catherine Cusset maintains, the autofiction writer is afraid of the effect that his own work will have on others.[21] The writer's moral decency generates a tension between the desire for truth and the fear of truth. 'The other, you, becomes an internal limit of autofiction' (Cusset 2012).

Religion

As well as the familial nucleus, young people are expected to integrate into the religious community. This is the effect of a revivalist Muslim religious discourse that became particularly prominent in the 1970s, after a period of secularisation that began earlier in the twentieth century. In the 1970s, President Sadat made it his aim to endow the state with an Islamic aura. He cultivated his public image as a pious Muslim, attributing to himself the title of 'the Believer President'. To this end, he increased Islamic programming in the media, schools and universitities, and cultivated relationships with religious leaders, such as religious scholars and the Shaykh of Al-Azhar. His encouragement of religious revivalism included a more liberal attitude towards Islamic groups, such as the Muslim Brotherhood (who were banned under Nasser) and the Islamic student associations, in order to counter the influence of pro-Nasser secular leftists. Members of the Muslim Brotherhood, who had been imprisoned in 1965 or gone into exile under Nasser's rule, were welcomed back into the country and allowed to create new media platforms to spread their ideology (Esposito 1984). Some writers have suggested that the fact that so many Egyptians spent some years during the 1970s and 1980s in the Gulf countries, where religion is more strictly observed, may have contributed to the Islamic revival in Egypt (Amin 2000: 41). This revival of Islamic tendencies has turned nonbelief into a serious taboo in Egypt. Samuli Schielke has shown in his anthropological study that publicly criticising core religious beliefs provokes disapproval and misunderstanding, may lead to forced divorce and loss of employment, and can result in imprisonment and assassination; therefore, many non-believers 'live fragmented lives with a high degree of duplicity' (Schielke 2012: 306). The spread of blogging and social networks has provided an outlet for non-religious views to be expressed in public. Indeed, the relative anonymity and freedom of the blog form encourages young people to assert and imagine a different approach to religion. At the same time, by going public, bloggers search for comfort and dialogue with their peers.

It is not rare to find accounts in which bloggers deal with religion with imaginative and playful attitudes; it is maybe thanks to this imagination and playfulness that the blogger is able to assert a more sincere, authentic religious view. For example, Bilal describes his relationship with God in the terms of game and casuality. In the entry 'al-Mushaf' ('The Quran', 10 November 2007), he writes that he and his girlfriend would put the Quran face down, open it randomly and read the sura on the page. After becoming bored with the game, they accidentally left the Quran outdoors. Later, they found the book in the corridor between the buildings, amidst the rubbish, a highly blasphemous image. In another entry, he mocks the conservative approach to religion and the way Islam is perceived by Western non-Muslims. This ironic attitude is shown in his dialogue with Mathieu, his American flatmate. While they sit together in front of a computer, Mathieu asks him: 'Do you have an objection if I use the mouse with my left hand?' ('il-ᶜId il-Shimal' ('The Left Hand'), 9 July 2007). The author is making fun of the fact that conservative Muslims refrain from using their left hand for regular actions, because it is said that the Prophet would only use it for cleaning himself. Mathieu thinks that this applies to every Muslim, including Bilal. The author/narrator does not add any narrative comment. However, the lines are followed by the picture of a waiter holding a glass of wine with his left hand, which adds emphasis to the blogger's sarcastic attitude towards religious fastidiousness.

Criticism of religion does not mean that all of these young bloggers become secular. Indeed, some of them, for example Emraamethlya, search for a more human, intimate relationship with God, based on a personal interpretation of religion, rather than the strict one suggested by religious conservatives. In the blog, she recounts her struggle with the realisation that she had desire for other women, a desire that is different from the social norm and is decried as being *ḥarām*, or forbidden. This in turn provoked a great amount of doubts regarding her faith and her relationship with God. Her first reaction was to acknowledge this desire, but then decide ultimately not to live it out, and to repress and contain her feelings.

> I don't deny that a strong conflict took place inside me the first time I felt attracted to women instead of men I was saying to myself 'no, this is not true, it is just a phase and it will pass it is just a change like all the other changes and turnabouts in teenage years' however days went by year after year teen age was over and nothing had changed first I was shocked I asked 'why?', a thousand and one whys were drilling my brain and there was no answer until I even asked to God 'Why?' ('Itsalaht Maᶜa Nafsi' ('I Was Reconciled with Myself'), 30 January 2006)

> منكرش أن صراعا قوي كان بيدور جوياه من يوم ما حسيت بإنجذابي نحو النساء دون الرجال و كنت بقول لنفسي لا مش صحيح دي اكيد فتره و حتعدي يعني تغير

> زي التغيرات و الأنقلابات بتاعت المراهقة بس كانت الأيام بتعدي و سنه ورا سنه خلصت المراهقة و مفيش حاجة أتغيرت في الأول أتصدمت و سألت ليه؟ ألف ليه و ليه كانت بتنخر في دماغي و مفيش إجابه حتى أني سألت ربنا ليه؟

Once she realised that she could not pray homosexuality away, and that her merciful God could not have created her sinful, Emraamethlya decided to ignore the religious teaching received by her parents and by the men of religion and to return to the original religious texts, to start her own personal research into and interpretation of the Quran, to find a personal way of reconciliation with God.

> I am an Arab and Muslim woman and like all Arab women, Muslim or Christian, I have learned since I was a child to fear God more than to love him. I learned how to fulfil the teachings of religion which were represented by what my Mum and my Dad said and which in turn they heard from the religious scholars who occupy a sacred place and whose sayings are not open for discussion. So, I researched a lot … and here I will try to answer the question that has been haunting me for a long time: is [lesbianism] *halal* or *haram*? ('al-Mithliyya al-nisaʾiyya fi 'l-ʾislam' ('Female Homosexuality in Islam'), 11 February 2006)

> أنا إمرأة عربية و مسلمة و مثل كل النساء العرب مسلمات أو مسيحيات تعلمت منذ نعومة أظافري أن اخاف الله أكثر من أن أحبه و تعلمت أن أنفذ تعاليم الدين المتمثلة فيما يقوله أبي و امي و التي يسمعناها [sic] من رجال الدين و الذين يحتلون مكانا مقدسا و كل ما يقولونه يكون غير قابل للنقاش. لقد بحثت كثيرا ...سوف احاول ان اجيب على السؤال الذي ظل يؤرقني لفترة طويلة هو : حلال أم حرام؟

Her personal research reinforces her faith in God rather than shakes it. She reaches the conclusion that her identity is the result of God's will, thus she has no choice other than to accept it. She points out that loving a person is not something that stands in opposition to being religious. In her words: 'We don't choose when we love, so what is it that hurts my religion if my heart beats for a woman, and I find happiness in her and I want to share my life with her.'[22]

Ahmed Naji addresses the question of religious identity in his early entries, despite the fact that he calls himself 'Iblis'. For example, in the entry

'Fi Mas'alat al-Salah' ('On the Question of Praying', 25 April 2005) he asks his audience why he sometimes feels the need to pray. The fact that the Devil confesses his need for prayer indicates that the Devil is still developing; his online personality is not a definite, stable one, rather it is being constructed over time with the support of the online community. In a later entry, Naji asserts that his attitude towards the big religious questions is not the arrogant certitude that is the hallmark of religion, but doubt. To express this, he used the example of the blind poet al-Maʿarri, known for his scepticism[23] ('ʾAn Takun Shakkakan ka-Khayal al-Zill' ('To be as Suspicious as a Shadow'), 27 April 2005).[24] In our interview, Naji claims that many members of the blogging community were hampered by questions of religious identity when they first entered the blogosphere. Unlike the offline world, the relative anonymity of the blogging community encouraged religious dialogue.

> Many bloggers were part of the Muslim Brotherhood organization. Others claimed to be 'atheist' or 'communists'. The blogosphere allowed us to talk freely about our religious identity without the fear of being accused or intimidated, as happens in offline society. Eventually, many bloggers, especially the most religious ones softened their religious views after an ongoing intellectual discussion with other bloggers.[25]

Therefore, it can be said that the Web has favoured the criticism of normative and fundamentalist religious thought in a way that was not possible before in offline media. It has validated a religious approach based on a personal interpretation of religion and an intimate relationship with God.[26]

The 'Family of Literature'

Another 'authority' that is often recurrent in bloggers' accounts is the figure of the literati, the Egyptian writer or intellectual. The fact that a great number of these bloggers articulate their relationship towards the 'literary fathers' indicates that they might have literary ambitions, and they aspire to enter into the cultural field.

Jacquemond writes that the relationships between older, more established writers and the younger ones within the Egyptian cultural field are often hierarchical. He quotes the Egyptian proverb, 'older by a day, wiser by a year', to indicate that the younger generation have to strive harder to find their place (2008: 169). Usually the power of senior generations is such that to gain access to the field, new entrants must constitute themselves as small, more or less homogeneous groups, and they tend to theorise their generation's diverse aesthetic experiment as 'revolutionary' to varying degrees. For example, Nael Eltoukhy aims a humorous critique at the famous Egyptian writer Alaa al-Aswany, whose style, in his view, is too 'realistic' and lacks literariness.[27] On 7 December 2007, Nael writes that he has just discovered that Al-Aswany inserts a character named 'Nail al-Tukhy', who works as a spy, into his novel *Shikaghu* (*Chicago*, 2007). In the blog entry, Nael imagines himself going to interview Al-Aswany and revealing to him that the real Nael is a journalist, and not a spy, causing him a big shock.

Jacquemond notices that relationships between generations are not necessarily ones of conflict (2008: 172). Since the 1950s and up to the present day, the most radical young authors have looked for, and found, material and moral support among older writers, who could facilitate their entry into the literary field. In fact, Muhammad Aladdin dedicates an entry to the Egyptian author Baha Taher, whose laudatory tone is already anticipated by the title: 'Fi Madih Bahaᵓ Tahir' ('In Praise of Baha Taher', 30 November 2006). He describes Baha as 'one of the most important of his literary fathers, who nurtured our generation with reading and thinking' and uploads a picture of himself and the writer sitting in a bookshop, portraying himself as a 'fan'. The same respect is also manifested by Aladdin towards the Egyptian writer Sonallah Ibrahim (15 April 2005), whom he elects as his mentor, the one who guides him through the difficult world of the Egyptian literary scene.[28] Several bloggers also dedicate entries to Naguib Mahfouz (30 June 2006), for example Amr Ezzat in 'Shaykhi' ('My Mentor', 8 September 2006) and Muhammad al-Hajj in 'Shahada ᶜan Mahfuz' ('Testimony about Mahfouz', 14 December 2010). Other bloggers, such as 'Sham3on' and Mahmud Hassan, upload pictures of Arab writers onto their blogs to express their admiration for them.

The Personal is Political

In this chapter, I have explored how Egyptian bloggers construct their identities on the blog and I have identified a main theme: 'the body'. The body can be set as the site of intersection between identity construction and other accounts concerning politics, religion, family and literature.

Blogging is driven by a quest for authenticity that pushes the bloggers to amass the pieces of their body and the scattered fragments of their identity. Following this quest for authenticity, bloggers write their body through the expression of emotions and feelings. At the same time, blogging is driven by a quest for imagination: bloggers tend to imagine different versions of their bodies that take the form of animals, objects and Egyptian goddesses. The identity is also fictionalised, in the sense that bloggers display only socially acceptable versions of themselves or tend to stress certain aspects of their personality, such as childish or rebellious instincts. These narratives are not meant to present a character that is different from the author, but rather to present dreams and ambitions that still pertain to the body, but that bloggers are hindered from presenting in offline society because of social, religious and political constraints. The importance bloggers give to the body is also related to their rejection of traditional authorities, which tend to impose their power on the body and to reject the human dimension of the self, that is, sexual instincts, emotions, body feelings.

The bloggers' tendency to share private issues online might be interpreted as a general tendency that affects modern societies, defined by the French philosopher Serge Tisseron as '*extimité*' (translated in English as 'extimacy'). 'Extimacy' consists of sharing with a relatively large group of people certain parts of oneself that were, up to that point, shielded from the gaze of others (and thus kept private). This tendency is motivated by the need for self-validation and the desire for approval through the gaze of the others (Tisseron 2003).

However, Tisseron's theory of extimacy partially explains why bloggers tend to display private issues in public. In fact, it must also be pointed out that in Egyptian society, this relative freedom can only be found online, while societal discourse is marked by more conservative tendencies. The body, in particular, is often the site of the inscription of social discipline and power (Mavelli 2012: 1058). Sherine Seykaly (2013) argues that in Egyptian society, 'power is so diffused that you live it on your own body, the flesh becomes the place where you are meant to be a consenting subject. Ethics, social status, social meaning are tied to the body.' Therefore, displaying private issues in public is often meant as an act of rebellion against social control and society's hypocritical tendency to hide the most 'ugly' aspects of society. Publicly exposing one's privacy thus may turn into a radical criticism of society. Bloggers aim at bringing about social change through self-disclosure. Therefore, just as feminist scholars have argued in relation to women body-writing, to write the body on the blog is therefore to engage in a political act as much as in a personal one. The feminist slogan quoted above, 'the Personal is Political',[29] may be very well applied in the Egyptian blogosphere, as both male and female bloggers write about their body as an act of rebellion towards patriarchal authority.

Bloggers' online narratives may be seen as a site of resistance. Bloggers expose a body that is tortured and violated by sexual harassment and police brutality. They claim the right to express amorousness and sexual desires that are natural attributes of the body, but are considered improper by society and religion. They question the power of established authorities in order to affirm their own views and beliefs. They legitimise different gender practices. By forcing the tortured body back into the public domain, they disclose the inscriptions of power/knowledge regimes onto the body, thus turning the body from an 'inscribed surface of events', at the mercy of the sheer power of the regime, into 'a source of resistance' (Mavelli 2012: 1059). They depict a body that is estranged by the social community it belongs to, because the society and the state do not pay any respect to emotions and bodily needs. The scars that bloggers carry on their bodies are personal, but at the same time they hint at a more general *malaise* that affects the entire society. There is no personal solution for it, if not denouncing it and speaking out.

This focus on the body illuminates the relation between the blogs and the 25 January revolution. One might argue that by breaking the fear barrier in the online sphere, bloggers have planted the seeds for a battle in offline reality, a battle in which Egyptian people have participated with their bodies.[30]

Several scholars have indeed celebrated Internet technology as a primary agent of the 25 January uprising, seemingly ignoring the fact that machines are managed by humans. On the opposite side, more recent studies have focused on the importance of the human body when analysing these political events. In his book *The Naked Blogger of Cairo* (2016), Marwan Kraidy maintains that the human body was central to the ways revolutionaries represented themselves and their opponents. Similarly, for Mavelli (2012), the fact that the picture of Khaled Said's brutalised body has managed to bring together millions of Egyptians, who took to the streets asking for dignity, means that the tortured bodies became the metaphor of a different kind of unity, a post-secular unity encompassing all Egyptians. Even before that, when Tunisian Mohamed Bouazizi set himself on fire, it was a desperate act, but also a powerful act, because it was a rejection of the State's capacity to exercise its power over the body (Seykaly 2013). Khaled Said's picture symbolised the body of Egypt – a body 'abused, raped and beaten by the state' (Mavelli 2012: 1072). During the Egyptian revolution, Egyptians reacted to this brutality by exposing their own bodies: they took to the streets knowing they could be raped, tortured or killed. Nonetheless, the massive amount of people willing to pay this price was a remarkable phenomenon. By going to the street, by rejecting sexual harassment, by demonstrating against the virginity test, Egyptian people have broken the fear of public shame.

In conclusion, by grounding the body in the blogosphere, bloggers have contributed to the rise of the 'individual', and the importance of human nature, as a political agent. By exposing their bodies, they have taken from the rulers and authorities the power to represent their subjectivity. However, we need to remember that the blogosphere, even if it is supposed to be a freer space, still reflects in a way the prejudice and constraints imposed in offline society. In her ethnographic study of Internet users in Kuwait, Wheeler asserts that 'online behavior is in part shaped by off-line variables' (2006: 189). While bloggers conceive the blog as a place of their own, in which they can feel free to talk about anything, they need to remember that, just as in Egyptian offline society, shame plays an important role. Keeping a social reputation is essential to the maintenance of personal and family honour. This must be remembered, especially when the bloggers use their real names and interact with the community in an offline setting. In their self-writing, Egyptian bloggers have to find a compromise between the fear of transparency and the desire for total self-disclosure. The solution to this question is often represented by the bloggers' reliance on fictional devices, whose function is to discourage the readers from attributing the events to the bloggers' own life. Alternatively, they sometimes portray only socially acceptable versions of themselves or practice self-censorship.

Notes

1 This view corresponds to a tendency in contemporary societies to encourage the expression of emotions as a way to reach our true self, 'for in their very naturalness they are perceived as breaking through the bonds of culture' (Lupton 1998: 88). D. Lupton explains that while Modern and Enlightenment-era intellectual schools discarded emotions, as they were considered to be the antithesis of reason and rationality and thus disruptive to the project of 'knowing the self', in recent years, with the rise of postmodernism, several theorists have argued that emotional experience is an essential and insightful conduit to knowledge (1998: 3). Stephan Guth has shown that there are several Middle Eastern postmodern novels that make fun of this search for authenticity and emotionality. For authors like Pamuk, for example, 'heroes having lost their individuality gain fun, if only to overcome the "imperative" of individuality, originality, or authenticity, which, from the age of Romanticism onwards, had restricted the possibilities of everyone who wanted to be solely "himself", i.e., as individualistic as possible.' See Stephan Guth (2007: 38), 'Individuality Lost, Fun Gained'.

2 Al-Baraa Ashraf defines the blogging community as 'a group of people put together by the need to confess' (29 January 2007). Ahmad Naji appreciates blogging because it allows him to 'speak openly (*al-būḥ*)' (see Chapter 2).

3 The 'body' is a recurrent theme in autofictional novels. This has charged French autofictional authors with being 'exhibitionists, shameless, and sexually obsessed'. In response to these accusations, Gasparini argues that the body displayed in these novels, is a body that very rarely enjoys pleasure, but rather suffers from illness, trauma, from the signs of old age (Gasparini 2008: 303).

4 In this discussion of embodied emotions and feelings, I am aware that there is a body of scholarship that, inspired by the Deleuzian theories of affect, makes a distinction between 'affects' and 'emotions'. While 'affect' refers to the precognitive sensory experience and its relationship to surroundings, 'emotions' are seen as culturally conscious constructs that emerge from them, such as anger, fear and joy. It is not my intention to engage in this discussion. Instead, I will follow Ann Cvetovich's use of terms such as emotions and feelings as generic terms for description, points of departure for a discussion, rather than for definition. In her book, *Depression: A Public Feeling*, these terms are indicated as 'the undifferentiated stuff of feeling that involves both body sensations and cognitive constructions of them, and that acknowledges body and mind as integrated' (Cvetovich 2012: 4).

5 For a discussion of the body in Arabic literature, see also Hoda el-Sadda's book chapter (El-Sadda 2012: 145–64) on the novels written by Egyptian women authors of the 1990s generation, in which the body figures as a main theme: 'The Personal is Political'. The novelist and scholar Sahar al-Mougy (al-Muji 1998) writes about the political significance of writing about the body for this generation in 'al-Kitaba ᶜan al-Jasad Nawᶜ Min al-Tamarrud' ('Writing about the Body is a Form of Rebellion'). See also Martina Censi (2016), *Le Corps dans le roman des écrivaines syriennes contemporaines* which explores the representation of the body in a selection of Arabic novels published (between 2004 and 2011) by six Syrian women authors.

6 Interview with the blogger. See the comment section in http://ma3t.blogspot.com/2006/10/blog-post_116213672466549323.html (last accessed 20 August 2017).

7 Likewise, in a post entitled 'Muhawala li-Tarjamat al-Haya' ('An Attempt at Translating Life', 9 December 2006), Rihab Bassam expresses her sense of fear as a woman concerning sexual harassment. The post recounts that while heading to a translation class at university, Rihab found a group of boys harassing girls. Disturbed, she hesitantly informed the university security guards. Later, when asked by her professor why she was not concentrating, she replies, 'I am scared (*ana khayfa*)'. As suggested by the post's title, Rihab uses her skills in translation in an attempt to translate life, and in a sense, recreate it. The contrast between the instructions she has to follow as a translator and what happens on the street gives a dramatic edge to the scene.

8 We find a similar attitude in the blog written by Rihab Bassam. Rihab's attachment to her childhood is echoed by her profile picture, depicting her as a child. The line captioning the picture says, '*mawlūdah li-l-ḥawādīt wa-shamm al-ward*' ('born for stories and to smell roses'). Likewise, in Nirmin Nizar's book-blog, the longing for childhood is expressed by invoking the image of Peter Pan. In her words: 'What excites me most in Peter Pan is that he is a child that refuses to grow up and he actually manages to remain a child. What most excites me about Wendy is that she wished to fly, and she did' (2008: 71). The book adapted from her blog is dedicated to Peter Pan. Similarly, Ahmad al-Fakharani writes on the lower banner of his blog-template, 'Ahmad al-Fakharani … writer, journalist, pharmacist, in a previous life … waiting to become Peter Pan in another life'.

9 Just like Mona, the blogger Zubayda describes her curly, messy hair as a metaphor for her subversive personality ('Wa-ma Baynahuma' ('Between the two of them'), 4 August 2009). The search for happiness and for a different self is also

expressed by Ghada Mahmud in the post 'Bayni wa-Bayni' ('Between me and me'), written in the colloquial; Ghada's search for a different self implies the imagination of a different body: straight hair, wings, tall and a childish look. Just as in Mona's passage quoted previously, the blogger explicitly suggests to the reader that this self-representation is fictional, although necessary to achieve a personal relief. In another passage, 'Hadhihi Raqsati Ana' ('This is my own dance'), Ghada imagines her body dancing freely for her lover. The use of the future tense throughout the passage expresses the blogger's strong wish for a different self and a visionary impulse. 'When I will dance for you, I will wear a red dress, my hair will be loose and my feet bare; I will wear only *kohl*, and I will teach you the magic of flamenco' (2008: 36).

10 The original Arabic is:

دا اللى صار وآدى اللى كان... مالكش حق.. ملكش حق تلوم عليا أهو

These verses and the title of the story are taken from the song by the Egyptian composer Sayyid Darwish (1892–1923), considered the father of Egyptian popular music.

11

* ليس للأحداث علاقة بصاحب المدونة

12 The *līf* is palm fibre used in lieu of a bath sponge. It is known for its rough texture and touch.

13 The deterioration of the body is a theme in several autofictional works. To mention just a few, we can think about Hervé Guibert's novels dealing with HIV, for example *À l'ami qui ne m'a pas sauvé la vie* (1990), published in English as *To the Friend Who Did Not Save My Life* in 1993. In the analysis of Guibert's works, Genon writes that autofiction is not a choice but a necessity: it translates the author's experience of alienation towards his own body; it allows him to distance himself and describe a body that is now transformed, that he cannot recognise any longer. See Arnaud Genon, 'Hervé Guibert: fracture autobiographique et écriture du sida' (Genon 2010).

14 Mona studied Zoology at the University of Cairo.

15 See Salah Jahin (2010), *Rubāʿiyyāt*, Cairo: Sphinx Agency.

16 بس كنت بنام وادامى العجله ولان خيالى واسع بحكم تجربه الكتابه انا كنت بنام فى اتجاه عكس رؤيه العجله لانهاالجسم الوحيد فى الشقه غيري

17 My title is a spin on the slogan 'turn on, tune in, drop out', a counterculture phrase used by Timothy Leary in 1967. It urged people to embrace cultural

changes through the use of psychedelics and by detaching themselves from existing conventions and hierarchies in society. My transposition indicates that Egyptian bloggers have used the Internet and blogging to break social conventions and detach themselves from mainstream society.

18 Even in his last speech to the nation, in February 2011, in which he announced that he would transfer some power to his deputy but would not step down until the election, Mubarak addressed his citizens saying, 'I am addressing the youth of Egypt today in Tahrir Square and across the country. I am addressing you all from the heart, a father's dialogue with his sons and daughters.' The speech is available at http://www.youtube.com/watch?v=l931zZcUbWU (last accessed 20 August 2017).

19 For a more detailed discussion of rebellion against patriarchal families in Arabic autobiography, see Tetz Rooke (1997: 237–68). See also H. Fähndrich (1995), 'Fathers and husbands'.

20 Al-Baraa says in the interview that his story is based on true events; however, he labelled it as untrue to prevent the readers from attributing it to his life.

21 Cusset writes that this limit of autofiction derives from an accident related to Doubrovsky's publication of the novel *Fils*. Doubrovsky's wife, Ilse, was tired of seeing him write only about the other women in his life, and asked him to write about their own relationship. He warned her that it would not be easy for her because he would write everything, a warning she accepted. As soon as he finished a chapter of his novel, he would send it to her to receive her feedback. Because of a visa problem, Ilse stayed in Paris while Serge went back to New York, and from New York he sent her the most challenging chapters in the book: the one about her abortions and tragic miscarriages, and the subsequent chapter detailing her consequential alcoholism and the ensuing domestic strife caused by the drinking. He was particularly pleased by this latter chapter; however, shortly after Ilse received it, she died. Although it was not proven, it is suggested that she committed suicide. On returning to Paris, Doubrovsky found an empty bottle of vodka in her fridge, and took it as a sign of relapse; additionally, Ilse had been taking anti-depressants. In the second part of the book, written shortly after her death, Doubrovsky finds himself questioning himself about her demise: 'Why?' 'Why did she do it?' 'How could she?' Over two hundred pages, the reasons he gives for her death are many. He addresses her alcohol addiction as the main cause. However, on page 572 he admits, 'My ink poisoned her, the game of truth is sometimes fatal' (Cusset 2012).

22 إننا لا نختار عندما نحب فماذا يضر ديني إن خفق قلبي لإمراة و اردت أن تشاركني حياتي و أجد سعادتي معها.

23 Al-Maarri taught that religion was a 'fable invented by the ancients'. Quoted in Reynold Alleyne Nicholson (1907: 318).

24 As mentioned in Chapter 2, '*khayāl al-ẓill*' is an expression used in the first title that Naji chose for his blog (*Yawmiyyat Khayal al-Zill* (*Diary of a Shadow Play*)). Therefore, the expression can be understood as self-referential. However, it must be noted that in Egyptian dialect, *khayal al-zill* is often used to mean just 'a shadow' rather than the technical meaning of 'shadow play'. This latter meaning seems more appropriate here.

25 Interview, March 2011.

26 This has already been argued by Albrecht Hofheinz in his article 'Nextopia' (2011).

27 The same critique of 'naïve realism' and lack of artistic quality is expressed by Sabry Hafez in regard to the novel *Yacoubian Building* by Al-Aswany. See Sabry Hafez (2006), 'ʿImarat Yaqubian'.

28 Sonallah Ibrahim had done the same with the writer Yusuf Idris. He submitted to him the manuscript of his novel *Tilka al-Ra'yha* (*The Smell of it*, 1966). Following Idris' suggestion, he reworked the text and changed the title and Idris offered to write a preface to the book (Jacquemond 2008: 172). Note also that Sonallah Ibrahim has acted as a defender for Ahmed Naji during the trial held in 2016.

29 One of the main inspirational figures in the tradition of writing the body in literature is Hélène Cixous, who called on women to 'write through their bodies, because only in writing lies the possibility of change, the space that can serve as a springboard for subversive thought, the precursory movement of a transformation of social and cultural structures' (quoted in El-Sadda 2012: 156).

30 An important episode in the history of the Egyptian blogosphere is the unveiling of Aliaa al-Mahdy on her blog in late 2011. On 27 May, she posted a naked picture of herself, as well as drawings of nudes. She attached the following text to the picture: 'Put on trial the artists' models who posed nude for art schools until the early 1970s, hide the art books, and destroy the nude statues of antiquity, then undress and stand before a mirror and burn your bodies that you despise to forever rid yourselves of your sexual hang-ups before you direct your humiliation and chauvinism and dare to try to deny me my freedom of expression.' Her blog and her Twitter account reached an incredible number of visits (Radsch

indicates her blog was viewed more than 1.1 million times and her picture on Twitter more than 14,000). After that, she left Egypt and lives in Europe at the moment. See Radsch (2012: 32), 'Unveiling the Revolution'. For an analysis of al-Mahdy's unveiling, see M. Kraidy (2016), *The Naked Blogger of Cairo*.

6

Blogging a Revolution: From Utopia to Dystopia

From the Blogosphere to Tahrir Square

While they serve to record, clarify and validate the self, blogs are also intended to be shared. Bloggers worldwide see blogging as a way of developing relationships with an online community, via linking back, waiting for signs of approval, acceptance, value. In fact, according to Miller and Shepherd (2004), 'what is truly novel in the blog is the ability to address simultaneously these dual yet mutually reinforcing purposes: to engage in self-expression in order to build community and to build community in order to cultivate the self'.

Initially, while writing about their personal feelings and frustrations, Egyptian bloggers were addressing an audience that was 'imagined', in the sense that, 'even if it was not founded on daily life interactions and strong interpersonal links, it shared the experience of instant publishing and participated in his [the blogger's] writing through feedback and comments' (Lampa 2004). Several bloggers looked at this community as a kind of utopian society because, unlike the offline Egyptian society that tends to suppress individuality and to annihilate personal differences, it included and encouraged a wide range of humanity. Also, as a result of this interactive element, bloggers discovered that most of the members of the community were affected by the same sense of alienation in society and dissatisfaction with the political regime. This is what encouraged them to keep blogging and to meet with other bloggers outside the virtual world.[1]

This is evidenced by the fact that Amr Ezzat, like many other bloggers, inserts pictures and writes accounts of bloggers' informal meetings (see Figure 16), and chronicles their participation in political and cultural campaigns.

For example, in his October 2006 entry 'Maᵓida Haqiqiyya' ('A Real Table', 7 October 2006), Amr describes a Ramadan *ifṭār* meeting among bloggers:

> It is so difficult to imagine that all those 'very different' people would gather around the same table! However, after a short time in each other's company at the virtual table, that became possible in the real world! This is the real innovation of the idea of blogging: the idea of an open universal forum without barriers!
>
> من الصعب تخيل أن يجتمع كل هؤلاء ' المختلفين جدا ' علي مائدة واحدة .
> و لكن بعد فترة , ليست بالطويلة , من الصحبة علي المائدة الافتراضية الواحدة ,
> أصبح ذلك ممكنا في العالم الحقيقي .هذا هو الإبداع الحقيقي لفكرة التدوين ..
> فكرة ذلك المنتدي الكوني المفتوح بلا حواجز.

Figure 16 The virtual table in the real world. Bloggers' *ifṭār* meeting held in Ramadan 2005. Source: http://mabadali.blogspot.no.

The presence of visual elements achieves a documentary function, as they act as pieces of evidence supporting the statement of the author. The picture also anchors his online character in the reality and in a precise social setting. Nonetheless, the verbal account is infused with the blogger's personal perceptions. The virtual/real table is presented as a utopian society without barriers within which different people peacefully coexist.

Soon, Amr also projects the dream of this community into the political realm. In the post 'ᵓAwwal Dukhulna li-l-Junayna' ('Our First Entrance to the Garden', 20 March 2006), Amr describes the bloggers' participation in the judges' strike in Tahrir in 2006.[2] In the first part of the account, he describes the street seller's astonishment at his request to buy an Egyptian flag to go to a political demonstration (and not to a football match, as was usual at that time). Then, once in the square, he describes the joy of being surrounded by his blogger friends. He writes that each of them took part in a different activity – writing, reading, studying, giving interviews, and painting – but all sat together, united, and singing Shaykh Imam's songs.[3] Using first-person-plural narration, which emphasises the blogger's affiliation to this community, Amr claims: 'It was as if we had become the owners of the square' (*badawnā naḥnu ka-asḥāb al-mīdān*). This post suggests that writing for Amr is a way of taking a picture of 'historical' moments such as this. In this way he and his friends can go back, read and enjoy the memories through reliving them. Additionally, by describing in detail the other bloggers' movements and actions, Amr reports his personal perception of them. The different activities performed by the members of the community represent their various inclinations and personalities. However, the act of singing together (political songs) suggests that, despite their differences, they all share the dream of political change. The picture of the Egyptian flag in Tahrir highlights that the blogger imagines the youths' '"conquest' of the square as a small step towards the takeover of the entire country.

Imagining a Revolution

Tahrir Square occupies a special place in bloggers' self-writing. The square is world famous for having hosted the 25 January 2011 political uprising and many additional protests that took place in the following years. But even before 2011, Tahrir Square had been the traditional site for numerous major protests and demonstrations over the years, including the 1977 Egyptian Bread Riots, and the March 2003 protest against the war in Iraq. It is not surprising, then, that driven by a sense of discomfort towards the current political situation, and at the same time by enthusiasm for collective political action, bloggers projected their imagination and ambitions on this particular place, far before 2011.

In March 2006, Ahmed Naji wrote a blogspot entitled 'al-Afyal Tatir wa al-Ghuzlan Tasbah' ('The Elephants Fly and the Gazelles Swim' in which he imagined Tahrir Square turning into a mythical, magical place. In his words:

> That day will come …
> When Tahrir Square will turn into a big lake, on whose river herons will graze [sic], fish will meet in the light of the sun, elephants will fly against

> Newton's laws and the weight that pulls them downwards, gazelles will swim in the lake, and he will smile from above his throne floating on the river. Life will not get better, or worse, but it will be different … there where gazelles swim and elephants fly.
>
> سيأتي ذلك اليوم..
> حين يصبح ميدان التحرير بحيرة كبيرة، على ضفتيها يرعى أبو قردان، و تستلقي الأسماك في ضوء الشمس، و تحلق الأفيال في حرية بعيداً عن قوانين نيوتن و ثقلها الذي يشدها للأسفل، ستعوم الغزلان في البحيرة، و سيبتسم هو من فوق عرشه الطافي على الماء. لن تصبح الحياة أفضل، و لن تصبح أسوء ، لكنها ستصير مختلفة..
> هناك حيث الغزلان تسبح و الأفيال تطير

In this passage, the square acquires fantastic traits. We can see the presence of animal characters, already pointed out in Chapter 5, but here the author includes terrestrial animals, such as gazelles and elephants. It is not specified who the character smiling while sitting on his throne is. The author does not explicitly express hope for the future, but the fact that the animals will free their bodies from the laws of gravity anticipates a desire for freedom and imagination.

Another similar but more catastrophic scenario is imagined by Mohammad Rabie on 30 October 2006. He imagines that he arrives in Downtown and finds that it has been taken over by the people. The people are stealing statues from the Pharaonic museum; others are occupying the American University and robbing the Omar Effendi department store[4] in Talaat Harb Street. The blogger himself contributes to the robbery of Omar Effendi, because finally he can obtain the electric tools he has always desired. He represents himself and his people as heroes, defeating capitalism and taking power of their own goods, history and knowledge.

A more epic account is written by Ahmad Gharbiyya on 20 January, just five days before the call for demonstrations:

> In a day not far from now we will enter Abdin Square victoriously on the back of our elephants, like Hannibal, we will defeat the flying creatures[5] … We will bear the first air strike, then we will take our screens and we will appear again … In our hands we will have stones, clubs and the helmets of the Central Security.

We will hit the ones who carry fire in their hands so they run … As for the big ones, we will send them back to Almaza Airport and Cairo East airport, where they came from.[6]

As for the petty ones and their assistants, their eyes will well up with tears and in the twinkle of an eye they will look kind and stupid. They will embrace the multitudes, so some of them would die and others survive. The regiments will come from every place: 6th of April[7] and 25th of January, the people of 6 October[8] will also march in, but as for the people of Tagammu[c9] most of them will be like rotten wood.[10] The people of the 15th of May[11] will come from the left, while the people of 10th of Ramadan[12] will come from the right.

A light will shine from the West, and the multitudes will think that this is the ship bringing the expatriates home, but then they will know who it is! Al-Baradei will appear from the light. He wears a helmet with two horns on his head, and in his hand a Blackberry with a screen that shines light toward the East. He will be borne by the roaring waves of hands, like a rock & roll star … Then, he would gain control. On that summer day, thin clouds will appear over Cairo, and people will find that nice, the whales that swim above the clouds will find that nice too. But as for the 30th of February[13] people, no one will see them although they will be in the eye of the storm.

في يوم ليس ببعيد سندخل إلىٰ ساحة عابدين علىٰ ظهور الأفيال منتصرين، كما حنّبعل سنهزم الطير الأبابيل..سنتحمل الضربة الجوية الأولىٰ و نتخذ السواتر ثم سنظهر..في أيدينا حجارة و شوم و خوذات الأمن المركزي
نقذف بها الذين في أيديهم النار المحرقة فيولون الأدبار..أما الكبار منهم فإلىٰ مطار الماظة و مطار شرق القاهرة لتكون نهايتهم حيث كانت بدايتهم
و أما الأعوان و الصغار فستدمع أعينهم و ترتسم البلاهة و الطيبة علىٰ وجوههم في غمضة عين، و سيحضنون الجموع، فيزهق بعضهم و يُستبقىٰ آخرون
و ستدخل الأفواج من كل مكان، 6 أبريل و 25 يناير، و شعب 6 أكتوبر كذلك سيزحف، لكن شعب التجمع أكثرهم خشب مسندة، شعب 15 مايو يأتي من الميسرة، و أما شعب 10 رمضان فمن الميمنة
ثم ينبلج في الغرب ضوء بعيد تحسبه الجموع سفينة الغرباء العائدين، حتىٰ يعلموا من هو
يظهر من وسط الضوء البرادعي، علىٰ رأسه خوذته ذات القرنين و في يده بلاكبري

> شاشته تشع نورا باهرا في اتجاه الشرق، محمولا فوق موج هادر من الأيادي كنجم
> روك أند رول، كلما واجهه جبل من الماء أو دوامة بلا قرار صاح «يا مُسقِّر شيّد هنا
> منارة عليها تمثال من نُحاس لتَسكُن الريحُ و يَستوي الموجُ»..حتىٰ يصير له الأمر
> في ذلك اليوم الصيفي سيظهر غمام فوق القاهرة فيستحسن الشعب ذلك، و كذلك
> الحيتان التي تسبح فوق الغمام
> أما 30 فبراير فلن يراهم إنسان رغم أنهم سيكونون في عين اللجة

The text contains many references to pre-Islamic and Islamic history, and also Egyptian contemporary history. There is also a play on words obtained by mixing names of Cairo suburbs with dates of historical events or political movements. Some expressions are drawn from the Quran, as indicated, which attributes a mythical, epic tone to the text. The reference to the political figure al-Baradei, in the guise of a rock star, enlightening the East with his Blackberry, possibly refers to the fact that Baradei made great use of online tools to inspire the grassroots 'Movement for Change'.

These texts show that bloggers have urged their peers to gather and protest in the square since 2006, when the idea of a possible revolution was still remote for many political observers. They have done so, not only through plain slogans and political messages, but also by using literary texts. Their use of metaphors and imaginary figures has contributed to shape the dream of Tahrir as a mythical place conquered by the youth.

The 25 January Revolution: The Dream Comes True

It is not surprising then that on his blog Amr describes the 25 January uprising as a victory of imagination over reality. When writing about the 25 January to 11 February protests that led to Mubarak's removal from power, Amr frequently uses the words '*al-khayāl*' (imagination) and '*ḥulm*' (dream). For example, in his article published both on his blog and in the independent newspaper *al-Masri al-Yawm*, entitled 'ᶜIndama Tarada al-Khayal al-Waqi' wa-Asqata al-Nizam' ('When Imagination Ousted Reality and Toppled the Regime', 15 February 2011), Amr writes that imagination is what brought people together, what convinced them that they deserved more than they had, what pushed them to go out and fight against the security forces; imagination was what gathered people together, both in the virtual and real worlds, from the first *Kifaya* demonstrations in 2004, to the rebellion for Khaled

Said's murder, and finally the uprising of 25 January. In another post, '[c]Ishu Kiraman Tahta Zill al-[c]Alam' ('Live with Dignity Under the Shadow of the Flag', 12 February 2011), Amr recounts that on 11 February he was in a taxi heading home, tired and depressed – but still trying to convince the taxi driver that it is important to continue the demonstration – when he heard the news on the radio that Mubarak had stepped down. Again, the sensation is described as 'a moment of confusion between dream and reality'. In the post 'Fi al-Watan al-Jadid' ('In the New Homeland', 14 February 2011), Amr quotes a song by the Egyptian artist Salam Yusri (Salām Yusrī): 'I don't feel a stranger in this new home, nor did I ever feel a stranger in the dream', re-affirming the idea that Mubarak's fall is for him the realisation of an old dream, something that he had always hoped to achieve but whose realisation he had ceased to expect.

The 25 January uprising appears in Amr's writing as the moment of completion of his process of self-finding and his final integration within the newly found community of friends. In his words:

> That's why I like protests: because they are an alternative to the loud insults deserved by the sons of a bitch; because I stand inside the cordon with the people I love, the cordon creates a moment of pure romance, a dreamy moment, a utopia; it is as if the cordon draws a line that separates us from the sons of a bitch. You know that I don't have big expectations with regard to humanity; which is why I am usually optimistic and happy with what I receive from the generous fates; I always forgive the sons of a bitch; but the protest is like a Sufi moment in which I am drawn close to the people and the things I love and I express my contempt for the people and things I hate.
>
> In the revolution we experienced many Sufi moments, which weren't planned, but this is what happened. I freaked out: I threw stones on the 25th while I screamed at the sons of a bitch, and I did the same thing on the 28th, and again on the 2nd of February but this time, I gritted my teeth and shouted even greater obscenities at the sons of a bitch, because this last time they hit me with a stone in the face. It was a minor injury but it was the first time they had gotten me. If I had been hit in the eye, I would be writing with one eye now: sons of a bitch.

ببساطة أحببت الاحتجاج دائما لأنه بديل عن السباب العالي الذي يستحقه ولاد الوسخة، ولأني في لحظة التظاهر والاحتجاج أكون مع من أحبهم داخل كردون، يصنع الكوردون لحظة خالصة رومانسية، حالمة ويوتوبية وكأن الكردون يرسم خطا فاصلا بيننا وبين عالم بنت وسخة. أنت تعرف أنه ليست لدي توقعات كبيرة فيما يخص الإنسانية، لذلك فإنني متفائل عادة وأفرح دائما بكل ما يجود به قدري السمح. متسامح مع ولاد الوسخة دائما، ولكن لحظة الاحتجاج كلحظة صوفية أنجذب فيها إلى ما أحب ومن أحب وأعبر عن احتقاري الحاد لما سواه وسواهم. في الثورة انفجرت لحظاتنا الصوفية، لم نقصد طبعا أن تنفجر أو أن تكون ثورة، ولكن هذا ماحدث. وانتابتني اللوثة: ألقيت حجارة يوم 25 يناير وأنا أهتف تجاه ولاد الوسخة، ثم ألقيت حجارة يوم 28 يناير وأنا أهتف يا ولاد الوسخة ثم ألقيت حجارة يوم 2 فبراير وأنا أجز على أسناني وأسب ولاد الوسخة بما هو أكثر بذاءة، لأنه في تلك المرة الأخيرة أصابوني بحجر في وجهي، إصابة طفيفة ولكنهم للمرة الأولى يتمكنون مني. لو كانت أصابت عيني لكنت الآن أكتب بعين واحدة .. ولاد وسخة

The protest is presented as both an individual and communal experience. He alternates the singular-first-person narration to tell about his own feelings and motives for demonstration, and the plural-first-person narration to express his own experience and expectations as well as those of his community of friends. Even when he talks about himself, he describes himself as close to the group of 'people he loves'. This group, enclosed and protected by the cordon, criticises and physically fights the 'sons of a bitch', that may be the ruling class, the mainstream intellectuals, the police and the security forces, but could also be more generally the society outside that has rejected him and his friends for following their dreams.

Reading this passage from a wider perspective, we can see that, just as the demonstration seemed to Amr and many other bloggers a Sufi experience, the whole blogging practice can be read as a mystical experience too: online self-writing is a way of abandoning outer laws and doctrinal, prescriptive values to start a new individual and collective experience. Just like the Sufi ascetics, Egyptian bloggers have developed their own personal approach to the world and at the same time have built a community based on the principles of humanity, non-violence and creativity.

Likewise, for Mona Seif, Tahrir is the place where she finds 'her community'. The community she had been imagining for a long time is now fleshed out in front of her eyes. Until this moment, Mona had tried to keep her anonymity. Many bloggers who took part in demonstrations could certainly find out who Maat was, since she had uploaded pictures of her family. After the 25 January uprising, Mona realised that she does not need a mask or an online counterpart anymore. The political demonstrations that ousted Mubarak's regime have brought the Truth (*mā^cat*) to Tahrir, to her people, have broken the fear of the public and the authorities. On 6 February 2011 Mona wrote a blog post, after the interview that she gave to *Aljazeera* had spread widely. The interview was conducted in the midst of the battle, and Mona broke down in tears while on TV. Her blog post, written in English, is a clarification that she was not crying out of fear, rather that in Tahrir she felt safe and protected:

> The center of Tahrir Square was safe. I could have stayed there to eat, sleep or even listen to music. I could have done all this and not even a flying rock could have harmed me, only because there were hundreds risking their lives out there for our safety. ('I was not Brave, I was Protected', 6 February 2011)

Tahrir is the place that turns her from a child into a mature woman. It is a place of self-finding and self-maturation. The turning point seems to be the fact that death is not a nightmare anymore, but normality. After the revolution, Mona can imagine her death without shivering and without seeking consolation in her mother.

> I was introduced to death again on Wednesday 2 February. In the middle of the square, while the sky rained fire, and in the midst of iron shields being drummed and gunshots, I made the acquaintance of death and was reconciled to it. … The square broke my fear of loneliness and death. The square embossed in my memory the faces of people whose names I shall never know, but whom I shall consider friends for life. … The death in the square does not scare me; it is forgetting the dead that scares me. ('al-Mawt fī 'l-Midān' ('Death in the Square'), 2 July 2011)

> اتعرفت على الموت تاني يوم الأربعاء ٢ فبراير،
> في وسط الميدان و السماء اللي بتمطر نار، و أصوات الخبط على الحديد، و ضرب النار..

اتصالحت مع الموت
...
الميدان كسر خوفي من الوحدة و من الموت
الميدان حفر جوايا صور و وشوش ناس يمكن عمري ما هأعرف أساميهم بس بقوا بالنسبالي صحبة عمر.
الميدان علمني احتمي بالاف الغرباء و أراهن معاهم بروحي على المجهول
الموت في الميدان مش بيخوف, لكن نسيان اللي ماتوا هو أكتر حاجة تخوف.

'Emraamethlya' was present in the square too. As expected by many readers, she also writes a short story set in Tahrir during the eighteen days of the 25 January uprising. The story depicts her attraction towards a girl she sees every day walking around in Tahrir, going from one tent to another to talk about politics, and occasionally standing in the square raising the slogan 'Down with Mubarak'.

> I remained silent. It was not the right time to talk, to get to know anyone, nor for the heart, mind or soul to fall in love, except for the love of this country, nor to fall for [beautiful] eyes, except for the eyes of the departed, whose pictures filled the square. ('Fi Qalb al-Midan' ('In the Heart of the Square'), 3 March 2011)

> فضلت ساكتة مكنش وقت كلام و لا معرفة مكنش وقت ينفع ينشغل فية القلب و العقل و الروح باي حب الا بحب البلد دي و عيون الا عيون اللي راحوا و صورهم مالية الميدان

'AZ', the author of the blog *A7lami al-Mob3athara* (*My Scattered Dreams*) points out that in those days (the eighteen days that extended from 25 January, when the demonstrations started, until 11 February 2011 on which day Mubarak resigned), the square was free from sexual harassment. This is how she describes her mood the day after Mubarak's resignation:

> This morning before leaving my house I changed my revolutionary kit … I dressed up, I put on a light perfume with a jasmine scent … I left the house and for the first time in my life I walked like a girl … I was walking with my head up and a smile on my face … for the first time nobody harassed me … and nobody was laughing at me because I was walking with a smile on

> my face … I am very happy with the post-revolutionary ethics, and I hope it lasts … Enough dirtiness! Time to be clean!
>
> النهارده قبل مانزل من البيت غيرت طقم الثورة....لبست واتشيكت وحطيت برفان خفيف بريحة الفل....نزلت من البيت بمشي بخطوه بناتي لأول مره في حياتي...كنت ماشيه رافعه راسي ومبتسمه..ولأول مره ماحدش يعاكسني...ولأول مره ماحدش يتريق عليا في الشارع عشان ماشيه مبتسمه..أنا مبسوطه جدا بأخلاق ما بعد الثورة واتمني انها تدوم...كفايه وساخه بقي خلونا ننضف

While these texts express optimistic feelings, the text 'Ihna Fen Ya Ibrahim' ('Where are we, Ibrahim?', 16 June 2011) written by Ahmed Naji already anticipates, in the form of a dialogue in Egyptian dialect, the sense of disorientation that affects the bloggers and the demonstrators in Tahrir at a later phase of the uprising. In this text, the narrator describes his arrival in Tahrir on 25 January, where he witnesses the presence of the security forces and some clashes between them and the demonstrators. However, his attention is grabbed by two men having the following conversation together: 'Where are we, Ibrahim? I don't know. Well, where has our plan gone? I don't know. Let's go and see there. No, not here. Where are we Ibrahim??' Significantly, the political uncertainty of the post-Mubarak political phase is expressed in terms of the disorientation of the body in space.

These perspectives on the writers' surroundings during the 25 January revolution contribute to ground the diary in a physical reality, to attribute authenticity to the narrative. These accounts illuminate the juncture of historical events and individual perception in online self-writing. They offer a different and important perspective on these large-scale events, and these perspectives may be used in contrast with the discourses of historians and authorities (Serfaty 2004: 107). However, these accounts are also informed by a personal perception of the author at a precise historical time. The utopian reality of Tahrir may seem outdated at this moment (April 2018), given the volatile political situation and the fast unfolding of recent political events. However, it still highlights the individual feelings of the eighteen days that have likely changed the history of Modern Egypt forever.

The Aftermath of the 25 January Revolution: A Demise of Blogging?

The utopic reality depicted by these bloggers in the immediate aftermath of the 25 January uprising was not going to last very long. After a period marked by enthusiasm and national pride among the Egyptian youth, the Egyptian political scene evolved into increased violence and polarisation. The government led by the Muslim Brotherhood President Muhammad Mursi in 2012 was overthrown by the military in July 2013 following mass protests, a year after he took office as the country's first democratically elected leader. Since 30 June 2013, the military has returned to power under the leadership of General, later President, al-Sisi. An authoritarian regime has been established; one far crueller than Mubarak's regime, with cases of imprisonment and torture increasing every day, and a devastating economic situation.[14] Since that date, young people have been deprived of all spaces, even that of virtual reality.

The report by *Freedom House* (2016) shows that online and offline censorship reached unprecedented levels in 2016, with twenty-one online news websites being blocked, VoiP calls over mobile connections also being blocked, a new cybercrime law being put in place, and a three-year prison sentence being handed to a twenty-two-year old for posting an image mocking the president. The report also maintains that: 'The Egyptian blogosphere has lost much of its vitality over the past few years'.[15]

One must remark that the question of the demise of personal blogging does not concern Egypt alone. Since 2010, several bloggers and observers worldwide have mourned the blog form and hailed its renaissance many times, to the point that Emma Beddington, author of the acclaimed blog *Belgian Waffle*, affirms in 2016: 'Blogging is dead: I've been reading about its demise for years.'[16] Therefore, a peek into how the blogs analysed in this study have changed since 2011 seems in place here. Even though exact data are difficult to get, it is possible to see that among the corpus of forty blogs analysed in this study, fifteen bloggers are still active to the present day (April 2018), three bloggers have restricted their access to 'private' (one needs to receive a password from the blog administrator in order to access it), one blogger has passed away (Al-Baraa Ashraf, R.I.P.), while fifteen stopped blogging between 2011 and 2014, and six bloggers stopped before 2011.

First of all, one must notice that the personal blogs that came into being to chronicle a particular life arc – as, for example, *al-Kanaba al-Hamra* (focusing on the author's life after the death of his mother) or *Yawimiyyat ᶜAnis* (dealing with the author's spinsterhood) – reached a natural end point as the author's circumstances changed, before the 2011 revolution, notwithstanding political circumstances. A number of authors also saw blogging as a means of developing certain skills towards a definite project, and stopped once they felt they were ready for it. For example, for Mohammad Rabie and Ahmad Abdalla, blogging was a training ground for writing. Rabie stopped in 2009 and devoted himself to write the novel *Kawkab ᶜAnbar* (*The Amber Planet*, 2010) that won the Sawiris Cultural Award in 2011. Ahmad Abdallah stopped in 2007 to dedicate himself exclusively to scriptwriting. In 2010, he finished the movie *Microphone*, which was awarded several prizes at cinema festivals worldwide.[17]

Undoubtedly, one of the reasons for the weakening of the blogging movement was the major competition with other social networks, like Twitter and Facebook. These services allow users to express themselves through short updates or single-click republishing. Their rise was further reinforced by the prevalence of smartphones, since mobile expression demands a short form, and the fast unfolding of political events. As Amr Ezzat pointed out in an interview in 2016, blogging had its own soul and rhythm, which was based on reflection (*taʾammul*). The events of the revolution demanded the expression of immediate feelings and actions; therefore, many abandoned regular blogging in favour of microblogging, preferring platforms, like Twitter, Facebook and Tumblr. These platforms also allowed more interaction, as it is much easier to write a comment on Facebook from your mobile or tablet, rather than posting a longer comment on a blog, which is easier to do while you are sitting in front of a PC.

Most bloggers agree that blogging is not dead, but the blogosphere has fragmented into a myriad of smaller communities. Back in 2006, the blogosphere was restricted to an urban, educated middle class that mainly oscillated between Cairo and Alexandria (see Chapter 2). As numbers of Internet users increased, it became more and more difficult for bloggers to address a specific audience. As the community was torn apart, bloggers like Abeer also lamented feeling uncomfortable with the level of exposure that blogging brings, finding more privacy in the novelist pact. This would explain why some bloggers have turned the privacy of their blog to a restricted audience. Again, this is not a purely Egyptian phenomenon. In the article 'What Were Blogs' published in *The New Republic*, Jeet Heer highlights the shift from a utopian community to the vanishing of a community in the US blogosphere.[18]

Possibly for this reason, several bloggers have joined forces and have created a number of platforms for collective blogging, where different bloggers post on the same website: examples are *Qoll: Didda al-Sawt al-Wahid* (*Say: Against One Voice*) or *Mada Masr*. On the latter, one can read posts that oscillate between investigative journalism, literary review, satirical cartoons, creative fiction and academic op-ed, available both in Arabic and English translation. Between 2014 and 2016, *Mada Masr* has been the victim of several attempts by the government at shutting it down, but it has managed to survive every time.[19] The platform has even managed to publish writing by the blogger Alaa Abdel Fattah from prison, in both Arabic and English.[20]

However, as numbers show, even though social networks and mobile devices have altered the frequency and mode of blogging practice, they have not necessarily led to its death. More than one third of the blogs analysed in this study are still active, but their authors post in a less frequent fashion. An example of this is Mona Seif's blog *Tanatif Ma^{c}at*. Following the revolution, Mona has started a parallel blog entitled *Tahrir Diaries*, to document victims of torture under the military regime. She uses Facebook and Twitter for her political activity. Nonetheless, she continues to blog, even though less frequently. Her blog *Tanatif Ma^{c}at* is still the platform where she can publish her drawings and her personal notes. For example, in 2014, Mona posted a letter on her blog sent by her brother Alaa from prison; only later was the letter republished on *Mada Masr* in both English and Arabic, and circulated widely.[21]

Undoubtedly, the changed political situation has had an influence on the contents of blog-writing. While in the pre-revolutionary phase blogging often expressed feelings of hope and the desire for change, in the post-revolutionary phase despair has become the predominant mood of writing. Indicative of this mood is the piece entitled 'My Only Words Are About Losing My Words', written and sent from prison by Alaa Abdel Fattah and published by *The Guardian* on the fifth anniversary of the revolution (2016). In this piece, the author explores feelings of impotence and surrender in contrast to the feelings of enthusiasm and hope that moved the blogging community in 2005. He concludes:

> But one thing I do remember, one thing I know: the sense of possibility was real. It may have been naive to believe our dream could come true, but it was not foolish to believe that another world was possible. It really was. Or at least that's how I remember it.

In an interview given to *as-Safir* in 2014, Ahmed Naji explains to the journalist that even though the blogging community that emerged from his generation, might have vanished, the Internet will continue to provide instruments of resistance because as long as there is power, there will be ways of fighting back.[22] Naji sees hope in the younger generations who use the Internet from their mobile phones and explore platforms such as Snapchat, Instagram, and so on. In his view, these will be their instruments of self-expression and resistance.

From the Blog to the (Dystopic) Novel

While technology evolves and blogging might be replaced by another medium, the aesthetics developed on the blogosphere have found their way into the novels published after the 2011 uprising. This will be described in what follows, focusing on the novels *Istikhdam al-Haya* (*Using Life*) written by Ahmed Naji and the novel *Bawlu* (*Paulo*) written by Youssef Rakha in 2016.

Istikhdam al-Haya *by Ahmed Naji*

This novel participates in the boom of dystopic writing that has taken place, especially in Egypt, after the Arab Spring. In her book *La fantascienza nella letteratura araba*, Ada Barbaro (2013) traces the early examples of dystopian writing in the play *Riḥla ilā al-Ghad* (*Voyage into the Future*), written by Tawfiq al-Hakim in 1957, and later, in 1982, in the novel *al-Sayyid min Ḥaql al-Sabānikh* (*The Man from the Spinach Field*) by Sabri Musa (Ṣabrī Mūsā). Examples of the dystopic novel could also be found before the 2011 uprising, such as in the novel *Utopia* by Ahmed Khaled Tawfiq (Aḥmad Khālid Tawfīq) published in 2010. However, in the tragic aftermath of the

Arab revolutions, the genre has been enriched by many other examples, among which are Ezzeddin Choukri Fishere's (ᶜIzz ad-dīn Shukrī Fishīr) *Bab al-Khurug* (*The Exit Way*, 2013), *Nisaʾ al-Karantina* (*Women of Karantina*, 2013) by Nael Eltoukhy (though with a more ironic take) and Basma ᶜAbd al-Aziz's (Basma ᶜAbd al-ᶜAzīz) *al-Tabur* (*The Queue*, 2015), and in 2016 the genre made its way into the running for the IPAF (International Prize for Arabic Fiction), with Mohammad Rabie's *ᶜUtarid* (*Otared*, 2015) an entry in the prize shortlist. This is not surprising, given that in the turbulent months after the uprising, the hope for democracy and greater social freedom was replaced by frustration and fear after the military's return to power in 2013.

As a work of dystopia, *Istikhdam al-Haya* offers a frightening vision of the future. It starts with the main character and narrator, Bassam, a forty-six-year-old Egyptian man, telling the reader that Egypt has been hit by a catastrophe, manifested in the form of a sandstorm and a series of earthquakes that have completely buried and destroyed Cairo. The city of Cairo, with its great heritage – civilisation, architecture, poetry and prose – has collapsed, causing an enormous loss in terms of human life and material goods. In the pages that follow we discover that a new capital has been built by a Society who controls world agriculture, and which manufactures everything, from machines to food to pornography, and produces electronic chips that can be implanted into the human brain to be connected to the rest of the world. In the chapters that follow, Bassam recounts the events that took place in previous years and that probably led to the catastrophe. The novel's futurist vision finds many references in contemporary reality. Indeed, we can find in it echoes of the Egyptian government's project of gradual abandonment of Cairo's old city and downtown and its aspiration to build a new capital city, a city of the future.[23]

As already mentioned in the Introduction, the publication of the novel has caused the author one year's imprisonment on account of damaging public morality. The charge was the result of reading the novel as a statement of truth, rather than a work of fiction. Writers and artists from all over the world raised a campaign for Naji's release between 2016 and 2017, which spread the news of his imprisonment online under the hashtag 'Against the Trials of Imagination' (*ḍidda muḥākimat al-khayāl*), and sent messages of protest to the Egyptian authorities. But so far, the debate surrounding the novel in the aftermath of the trial has focused on the presence of sexual elements and vulgar expressions, neglecting the fact that the novel contains many of the traits that could already be found on Naji's blog, *Wassiᶜ Khayalak*, including the autofictional reading pact, hybridity, interactivity and multimediality.

First of all, just like the blog, the novel could be read as 'autofiction', as it plays with the supposed identity of the author and main character. Bassam, the main character, is 'Beso' (Bēsō) to his friends, which is the same name that was attributed to Naji on the blogosphere as a shortening for his pseudonym Iblis (see Chapter 2). At some point in the narration, Bassam writes that in his twenties he used to have a blog. Also, he is living in 6th October, a city to which Naji dedicates several entries on his blog.[24] The text also includes a significant body of footnotes, which provide the readers with additional information about the characters, places and books mentioned in the narration, thus blurring further the border between fictional and non-fictional works. The hybridity is demonstrated by the fact that the novel is composed of both prose and graphic sketches, drawn by the Egyptian artist Ayman al-Zorkany (Ayman al-Zurqānī). In some sense, the novel also embodies the multimedia and interactive nature of the blog, as its contents travel outside the pages of the book and require the active involvement of the reader: the novel's release was coupled with an art exhibition held at Town House in Cairo in which Naji and al-Zorkany showed the art drawings and invited their 'fans" to draw their own comics or to colour the ones hanging on the walls. The graphics and text of the chapter 'al-Raqs al-Akhir li-l-Dhabab al-Ist al-Zarqaᵓ' ('The Last Dance of the Blue Anus Fly', 29–31) have also been turned into a short movie.

Like the blog, the novel's structure is fragmentary; it is not built around a coherent plot. In the opening of the text, Bassam alerts the readers that what they are reading is

> no more than a collection of papers and memories gathered in secret, over a number of years, by a lonely old man. It is a lengthy epistle addressed to the past, an act of narrative trickery in the form of a travel guide.[25]

Indeed the narration oscillates between accounts of the reality contemporary to Bassam, and Bassam's flight of mind that take us back to Egypt in the aftermath of the Arab uprising. Here we meet Bassam and his friends, striving to survive in the alienating city of Cairo. The openness of the novel is emphasised by the fact that it also has an open ending. In the final pages, we find Bassam being the guardian of 6th of October city, giving his last goodbye to Muna May (Munā Mayy), the only friend who remains alive after the catastrophe, and heading south with his car, letting the reader imagine the continuation of his trip in this futuristic Cairo.

The novel also relates to the blog in terms of language. Like the blog, it includes a mix of vernacular, standard Arabic and obscene expressions. The inclusion of these obscenities in the novel was the reason behind the resentment of the citizen who sued Naji and whose case was upheld by the judiciary.

While offering a frightening vision of the future, the novel also re-evaluates the 25 January revolution, not as a utopic moment, but rather as a moment of illusion for him and his friends: an illusion sparked by their active involvement in the uprising and the attention they received by the media, only to be forgotten soon after. According to Moylan and Baccolini, editors of the book *Dark Horizons: Science Fiction and the Dystopian Imagination* (2003), the hybridity and openness of the novel and the historical awareness of the main character, qualifies a dystopic novel as a work of 'critical dystopia', that is, a novel that offers a bleak future scenario, while still creating some hope for the future. Therefore, they argue that with their permeable borders, their questioning of generic conventions, and their resistance to closure, 'critical dystopia novels represent one of the preferred sites of resistance politics' (2003: 7). Naji's novel shows that even though the blog has transmuted into a dystopic novel, its fragmented, open structure and original style still gives a glimpse of hope between the pages.

Bawlu (Paulo, *2016) by Youssef Rakha*

A further indication of how blogging continues to impact print literature may be found in the novel *Bawlu* (*Paulo*, 2016) by the Egyptian author Youssef Rakha, published in 2016.

Bawlu is the second part of a trilogy of novels rotating around a group of poets of the 1990s generation and their relation to the revolution of 2011. The first novel, *Al-Tamasih* (*The Crocodiles*, 2012), is narrated by the poet Youssef (Yūsuf), named after the author, and is written in short poetry stanzas. It focuses on the period from 1997 to 2002, telling the story of the formation of a secret poetic group and the tragic death of one of its members, Nayf (Nayf). Alternatively, *Bawlu* can be classified as a murder story.

The novel is written in the form of a blog entitled *al-Asad ᶜAla al-Haqq* (*The Lion is Right*), published online on 14 August 2013, the date of the Rabᶜa massacre, in which the Egyptian security forces killed hundreds of supporters of the ousted president Muhammad Mursi.[26] The blog's author, as well as the novel's narrator and main character, is ᶜAmir, aka Paulo (Bāwlū), one of the members of the 'Crocodile's group'. Paulo starts his blog in mid-2012 following the discovery of the body of a woman, savagely knifed, in his place of work. Through the blog, Paulo confesses his view of the revolutionary events, his dreams, encounters, and his secret affiliation to the Egyptian security forces. Through the blog fragments, we get to know that Paulo has strong links to the vibrant and pro-revolutionary cultural scene in Cairo as well as to the Egyptian security apparatus before and during the time of the revolution. The Downtown bookstore he manages, and where he takes nude photographs of his lovers, is also the same place from which he conducts clandestine meetings and collects information from unsuspecting sources, and tortures his enemies, especially those affiliated to the Muslim Brotherhood.

The novel shares many features with the autofictional blogs analysed in this study. The first, obviously, is that it is presented in the form of a blog itself. And indeed, as pointed out by Asmaa Abdallah in her review of the novel (16 February 2017) published on the blog *Arabic Lit in English*, 'it reads more like a blog than like a novel', as it shares with blogs its fragmentary structure and an ever-looping circular order. The chapters are organised as fifty-nine blog entries, divided into four categories – Dreams, Events, Movies and Meetings – but the distinction between the categories is often blurred. Some meetings and movies read more as if they were dreams, or rather nightmares, and some dreams are in fact an account of real events, followed by Paulo's opinion of them. In addition, the narration constantly shuttles back and forth, re-telling the same events differently.

Like autofictional blogs, the novel plays with the supposed identity of the author as the main character and narrator. Again, as shown above in *Istikhdam al-Haya*, the main character shares many life-traits with the author. The story is told in first person by Paulo himself as a confession, and in some instances Paulo addresses the security officer that he imagines will find the file. Like the author, Paulo is a poet of the 1990s generation and a photographer, who hangs out in the intellectual milieu of Downtown Cairo. Real characters and events are mentioned in the narration, such as the author engaging in a conversation with the novelist Nael Eltoukhy, or the award of the IPAF to Baha Taher (Bahāʾ Ṭāhir) in 2008. Juxtaposed with this factual element, there is the magical appearance of a lion, which is heard roaring in the square, a reference that continues from *The Crocodiles*, where the poets were obsessed with Allen Ginsberg's poem 'The Lion for Real'. There are also snakes; a tribal figure Mitri (Mītrī), whose supernatural powers are unexplained; and the appearance and disappearance of Nayf's body. These characters and occurrences, along with Paulo's questionable ethics, throw doubt on his credibility as a narrator. There is also the fact that he is convinced he is the unknown leader of the revolution, although he admits to contributing to the counter-revolution as well.

The most remarkable element of similarity between the blog and the novel *Bawlu* is the literary use of Mixed Arabic. In the foreword, we read that the blog has been found by police officers, who, as they annotate in their report, have re-arranged the entries in chronological order; however,

> We have been careful to pass them on as found, while noting that the shameful obscenities, vulgar expressions, and indefensible defamation of sacred beliefs and symbols contained herein (not to mention the slanders directed at religious and national identity) are punishable by law.[27]

This fictional device is meant to justify the particular style that the author uses in this novel.

In most of the narration, Paulo mixes elements from the high variety of Arabic (FU), spoken variety (AM) and English. The grammar follows the FU norms, as for example the future tense is achieved by adding the prefix س to the present tense and the negation follows the FU parameters (*lam* + jussive). Both the complementisers *inna* and *anna* are present, while in AM only *inna* is generally used. The demonstratives are used in their FU form (*hādhā, hādhihi*). However, we also find both lexical and syntactical elements from AM. It occurs often in the use of the active participle to indicate a present continuous action (instead of present tense) and of *kāna*

+ active participle (*kunnā muṣaddiqīn*) to indicate a past continuous action. There are a number of English words that are transcribed in Arabic letters, such as *labtūb* (laptop), *hard al-kumbiyutir* (hard drive), *fūldir* (folder). The sentences are quite short and carry an oral flavour. The mix of the elements in Paulo's internal monologue is probably meant to represent a written form of the so-called '*ᶜāmmiyyat al-muthaqqafīn*', a mixed register that, according to Badawi (1973), characterises literate people in Egypt. This gives an oral flavour to his narration. The presence of these elements also contributes to giving the narration a sense of immediacy. The written narrative appears as a long stream of consciousness that Paulo addresses to himself and to the officer.

Even though Rakha uses the blog as a fictional device, his use of mixed Arabic differs from the one found in blogs and described in Chapter 3. A blogger's use of mixed styles of Arabic is mainly based on code-switching, intra-sentence and extra-sentence between AM and FU. Instead, Rakha's experimentation with language should be seen as in line with a tradition of authors who have tried to coin a third language, or to find compromises between the spoken variety and the written variety, such as Tawfiq al-Hakim's linguistic experiment mentioned above in Chapter 3.

The passages in which mixed styles of Arabic are used are alternated with others, written in high style, using long sentences and sometimes archaic vocabulary. In a footnote, the author explains that he paraphrases the *Book of Jeremiah*, a collection of prophetical writings from the Old Testament. Paulo, indeed, compares himself to the Biblical prophet Jeremiah, in that he thinks that he himself is a prophet, who is delivering his own kingdom into the enemy's hands, following the order of his Lord.[28] Furthermore, the style changes dramatically in the end. After recounting his work as a spy for the secret service, the torture that he has inflicted on his enemies, the sexual violence inflicted on his lover Moon, Paulo confesses the truth concerning Moon's murder: Moon was killed by the spirit of a Masai that magically entered into his own office. Here the style shifts to plain oral variety. This is evidenced by the use of demonstratives *dī* and *dā*, the relative *illī* and the negation prefix *mish*. Here, even the orthography changes to the AM variety. The shift to complete AM may indicate the total psychological collapse of the intellectual.

Overall, we could say that the use of this mixed style may be functional in the depiction of the main character. Paulo is a crazy murderer who hides behind the mask of a distinguished intellectual. It is impossible to find logic behind his actions. The linguistic schizophrenia (Suleiman 2004: 43) found in the novel equals Paulo's schizophrenia and the shadiness of the characters that surround him. Given that this is a blog about the revolution, one would hardly expect its author to be an informant, since this medium has generally been reserved for the pro-revolutionaries defending and romanticising the uprising. Here, however, Rakha seems to do the very opposite, showing another side that is disillusioned, violent and very much anti-change. Nonetheless, the fact that this novel has been longlisted in the IPAF in 2016, the most prestigious prize in Arabic literature, may give us hope that a change of attitude towards linguistic register choices in literature may take place in the near future. No doubt autofictional blogs have sown the seeds for this kind of change.

Notes

1 Interview, Cairo, April 2011. Khamis and al-Nawawy point out that blogging in Egypt provided a tool for 'bridging' and bonding (2013: 214), as it brought together like-minded souls who shared particular backgrounds, hobbies or interests.

2 In 2006 Egypt's judges mobilised for the independence of the judiciary. The judges made a potent case against the regime, alleging corruption and malpractice in the electoral system and demanding freedom from political influence in the judicial system. Bloggers, who had themselves reported these irregularities from inside and outside polling stations, participated in this protest. See R. El-Mahdi and P. Marfleet (eds) (2009: 99), *Egypt: The Moment of Change*.

3 ᶜIsa Ahmad Muhammad Imam (ᶜĪsā Aḥmad Muḥammad Imām) or al-Shaykh Imam (al-Shaykh Imām; 2 July 1918–7 June 1995) was a famous Egyptian composer and singer. For most of his life, he formed a duo with the famous Egyptian colloquial poet Ahmad Fuʾad Nijm (Aḥmad Fuʾād Nijm). Together, they became known for their political songs in favour of the poor and the working classes.

4 A chain of department stores owned by the Egyptian State that in the 1960s had a major cultural significance for the Egyptian middle class. It was sold to a Saudi entrepreneur in 2006, shortly before the blogger wrote this entry, and was then bought back by the State in 2011.

5 The invaders of Arabia, according to historical anecdotes, came riding elephants. That year was called the 'year of the elephant' (AD 570) by the pre-Islamic Arabs. They wanted to destroy the Kaaba, and God sent the *abābīl* birds to attack them. The story is mentioned in the Quran and was supposed to have happened in the pre-Islamic era.

6 Names of military airports.

7 Name of anti-Mubarak political movement.

8 A suburb of Greater Cairo, named after 6 October 1973, the date the Egyptian army launched a war against the Israelis to liberate Sinai, occupied by them since 1967. The date is still celebrated today as a national holiday.

9 Al-Tagammu[c] al-Khamis is the name of a Cairo suburb, also called New Cairo, mostly inhabited by the well-off. It is also the short name for the National Progressive Unionist Party (*Ḥizb al-tagammu*[c] *al-waṭanī al-taqaddumī al-waḥdawī*), a left-wing party established in 1977.

10 A Quranic expression, 63:4.

11 Date of Sadat's self-claimed revolution against the remnants of Nasser's regime, known as '*thawra al-taṣḥīḥ*' ('Rectification Revolution).

12 Name of a new city at the perimeter of Greater Cairo, named after the date of the launch of the Egyptian attack on Israeli occupation forces in Sinai in 1973; it is the same date as 6 October 1973 in the Arabic calendar.

13 Name of a fake political movement set up by bloggers. It started as a joke (they gave their movement a non-existent date to make fun of real political movements such as 6th of April) but then, during the uprising, they gathered around a tent called 30th of February. Thus, as shown by this imaginative description of the revolution, we can see their imagination turning into reality.

14 See, for example, the report by Amnesty International concerning the deterioration of freedom of expression and other human rights between 2016 and 2017: https://www.amnesty.org/en/countries/middle-east-and-north-africa/egypt/report-egypt (last accessed 28 August 2017).

15 The full report can be accessed at https://freedomhouse.org/report/freedom-net/2016/egypt (last accessed 28 August 2016).

16 E. Beddington (2016), 'Personal Blogging has Declined in Popularity but it Will Never be Obsolete'. On 16 July 2014, *The Guardian* points to statistics showing that the number of blogs started by teens has halved since 2006, and massively declined among millennials. See https://www.theguardian.com/commentisfree/2014/jul/17/should-we-mourn-the-end-of-blogs (last accessed 28 August 2017).

17 See Mia Jankowicz's review of the movie published in *Mada Masr* (1 March 2014): https://www.madamasr.com/en/2014/03/01/feature/culture/egypts-cinematic-gems-microphone (last accessed 28 August 2017).

18 In his words, 'At the height of the blogging craze, there were even utopian claims made on its behalf: Blogging would give us (finally) the Republic of Letters that the Enlightenment promised, a world where everyone could be a writer and find an audience – an interconnected network where, in true McLuhanesque fashion, a divided world would become a unified global village ... But the feeling of community and camaraderie in pioneering a new medium – the fellowship of the hyperlink – is no longer palpable' (Heer 2016).

19 On the last attempt by the government to shut the website down, see Mohammed Hamama (2017), '24 hours later: What we know about the blocking of Mada Masr's website'.

20 The articles are available at https://www.madamasr.com/en/contributor/alaa-abd-el-fattah (last accessed 28 August 2017).

21 See https://www.madamasr.com/en/2014/01/23/feature/politics/a-letter-from-alaa-abd-el-fattah-to-his-sisters (last accessed 27 August 2017).

22 'al-Mudawwanat Intahat wa Muqawamat al-Sulta Satakun ᶜAbar Wasa᾿it Jadida' ('The Blogs are Finished, and the Resistance to Power will take place via New Media'), *as-Safir*, 4 August 2015, http://shabab.assafir.com/Article/12838 (last accessed 28 August 2017).

23 In her article, 'Personal Reflection on Enduring Daily Life', Mona Abaza writes about how construction companies fill the city and social networks with advertisements pushing citizens to invest in futuristic villas in the new satellite city built in the desert, and therefore 'grasp their last chance of breathing' (Abaza 2016).

24 See, for example, the entry ᾿Uctuber, Leih?' ('October, Why?', 16 August 2008) in which Naji explains that what led him to move to this area was its emptiness, the absence of history, nostalgia or memories. In this area, the blogger feels as though every day is a blank page to be written in the evening and deleted again the following morning.

25 Translation by Ben Koerber, *Using Life*, 2017: 2.

26 On 14 August 2013, Egyptian security forces and the army under the command of General Abdel Fattah el-Sisi raided two camps of protesters in Cairo: one at al-Nahda Square and a larger one at Rabaa al-Adawiya Square. The two sites had been occupied by supporters of ousted President Muhammad Morsi, who had been removed from office by the military a month earlier in response to large

demonstrations against him. The raids were described by Human Rights Watch as 'one of the world's largest killings of demonstrators in a single day in recent history'. According to Human Rights Watch, a minimum of 817 people, and more likely over 1,000, died during the dispersal. The full report is available at https://www.hrw.org/report/2014/08/12/all-according-plan/raba-massacre-and-mass-killings-protesters-egypt (last accessed 23 April 2018).

27 Translation is currently in process by Robin Moger. Mohammad Rabie, who currently works as editor at Dar al-Tanwir, the actual publishing house which released the novel, has told me that the novel has not undergone any editing, except for typos.

28 Jeremiah, a Judaean prophet, appears to have received his call to be a prophet in the thirteenth year of the reign of King Josiah (627/626 BC) and continued his ministry until after the siege and capture of Jerusalem by the Babylonians in 586 BC. Many of his oracles concerned the turbulent events of his times. He warned his people against the sin of apostasy, the moral and religious corruption of Jerusalem, and he advocated his people to surrender to the Babylonians. An unusual feature of this book is the 'confessions' of Jeremiah, a group of individual laments reflecting the personal struggles precipitated by the prophet's role as the spokesman of a message so unpopular that it evoked imprisonments and threats to his life. See T. R. Hobbs (1972), 'Some Remarks on the Composition and Structure of the Book of Jeremiah'.

Conclusion: A New Literary Genre and a Social Uprising

This work aimed to study the impact of the Internet medium on the Arabic literary sphere. To this end, I roamed the Arabic Web in search of online venues in which one could find original, creative forms of literary expression. I found that, since Internet facilities were introduced to the Arab world at the end of the 1990s, several intellectuals grasped the potential of the medium to renovate the field of Arabic literature, which at that time was hampered by censorship, lack of distribution and a limited readership. Thanks to their efforts, a virtual literary sphere came to the fore, which included online literary journals, literary websites, e-publishing houses, online bookshops, libraries and reading clubs as well as the Internet Writers Union.

The development of Web 2.0 and the implementation of tools for blogging in Arabic in 2004 gave a democratic boost to Arabic digital expression. It afforded everybody the opportunity to create an online page for free and to link with other users. In the Arab region, the Egyptian blogosphere distinguished itself by its large number of participants (both male and female), their active roles, both online and offline, and its uncensored nature. Since 2005, many young people, including both amateur and more experienced writers, started blogging as a form of self-expression and literary experimentation, attracted by the uncategorised nature, relative freedom and interactive and aesthetic possibilities set by the medium. The personal blog emerged as a writing genre whose literary significance was worthy of investigation.

In order to explore the literary features of this form, I have analysed forty personal blogs written by Egyptians between 2005 and 2011. Among them, six were chosen as case studies and analysed more closely, following the chronological order of the posts. For the entire sample of blogs, I have combined a close reading of the texts with interviews conducted with the authors. I have investigated the paratext of blogs, narrative strategies, the interaction between authors and readers, linguistic and stylistic choices, and recurrent themes in the bloggers' self-presentation. In the interviews, I have inquired about the bloggers' reasons for blogging, the effect of fictional self-construction on their daily life, and how blogging helped them to depict their internal world (their emotions and bodies) and to deal with the constraints of the outside reality, including their families and social groups, traditional religious authorities and the spheres of politics and professional life.

The interviews have shown that the authors of these blogs mainly belong to globalised upper-middle-class urban youth. In comparison with the results found in Peterson's (2011) and de Koning's (2009) studies, I have shown that the members of this globalised youth not only visit shopping malls and Western-style coffee shops but also use the Internet as a tool of self-expression and socialisation.

As for their blogs, the six blogs analysed as case studies present a number of literary features that brings them close to 'autofiction', a literary form that originated in France in the 1970s and later spread worldwide. This genre is distinguished by an oxymoronic reading pact, created by combining the novelistic format with the onomastic identity of the author/narrator/main character that is usually found in an autobiography. The result of this reading pact is the readers' uncertainty concerning the ontological status of the story that in turn encourages them to take an active role in the interpretation of the text. In the six Egyptian blogs analysed, the autofictional pact is created in a slightly different way. On the blog, the reading pact is unclear, but readers tend to read it as a factual account. To this end, the six bloggers adopt several narrative strategies that tend to confuse the readers' expectations, and involve them in a more active reading. This could include: the adoption of a pseudonym (a strategy adopted as a means of ensuring personal safety only by the author of the blog *Diary of a Gay Woman*); the use of a self-conscious narrator that signals that the story might be fictional; the insertion of audio and visual elements; the fragmentation of the life story across time and space; and the use of a literary language. The readers participate in the blog in several ways. Firstly, they are called upon to discover the identity behind the screen. Secondly, readers have to make their own way through the labyrinth of the open, multimedia text, by reading text together with pictures, selecting links and browsing different pages, and playing music and videos. Thirdly, readers are invited to return to the narration, as the blog is continuously updated; new pieces are added to the main story over time. Fourthly, readers can continuously interact with and contribute to the plot of the blog by adding their own stories in the comment section. Fifthly, readers sometimes replace traditional gatekeepers, as they want to have a say in the visual layout of the blog and the stylistic features of the narrative, and they often criticise the bloggers for exposing some controversial issues in public.

By establising an autofictional pact, bloggers, both male and female, feel free to talk about themselves in a way which would not be allowed in the offline realm. They expose their body through the expression of emotions and feelings, such as fear, anger, frustration, alienation towards the state and society, pain, sexual desires and amorousness. These emotions and feelings are considered to be the essence of a subjectivity that has been lost or repressed in real life. In addition, the screen also inspires the expression of dreams and fantasies, memories and aspirations; here the body takes the shape of animals, Ancient Egyptian icons, objects, or a Peter Pan-style character. In some cases, bloggers impose on themselves other kinds of constraints, such as self-censorship: their 'fictionalised identities' are often socially situated and reflect the same gender roles found in real life.

I have discussed how the expression of these private feelings on the public platform of the blog may be seen as a general tendency towards 'extimacy' (Tisseron 2003) that is spreading in societies worldwide in response to a need for public support and social confirmation. However, I have also argued that by writing about their body, bloggers denounce and reject the power that the outside society imposes on them. In this way, the autofictional blog complicates the distinction between the 'literary' and the 'political', 'individual' and 'community', 'private' and 'public'. In other words, these blogs should be studied as both a new literary genre and a social uprising.

For the bloggers analysed in this study, blogging could be seen as a move towards individuality, a means of getting rid of the bonds of loyalty that link the bloggers to their traditional social group and focus on one's own self. At the same time, it is also a means of connecting with a new social group that shares the same values and the same interests. Significantly, this community in Egypt has become connected both online and offline, as shown by the numerous pictures and accounts of bloggers meetings uploaded on the blogs. By relying on this community, bloggers have introduced into the public sphere themes that could not be easily discussed before in societal discourse, for example, sexual harassment, atheism and homosexuality. As such, they have prepared the ground for an exposure of the body in real life, a rejection and mocking of the authorities that climaxed in the 25 January political uprising and continues to the present day. However, over time, this community has gradually enlarged and fragmented, turning from a utopian reality into a mirror of the controversies and debates found in outside society. As a result, bloggers have tended towards a restriction of the privacy of their blogs, or have stopped blogging, as in the case of Abeer Soliman, for fear of a dangerously complete exposure to the society offline.

The liberation of the body, as anti-authoritarian attitude, is also achieved through the invention of a new language, reflecting an effort by a younger generation of Egyptians to redefine their identities and to distance themselves from the language used by the religious, political and literary authorities. Bloggers mix formal and informal varieties of Arabic, with youth slang and English. This linguistic practice differs from the ones identified by previous scholars in social networks and email conversations because it combines a pursuit of literariness with the desire to connect with their peers. It also differs from the language choices in Arabic literary works produced in previous decades: for example, the use of vernacular in the texts is not just limited to dialogue. This language has proven attractive for online readers. It has also started to infiltrate into the novelistic genre, as shown in my analysis of Youssef Rakha's novel *Paulo* (2016) in Chapter 6.

Furthermore, the political stance of the bloggers can be seen in their rejection of traditional literary genres, particularly the novel, because, as claimed by Ahmed Naji, it is seen as the artistic expression of a 'rotten' nation and of an older artistic generation with which they often cannot identify. However, it is significant that some of them, including Naji, make the jump to novelistic writing after achieving fame through the blog form. The shift to novelistic writing may be due to the fact that blogging is an artistic form that resists commodification, because of its interactive nature, labyrinthine structure, intrinsic reliance on the present and continuous updating (Himmer 2004). This shift can also be attributed to the fact that print publishing still acquires a higher level of prestige, at least while society fails to give a similar level of recognition to digital forms of literature. This shift towards print ends up confirming Jacquemond's arguments that the novel still remains the most legitimate genre in Arab literary production (Jacquemond 2008: 217). Nonetheless, the blog continues to have an impact on novelistic production. The analysis of the novel *Istikhdam al-Haya* by Naji has shown that the novel, like the blog, is based on an autofictional pact, it presents a fragmented structure, mixed registers of Arabic and it includes both visual and textual elements.

The evaluation of these blogs from a historical literary perspective shows that the autofictional blog, in some ways, continues the role played by the autobiographical novel or novelised autobiography in the early twentieth century. Like the authors who wrote their autobiography in the early to mid-twentieth century, bloggers use the fictional cover as a way to expose their body, thoughts and emotions, usually considered private. At the same time, the relative freedom granted by the medium allows blog authors to push further some of the innovations introduced by the Egyptian writers of the 1990s generation through self-publishing: the breaking of taboos, innovations in terms of language and style, and a marked blurring of fiction and non-fiction. In addition, the interactivity afforded by blogging has helped intellectuals to re-establish connections with the public sphere and to communicate with their readers, a connection that was lost in recent decades, particularly the 1990s. Autofictional blogs and other forms of online literary manifestations may be seen as the expression of globalised youth, who are willing to rise from the ruins of previous decades and to reconnect with their own bodies and imaginations; youth who are fed up with the isolated intellectual circles and power games that afflict the cultural field. Rather, they want to catch up with global trends to bring society forward. In order to do so, they are aware that they have to find new voices, new language, and new forms of literature to depict the reality they live in, and imagine a better one. Failing to recognise these efforts means also failing to understand the political uprisings that have shaken the Arab world since 2005, and the changes that Arabic societies are undergoing at the moment. Like the events on the political scene, one could think that this developing cultural process may pass through very difficult phases, and may still take years in order to result in a more stable situation.

Over time, the blogging movement has lost its cohesion. Some bloggers attribute this to technological changes (and the shift from computer tools to mobile tools, like smartphones and tablets, which encourage the use of micro-blogging platforms) and to the worsening political situation (with the return of the military to power and the intensification of censorship on the Internet). However, blogging platforms are being replaced by other platforms, like Facebook, Twitter, Snapchat, Instagram, Tumblr, and so on, where one could still find the aesthetics developed in the blogosphere.

In the future, I wish to see more studies exploring the field of Arabic digital literature as a crucial component of Arabic literary expression. These studies would benefit from both a diachronic and synchronic perspective. From a diachronic perspective, the impact of the Internet on Arabic literature should be studied in comparison with the effect of other writing technologies, such as print. History may show us that what we are witnessing is not so new, and might provide suggestions and evaluations for the future. From a synchronic perspective, online literature needs to be integrated into the study of contemporary Arabic literature. In addition, blogs need to be allied with new emerging artistic forms, such as comics, graffiti or hip-hop music. These forms of expression are leading the Arabic cultural field to new and fascinating directions, modifying our understating of what literature was, what it is now, and what it does.

Works Cited

Aarseth, Espen J. (1997), *Cybertext: Perspectives on Ergodic Literature*, Baltimore: Johns Hopkins University Press.

Abaza, Mona (2011), 'Art, Subcultures and the Reinvention of Public Space in Egypt', *Ahram English*, 24 July, http://english.ahram.org.eg/NewsContentPrint/4/0/17201/Opinion/0/Art,-subcultures-and-the-reinvention-of-public-spa.aspx (last accessed 27 August 2017).

Abaza, Mona (2016), 'Cairo: Personal Reflections on Enduring Daily Life', *Journal of Arabic and Islamic Studies*, 16, 234–52, http://www.hf.uio.no/ikos/forskning/publikasjoner/tidsskrifter/jais (last accessed 3 September 2017).

Abboud-Haggar, Soha (2010), 'Linguistic Varieties in Twenty-First Century Arabic Novels: An Applied Study', in R. Bassiouney (ed.), *Arabic and the Media: Linguistic Analysis and Application*, Leiden: Brill, 201–15.

^{c}Abd al-^{c}Azim, Ahmad (2011), 'Al-Mudawwana al-Iliktruniyya … tahawwulat al-sard al-mu^{c}asir' ['The weblog … transformation in contemporary narration'], *Fusul: Majallat al-Naqd al-Adabi* [*Fusul: The Journal of Literary Criticism*], 79, 157–77.

^{c}Abd al-Mun^{c}im, ^{ɔ}Ibrahim ^{c}Ala^{ɔ} (2011), 'al-Rihan ^{c}ala Basatat al-Mutakhayyil: Qirā^{ɔ}a fi Jamaliyyat al-Wasf fi Mudawwanat ^{ɔ}Aruzz bi-Laban li-Shakhṣayn li-Riḥāb Bassām' [Bet on the simplicity of imagination: a reading of the blog *Rice Pudding for Two* by Rihab Bassam], *Fusul: Majallat al-Naqd al-Adabi* [Fusul: The Journal of Literary Criticism], 79, 143–56.

Abdel Fattah, Alaa (2016), 'Jan 25, 5 years on: The only words I can write are about losing my words', *Mada Masr*, 24 January, https://www.madamasr.com/en/2016/01/24/opinion/u/jan-25-5-years-on-the-only-words-i-can-write-are-about-losing-my-words (last accessed 26 June 2017).

Abdel-Messih, Marie Thérèse (2009), 'Hyper Texts: Avant-gardism in Contemporary Egyptian Narratives', *Neohelicon*, 36 (2), 515–23.

Abdulla, Rasha (2007), *The Internet in the Arab World: Egypt and Beyond*, New York: Peter Lang.

Abdulla, Rasha (2008), 'Arabic Language Use and Content on the Internet', Report presented to the Bibliotheca Alexandrina, http://www.bibalex.org/a2k/attachments/references/dr.%20rasha%20en.pdf (last accessed 2 September 2017).

Abou-Chakra, Chirine (2008), 'Usages et rencontres des homosexuels beyrouthins sur internet', in Y. Gonzalez-Quijano and C. Varin (eds), *La société de l'information au Proche-Orient, Internet au Liban et en Syrie*, http://www.cemam.usj.edu.lb/sipo/ouvrage_sipo_pdf/10.pdf (last accessed 2 September 2017).

Adams, Hazard (1987), 'Titles, Titling, and Entitlement To', *Journal of Aesthetics and Art Criticism*, 46, 7–21.

al-Abd, Muhammad, *et al.* (eds) (2011), 'Al-Mudawwinun Yataḥaddathun: Shahadat min Qalb Mujtama^{c} al-Tadwin al-Misri wa-l-^{c}Arabi' ['The bloggers speak: Testimonies from the heart of the Egyptian and Arabic blogging society'], *Fusul: Majallat al-Naqd al-Adabi* [*Fusul: The Journal of Literary Criticism*], 79, 234–62.

al-Ghafari, Iman (2003), 'Is there a Lesbian Identity in Arab Culture?', *Al-Raida*, Lebanese American University, 20 (99), Fall, 86–90, http://inhouse.lau.edu.lb/iwsaw/raida099/EN/p84-90.pdf (last accessed 2 September 2017).

al-Ghitani, Gamal (2009), 'Adab al-Kliniks', *Akhbar al-Adab*, 19 August.

al-Muji, Sahar, see El-Mougy, Sahar.

al-Muji, Sahar (1998), 'al-Kitaba ^{c}an al-Jasad Naw^{c} min al-Tamarrud' ['Writing about the body is a form of rebellion'], *al-Anba*$^{\circ}$, 7883, 29 April, http://saharelmougy.com/?cat=17 (last accessed 9 September 2013).

al-Muji, Sahar (2004), 'Naḥnu Iil bi-la Qurra$^{\circ}$ wa-Riwayatuna la Tasluh lil-Sinima' ['We are a generation without readers and our novels do not suit cinema'], *al-Qahirah*, 27 April, http://saharelmougy.com/?cat=17 (last accessed 2 September 2017).

al-Muji, Sahar (2008), 'Riḥab Bassam', *Al-Misri al-Yawm*, 2 March, http://www.almasry-alyoum.com/article2.aspx?ArticleID= 95737 (last accessed 2 September 2017).

al-Sahrawi, al-Azhar (2007), 'Al-adab al-Tafa^{c}uli fi Daw$^{\circ}$ al-Talaqqi' ['Interactive literature in the light of reception'], *Al-Rafid*, 120, August, 80–4.

Al-Samman, Hanadi (2008), 'Out of the Closet: Representation of Homosexuals and Lesbians in Modern Arabic Literature', *Journal of Arabic Literature*, 39 (2), 270–310, www.jstor.org/stable/25597977 (last accessed 22 August 2017).

al-Sherif, Nehal (2008), 'On the Threshold of Maat', *Egyptian Mail*, 3 June, 12, http://www.ahdafsoueif.com/Articles/Maat.pdf (last accessed 26 June 2017).

al-Tukhi, Na'il, see Eltoukhy, Nael.

al-Tukhi, Na'il (2008), 'Al-Kanaba al-Hamra: Muhawala li-Rtifa[c] Daraja Fawqa al-Waqi[c]' ['The Red Sofa: An Attempt at Getting One Degree Beyond Reality'], *Akhbar al-Adab*, 15 July, 788–9.

Alberca, Manuel (1996), 'El pacto ambiguo: ¿Es literario el género autobiográfico?' *Boletín de la Unidad de Estudios Biográficos*, 1, 9–18.

Allan, Michael (2012), 'How Adab Became Literary: Formalism, Orientalism and the Institutions of World Literature', *Journal of Arabic Literature*, 43, 172–96.

Allen, Roger (2000), *An Introduction to Arabic Literature*, Cambridge: Cambridge University Press.

Allen, Roger, and Hillary Kilpatrick (eds) (1995), *Love and Sexuality in Modern Arabic Literature*, London: Saqi Books.

Amin, Galal (2000), *Whatever Happened to the Egyptians*, Cairo: AUC Press.

Amin, Galal (2011), *Egypt in the Era of Hosni Mubarak, 1981–2011*, Cairo: AUC Press.

Amir-Ebrahimi, Masserat (2008), 'Transgression in Narration: The Lives of Iranian Women in Cyberspace', *Journal of Middle East Women's Studies*, 4 (3), Fall, http://muse.jhu.edu/journals/journal_of_middle_east_womens_studies/v004/4.3.amir-ebrahimi.html (last accessed 2 September 2017).

Anishchenkova, Valerie (2014), *Autobiographical Identities in Contemporary Arab Culture*, Edinburgh: Edinburgh University Press.

Anonymous (2003), *Arab Human Development Report 2003: Building a Knowledge Society*, http://hdr.undp.org/en/content/arab-human-development-report-2003 (last accessed 20 June 2017).

Anonymous (2004), 'In a Time of Torture: The Assault on Justice in Egypt's Crackdown on Homosexual Conduct', *Human Rights Watch Report*, http://www.hrw.org/sites/default/files/reports/egypt0304_0.pdf> (last accessed on 3 September 2018).

Anonymous (2010), *Egypt: Amnesty International Report*, http://www.amnesty.org/en/region/egypt/report-2010 (last accessed 2 September 2017).

Armbrust, Walter (2003), 'Bourgeois Leisure and Egyptian Media Fantasies', in D. Eickelman and J. Anderson (eds), *New Media and the Muslim World: The Emerging Public Sphere*, Bloomington: Indiana University Press, 106–32.

Armbrust, Walter (2012), 'A History of New Media in the Arab Middle East', *Journal for Cultural Research*, 16 (2–3), 155–74, http://dx.doi.org/10.1080/14797585.2012.647666 (last accessed 3 September 2017).

Awn, Peter J. (1983), *Satan's Tragedy and Redemption: Iblis in Sufi Psychology*, Leiden: Brill.

Badawi, El-Said (1973), *Mustawayat al-Lugha al-ᶜArabiyya al-Muᶜasira fi Misr*, Cairo: Dar al-Maᶜarif.

Badawi, El-Said, and Martin Hinds (1986), *A Dictionary of Egyptian Arabic*, Beirut: Librairie du Liban.

Barbaro, Ada (2013), *La fantascienza nella letteratura araba*, Rome: Carocci.

Bassiouney, Reem (2010), 'Redefining Identity through Code Choice in *al-Ḥubb fī al-Manfā* by Bahāᵓ Ṭāhir', *Journal of Arabic and Islamic Studies*, 10, 101–18, http://www.lancs.ac.uk/jais/volume/docs/vol10/v10_05_Bassiouney_101-118.pdf (last accessed 2 September 2017).

Bauman, Zygmunt (2002), 'Individually, Together', in U. Beck and E. Beck-Gernsheim (eds), *Individualization*, London: Sage.

Beddington, Emma (2016), 'Personal Blogging has Declined in Popularity but it Will Never be Obsolete', *The Pool*, 26 September, https://www.the-pool.com/life/life-honestly/2016/38/emma-beddington-on-the-demise-of-blogging (last accessed 28 August 2017).

Behrendt, Poul (2006), *Dobbeltkontrakten. En æstetisk nydannelse* [*The Double Contract: A newly created aesthetic concept*], Copenhagen: Gyldendal.

Bennet, Daniel (2011), 'A "Gay Girl in Damascus", the Mirage of the "Authentic Voice" – and the Future of Journalism', in R. Keeble and J. Mair (eds), *Mirage in the Desert? Reporting the Arab Spring*, London: Abramis, 187–95.

Bjørnsson, Jan Arild (2010), *Egyptian Romanized Arabic: A Study of Selected Features from Communication Among Egyptian Youth on Facebook*, MA thesis, University of Oslo, IKOS, https://www.duo.uio.no/bitstream/handle/10852/24250/Bjoernsson_master.pdf?sequence=1 (last accessed 2 September 2017).

Burgelin, C., I. Grell and R. Yves-Roche (eds) (2010), *Autofiction(s)*, Lyon: PUL.

Calvert, Clay (2000), *Voyeur Nation: Media, Privacy, and Peering in Modern Culture*, New York: Basic Books.

Censi, Martina (2016), *Le Corps dans le roman des écrivaines syriennes contemporaines*, Leiden: Brill.

Cohen-Mor, Dalya (ed. and trans.) (2005), *Arab Women Writers*, Albany: State University of New York Press.

Corrao, Francesca (1996), *Il riso, il comico e la festa al Cairo nel XIII secolo: il teatro delle ombre di Ibn Dāniyāl*, Rome: Ipocan.

Cusset, Catherine (2012), 'The Limits of Autofiction', paper presented at *Conference on Autofiction, April 19–21, 2012, New York University*, http://www.catherinecusset.co.uk/wp-content/uploads/2013/02/THE-LIMITS-OF-AUTOFICTION.pdf (last accessed 2 September 2017).

Cvetovich, Ann (2012), *Depression: A Public Feeling*, Durham, NC: Duke University Press.

Daoudi, Anissa (2011), 'Globalization, Computer-Mediated Communications and the Rise of e-Arabic', *Middle East Journal of Culture and Communication*, 4, 146–63.

Darrieussecq, Marie (1996), 'L'Autofiction, un genre pas sérieux', *Poétique*, 107, 369–80.

Darrieussecq, Marie (2007), 'Je est un autre', in A. Oliver (ed.), *Ecrire l'histoire d'une vie*, Rome: Spartaco.

Darwish al-Liban, Sharif (2011), 'Qiraʾa fī Zahirat al-Tadwin al-Iliktruni' ['Reading in the phenomenon of web logs'], *Fusul: Majallat al-Naqd al-Adabi* [*Fusul: The Journal of Literary Criticism*], 79, 82–100.

Davies, Humphrey T. (2001), 'Dialect Literature', in Edzard Lutz and Rudolf de Jong (eds), *Encyclopedia of Arabic Language and Linguistics*, online edn (Leiden: Brill), http://dx.doi.org/10.1163/1570-6699_eall_EALL_COM_0086 (last accessed 18 July 2018).

Dawson, Thomas A. (2008), 'Queering Sex and Gender in Ancient Egypt', in C. Graves-Brown (ed.), *Sex and Gender in Ancient Egypt*, Swansea: Classical Press of Wales.

de Koning, Anouk (2009), *Global Dreams*, Cairo: AUC Press.

De Moor, Ed (1998), 'Autobiography, Theory and Practice: The Case of al-Ayyam', in R. Ostle, E. de Moor and S. Wild (eds), *Writing the Self*, London: Saqi, 128–38.

Deleuze, Gilles, and Félix Guattari (with Robert Brinkley) (1983), 'What is Minor Literature', *Mississippi Review*, 11 (3), (Winter/Spring), 13–33.

Doss, Madiha (2004), 'Cultural Dynamics and Linguistic Practice', in M. AbdelRahman, M. Rouchdy and I. Hamdy (eds), *Cultural Dynamics in Contemporary Egypt, Cairo Papers in Social Science*, 27 (1–2), 51–68.

Eid, Mushira (2002), 'Language is a Choice: Variation in Egyptian Women's Written Discourse', in A. Rouchdy (ed.), *Language Contact and Language Conflict in Arabic: Variations on a Sociolinguistic Theme*, London: RoutledgeCurzon, 203–32.

El-Ariss, Tarek (2010), 'Hacking the Modern: Arabic Writing in the Virtual Age', *Comparative Literature Studies*, 47 (4), 533–48.

El-Ariss, Tarek (2012), 'Fiction of Scandals', *Journal of Arabic Literature*, 43, 510–31.

El-Ariss, Tarek (2013), *Trials of Arab Modernity*, New York: Fordham University Press.

El-Enany, Rasheed (1993), *Naguib Mahfouz: The Pursuit of Meaning*, London: Routledge.

El-Katatney, Ethar (2008), 'Egyptian Spinsters and Old Maids Sitting Happily on the Shelf', *Muslima Media Watch*, http://muslimahmediawatch.org/2008/12/egyptian-spinsters-and-old-maids-sitting-happily-on-the-shelf/ (last accessed 2 September 2017).

el-Mahdi, Rabab, and Philip Marfleet (2009), *Egypt: The Moment of Change*, Cairo: AUC Press.

El-Mougy, Sahar, see al-Muji, Sahar.

El-Mougy, Sahar (2011), 'The Voice of the Egyptian Expatriates in Egypt: A Reading of "Imbaba Bridge" Blog as Resistance Literature', in S. A. Kamel and H. Gindi (eds), *The Marginalized (Proceedings of the 10th International Symposium on Comparative Literature)*, Cairo: Department of English Language and Literature, Cairo University, 159–81.

El-Sadda, Hoda (2010), 'Arab Women Bloggers: The Emergence of Literary Counter publics', *Middle East Journal of Culture and Communication*, 3, 312–32.

El-Sadda, Hoda (2012), *Gender, Nation and the Arabic Novel. Egypt, 1892–2008*, New York: Syracuse University Press.

El-Sayed, Amany M. (2010), 'Arab Online Book Clubs: A Survey', *IFLA Journal*, 36 (3), 235–50, http://ifl.sagepub.com/content/36/3/235.abstract (last accessed 2 September 2017).

Enderwitz, Susanne (1998a), 'Public Role and Private Self', in R. Ostle, E. de Moor and S. Wild (eds), *Writing the Self*, London: Saqi, 75–81.

Enderwitz, Susanne (1998b), 'From Curriculum Vitae to Self-Narration: Fiction in Arabic Autobiography', in S. Leder (ed.), *Story-Telling in the Framework of Non-Fictional Arabic Literature*, Wiesbaden: Harrassowitz, 1–19.

Esposito, John. L. (1984), *Islam and Politics*, Syracuse: Syracuse University Press.

Etling, Bruce, Rob Faris, John Palfrey and John Kelly (2009), 'Mapping the Arab Blogosphere: Politics, Culture and Dissent', *Berkman Center Research Publication*, 6, http://cyber.law.harvard.edu/publications/2009/Mapping_the_Arabic_Blogosphere (last accessed 2 September 2017).

Fähndrich, Hartmut (1995), 'Fathers and Husbands: Tyrants and Victims in some Auto-Biographical and Semi-Autobiographical Works from the Arab World', in R. Allen and H. Kilpatrick (eds), *Love and Sexuality in Modern Arabic Literature*, London: Saqi, 106–15.

Farghali, Ibrahim (2008), 'Kitaba Iftiradiyya Hassasa Tantaqil lil-Waraq' ['Sensitive Virtual Writing Turns into Paper'], *Al-Nahar*, 15 March.

Faris, David (2015), *Dissent and Revolution in the Digital Age*, London: I. B. Tauris.

Feneey, John (1999), 'Shadows of Fancy', *Aramco World*, 50 (2), March/April.

Ferguson, Charles A. (1959), 'Diglossia', *Word*, 15, 325–40.

Ferreira-Meyers, Karen (2012), 'Autofiction: Imaginaire and Reality: An Interesting Mix Leading to the Illusion of a Genre?', *Caietele Echinox*, 23, 103–16, http://phantasma.ro/wp/?p=4365 (last accessed 2 September 2017).

Fisher, John (1984), 'Entitling', *Critical Inquiry*, 11, 288–9, http://www.jstor.org/stable/1343396 (last accessed 2 September 2017).

Fitzpatrick, Kathleen (2007), 'The Pleasure of the Blog: The Early Novel, the Serial and the Narrative', in T. Burg and J. Shmidt (eds), *Blogtalks Reloaded*, Wien: Books on Demand, http://machines.pomona.edu/dossier/files/2009/10/fitzpatrick-blogtalk.pdf (last accessed 2 September 2017).

Gasparini, Philippe (2004), *Est-il Je? Roman autobiographique et autofiction*, Paris: Éditions du Seuil.

Gasparini, Philippe (2008), *Autofiction: une aventure du langage*, Paris: Éditions du Seuil.

Genette, Gérard (1997), *Paratexts: Thresholds of Interpretation*, Cambridge: Cambridge University Press.

Genon, Arnaud (2009), 'L'autofiction dans la littérature maghrébine. Entretien avec M'hamed Dahi', http://www.autofiction.org/index.php?post/2009/08/27/L-autofiction-dans-la-litterature-maghrebine (last accessed 2 September 2017).

Genon, Arnaud (2010), "Hervé Guibert: fracture autobiographique et écriture du sida", in C. Burgelin, I. Grell and R. Yves-Roche (eds), *Autofiction(s)*, Lyon: PUL, 187–206.

Gonzalez-Quijano, Yves (1998), *Les Gens du livre*, Paris: CNRS Editions.

Gonzalez-Quijano, Yves (2012), *Arabités numériques: Le printemps du Web arabe*, Paris: Actes Sud.

Guth, Stephan (1998), 'Why Novels – Not Autobiographies', in R. Ostle, E. de Moor and S. Wild (eds), *Writing the Self*, London: Saqi, 139–47.

Guth, Stephan (2007), 'Individuality Lost, Fun Gained: Some Recurrent Motifs in Late Twentieth-Century Arabic and Turkish Novels', *Journal of Arabic and Islamic Studies*, 7, 25–49, http://www.uib.no/jais/v007/GuthPP.pdf (last accessed 2 September 2017).

Guth, Stephan (2010), 'Politeness, Höflichkeit, ᵓAdab: A Comparative Conceptual-Cultural Perspective', in L. Edzard and S. Guth (eds), *Verbal Festivity*, Wiesbaden: Harrassowitz, 1–29.

Guth, Stephan (2013), 'Novel, modern Arabic', in K. Fleet, G. Krämer, D. Matringe, J. Nawas and E. Rowson (eds), *Encyclopedia of Islam*, 3rd edn, http://dx.doi.org/10.1163/1573-3912_ei3_COM_27115 (last accessed 3 September 2017).

Habib, Samar (2007), *Female Homosexuality in the Middle East*, New York: Routledge.

Hafez, Sabry (1993), *The Genesis of Arabic Narrative Discourse*, London: Saqi.

Hafez, Sabry (2000), 'The Novel, Politics and Islam', *New Left Review*, 5 (September–October), https://newleftreview.org/II/5/sabry-hafez-the-novel-politics-and-islam (last accessed 2 September 2017).

Hafez, Sabry (2006), 'ᶜImarat Yaqubian: al-Tanmit al-Sardi wa-l-Khibra al-Samaᶜiyya, wa adab al-Talsin al-Siyasi' ['Yacoubian Building: narrative of types, hearsay knowledge, and the literature of political tongue-wagging'], *Cinema Isis*, 17 August, http://www.cinemaisis.blogspot.com/2006/08/blog-spot_17.html.

Hafez, Sabry (2007), *The Quest for Identities*, London: Saqi.

Hafez, Sabry (2010), 'The New Egyptian Novel: Urban Transformation and Narrative Form', *New Left Review*, 64 (July–August), http://newleftreview.org/II/64/sabry-hafez-the-new-egyptian-novel (last accessed 2 September 2017).

Hafez, Sabry (2011), 'The Aesthetics of the Closed Horizon: The Transformation of the City and the Novel in Egypt Since 1990', in S. Guth and G. Ramsay (eds), *From New Values to New Aesthetics: Turning Points in Modern Arabic Literature, vol. II: Postmodernism and Thereafter*, Wiesbaden: Harrassowitz, 109–38.

Hafez, Sabry (2017), 'Cultural Journals and Modern Arabic Literature: A Historical Overview', *Alif: Journal of Comparative Poetics*, 37, Cairo: AUC Press.

Hamama, Mohammed (2017), '24 hours later: What we know about the blocking of Mada Masr's website', *Mada Masr*, 26 May, https://www.madamasr.com/en/2017/05/26/feature/politics/24-hours-later-what-we-know-about-the-blocking-of-mada-masrs-website (last accessed 28 August 2017).

Hamilton, Susan (1992), 'Pets and Scientific Subjects: Construction of the Animal Body in Victorian Anti-Vivisectionist Periodicals', in A. Purdy (ed.), *Literature and the Body*, Amsterdam: Rodopi.

Haraway, Donna (1991), 'A Cyborg Manifesto: Science, Technology, and Socialist-Feminism in the Late Twentieth Century', in D. Haraway, *Simians, Cyborgs and Women: The Reinvention of Nature*, New York: Routledge, 149–81.

Heer, Jeet (2016), 'What were Blogs', *New Republic*, 24 August, https://newrepublic.com/article/136272/what-were-blogs-death-gawker-blogging (last accessed 28 June 2017).

Herrera, Linda (2012), 'Youth and Citizenship in the Digital Age: A View from Egypt', *Harvard Educational Review*, 82 (3), 333–52.

Himmer, Steve (2004), 'The Labyrinth Unbound: Weblogs as Literature', in L. Gurak, S. Antonijevic, L. Johnson, C. Ratliff and J. Reyman (eds), *Into the Blogosphere*, Minnesota: University of Minneapolis, http://blog.lib.umn.edu/blogosphere (last accessed 2 September 2017).

Hobbs, T. Ray (1972), 'Some Remarks on the Composition and Structure of the Book of Jeremiah', *The Catholic Biblical Quarterly*, 34 (3), 257–275, www.jstor.org/stable/43713304.

Hofheinz, Albrecht (2005), 'The Internet in the Arab World: Playground for Political Liberalization', *International Politics and Society*, 3, 78–96, http://www.fes.de/IPG/IPG3_2005/07HOFHEINZ.PDF (last accessed 2 September 2017).

Hofheinz, Albrecht (2007), 'Arab Internet Use: Popular Trends and Public Impact', in Naomi Sakr (ed.), *Arab Media and Political Renewal: Community, Legitimacy and Public Life*, London: I. B. Tauris, 56–79.

Hofheinz, Albrecht (2011), 'Nextopia: Revolution 2.0', *International Journal of Communication*, 5, 1417–34, http://ijoc.org/index.php/ijoc/article/view/1186/629 (last accessed 2 September 2017).

Hugueny-Leger, Elise (2011), 'Autofiction and Technology: Broadcasting the Self in Contemporary French Literature', presentation given at *Conference: Technologies of the Self, September 2011, Cork.*

Ibadah, Mustafa (2008), 'Mudawwanat: Kitaba Jadida aw Ihtijaj Ijtima^c^i?' ['Blogs: a new (form of) writing or a social uprising?'], *Al-Ahram al-^c^Arabi*, 11, 22 March, 48–52.

Ibrahim, Zeinab (2010), 'Cases of Written Code-Switching in Opposition Egyptian Newspapers', in R. Bassiouney (ed.), *Arabic and the Media*, Leiden: Brill, 23–45.

Jacquemond, Richard (2008), *Conscience of the Nation: Writers, State and Society in Modern Egypt*, Cairo: AUC Press. [Original French version: *Entre scribes et écrivains: Le champ littéraire dans l'Égypte contemporaine*, Arles, 2003.]

Jacquemond, Richard (2016), 'Ahmed Naji, the Use of Life and the Zombies', *Mada Masr*, 23 February, https://www.madamasr.com/en/2016/02/23/opinion/culture/ahmed-naji-the-use-of-life-and-the-zombies (last accessed 3 September 2017).

Jahin, Salah (2010), *Rubā^c^iyyāt*, Cairo: Sphinx Agency.

Jones, Elizabeth H. (2009), 'Autofiction: A Brief History of a Neologism', in R. Bradford (ed.), *Life Writing*, Basingstoke: Palgrave Macmillan, 174–84.

Junge, Christian (2011), 'Emotions in Postmodernism and Beyond: Autobiographic Metafiction in Two Egyptian Novels of the 1990s', in S. Guth and G. Ramsay (eds), *From New Values to New Aesthetics: Turning Points in Modern Arabic Literature, vol. II: Postmodernism and Thereafter*, Wiesbaden: Harrassowitz, 139–66.

Jurkiewicz, Sarah (2018), *Blogging in Beirut: An Ethnography of a Digital Media Practice*, Bielefeld: Transcript.

Kendall, Elizabeth (2006), *Journalism, Literature and the Avant-Garde: Intersection in Egypt*, London/New York: Routledge.

Khamis, Sahar, and Mona el-Nawawy (2013), *Egyptian Revolution 2.0; Political Blogging, Civic Engagement, and Citizen Journalism*, London: Palgrave McMillan.

Khamis, Sahar, and Katherine Vaughn (2011), 'Cyberactivism in the Egyptian Revolution: How Civic Engagement and Citizen Journalism Tilted the Balance', *Arab Media and Society*, 14 (Summer), http://www.arabmediasociety.com/?article=769 (last accessed 2 September 2017).

Klinenberg, Eric, and Claudio Benzecry (2005), 'Cultural Production in a Digital Age', *Annals of the American Academy of Political and Social Science*, 597, 6–18.

Koning, Anouk de, see de Koning, Anouk.

Kraidy, Marwan (2016), *The Naked Blogger of Cairo*, Cambridge, MA: Harvard University Press.

Kulesz, Octavio (2011), *Digital Publishing in Developing Countries*, International Alliance of Independent Publishers, http://alliance-lab.org/etude/?lang=en (last accessed 4 July 2018).

Lable, I., J. M. Kelley and J. Ackerman (2010), 'The Role of the Couch in Psychoanalysis: Proposed Research Designs and Some Preliminary Data', *Journal of the American Psychoanalytic Association*, 58, 861–87, http://www.ncbi.nlm.nih.gov/pubmed/21300629 (last accessed 2 September 2017).

Lampa, Graham (2004), 'Imagining the Blogosphere: An Introduction to the Imagined Community of Instant Publishing', in L. Gurak, S. Antonijevic, L. Johnson, C. Ratliff and J. Reyman (eds), *Into the Blogosphere: Rhetoric, Community and Culture of Weblogs*, http://blog.lib.umn.edu/blogosphere/imagining_the_blogosphere.html (last accessed 2 September 2017).

Langrange, Frederic (2000), 'Male Homosexuality in Modern Arabic Literature', in M. Ghoussoub and E. Sinclaire-Webb (eds), *Imagined Masculinities*, London: Saqi, 169–98.

Langrange, Frederic (2010), 'Arabies malheureuses, corps, désirs et plaisirs dans quelques romans saoudiens récents', *Revue de Littérature Comparée*, 1, 101–18.

Laouyen, Mounir (1999), 'Autofiction: une réception problématique', *Fabula*, http://www.fabula.org/forum/colloque99/PDF/Laouyen.pdf (last accessed 2 September 2017).

Laouyen, Mounir (2002), 'Préface', *Esprit Créateur*, 42 (4), 3–7, https://muse.jhu.edu/article/264874N1, (last accessed 4 July 2018).

Lecarme, Jacques (1993), 'L'autofiction: un mauvais genre?', in *Autofictions & Cie* (Colloque de Nanterre, 1992), RITM (Recherches Interdisciplinaires sur les Textes Modernes), 6, 227–49.

Lejeune, Philippe (1975), *Le pacte autobiographique*, Paris: Éditions du Seuil.

Lejeune, Philippe (2000), *Cher Écran*, Paris: Éditions du Seuil.

Lentin, Jérôme (2012), 'Reflections on Middle Arabic', in G. Mejdell and E. Lutz (eds), *High vs. Low and Mixed Varieties. Domain, Status and Function across Time and Languages*, Wiesbaden: Harrassowitz, 32–51.

Lentin, Jérôme (2013), 'Middle Arabic', in E. Lutz and R. de Jong (eds), *Encyclopedia of Arabic Language and Linguistics*, online edition, http://referenceworks.brillonline.com/entries/encyclopedia-of-arabic-language-and-linguistics/middle-arabic-COM_vol3_0213?s.num=0&s.q=middle+arabic (last accessed 2 September 2017).

Lenze, Nele (2012), *Telling Stories Online in the Gulf: Prolegomena to the Study of an Emerging Form of Arabic Literary Expression*, PhD thesis, Institutt for kulturstudier og orientalske språk (IKOS), University of Oslo.

Lupton, Deborah (1998), *The Emotional Self*, London/Thousand Oaks/New Delhi: Sage Publications.

Lynch, Mark (2007a), 'Blogging the New Arab Public', *Arab Media and Society*, 1, http://www.arabmediasociety.com/?article=10 (last accessed 2 September 2017).

Lynch, Mark (2007b), 'Young Brothers in Cyberspace', *Middle East Report*, 245 (37), http://www.merip.org/mer/mer245/young-brothers-cyberspace (last accessed 2 September 2017).

Malti-Douglas, Fedwa (1988), *Blindness and Autobiography: Al-Ayyām of Ṭāhā Ḥusayn*, Princeton, NJ: Princeton University Press.

Massad, Joseph (2007), *Desiring Arabs*, Chicago: University of Chicago Press.

Mavelli, Luca (2012), 'Postsecular Resistance, the Body, and the 2011 Egyptian Revolution', *Review of International Studies*, 38 (5), 1057–78.

McNeill, Laurie (2003), 'Teaching an Old Genre New Tricks: The Diary on the Internet', *Biography*, 26 (1), 24–47, https://muse.jhu.edu/journals/biography/v026/26.1mcneill.html (last accessed 2 September 2017).

Mehrez, Samia (2008), *Egypt's Culture Wars*, Cairo: AUC Press.

Mejdell, Gunvor (2006a), *Mixed Styles in Spoken Arabic in Egypt*, Leiden: Brill.

Mejdell, Gunvor (2006b), 'The Use of Colloquial in Modern Egyptian Literature: a Survey', in E. Lutz and J. Retsö (eds), *Current Issues in the Analysis of Semitic Grammar and Lexicon*, II, Wiesbaden: Harrassowitz, 195–213.

Mejdell, Gunvor (2008), 'What is Happening to *lughatunā l-gamīlah*? Recent Media Representations and Social Practice in Egypt', *Journal of Arabic and Islamic Studies*, 8, 108–24.

Mejdell, Gunvor (2011), 'Luġa wusṭā', in Lutz Edzard and Rudolf de Jong (eds), *Encyclopedia of Arabic Language and Linguistics*, online edition, Leiden: Brill, http://dx.doi.org/10.1163/1570-6699_eall_EALL_SIM_000004 (last accessed 20 April 2018).

Miller, Carolyn, and Dawn Shepherd (2004), 'Blogging as a Social Action: A Genre Analysis of the Weblog', in L. Gurak, S. Antonijevic, L. Johnson, C. Ratliff and J. Reyman (eds), *Into the Blogosphere*, Minneapolis: University of Minnesota, http://blog.lib.umn.edu/blogosphere (last accessed 2 September 2017).

Mina, Nima (2007), 'Blogs, Cyber-Literature and Virtual Culture in Iran', *George C. Marshall European Center for Security Studies*, Occasional Paper no. 15, http://www.marshallcenter.org/mcpublicweb/mcdocs/files/College/F_Publications/occPapers/occ-paper_15-en.pdf (last accessed 2 September 2017).

Moaddel, Mansour, and Stuart A. Karabenick (2008), 'Religious Fundamentalism Among Young Muslims in Egypt and Saudi Arabia', *Social Forces*, 86 (4), 1675–710.

Montremy, Jean-Maurice de (2002), 'L'Aventure de l'autofiction', *Le Magazine littéraire*, (May), 62–4.

Moor, Ed de, see De Moor, Ed.

Moylan, Tom, and Raffaella Baccolini (eds) (2003), *Dark Horizons: Science Fiction and the Dystopian Imagination*, London/New York: Routledge.

Naji, Ahmad (2010), *al-Mudawwanat: Min al-Bust ila al-Twit* [*Blogs: From Post to Tweets*], Cairo: ANHR Press.

Nelson, Meredith (2006), 'The Blog Phenomenon and the Book Publishing Industry', *Publishing Research Quarterly*, 22 (2), 3–26.

Nicholson, Reynold Alleyne (1907), *A Literary History of the Arabs*, London: Routledge.

Nordenson, Jon (2017), *Online Activism in the Middle East: Political Power and Authoritarian Governments from Egypt to Kuwait*, London: I. B. Tauris.

Nordenson, Jon (2010), *We Want Five! – Kuwait, the Internet, and the Public Sphere*, Saarbrücken: Lambert Academic Publishing.

Osell, Tedra (2007), 'Where are the Women: Pseudonymity and the Public Sphere, Then and Now', *Scholar and Feminist Online*, 5 (2), http://sfonline.barnard.edu/blogs/osell_03.htm (last accessed 2 September 2017).

Otterman, Sharon (2007), 'Publicizing the Private: Egyptian Women Bloggers Speak Out', *Arab Media & Society*, 1, http://www.arabmediasociety.com/topics/index.php?t_article=28 (last accessed 2 September 2017).

Palfrey, John, and Urs Gasser (2008), *Born Digital*, New York: Basic Books.

Palfreyman, David, and Muhammed Al-Khalil (2007), 'A Funky Language for Teenzz to Use. Representing Gulf Arabic in Instant Messaging', in B. Danet and S. C. Herring (eds), *The Multilingual Internet: Language, Internet, and Communication Online*, Oxford: Oxford University Press, 43–63.

Peeters, Heidi (2007), 'The Networked Self: Autofiction on MySpace', *Image & Narrative*, 19, http://www.imageandnarrative.be/autofiction/peeters.htm (last accessed 18 July 2018).

Pepe, Teresa (2011), 'From the Blogosphere to the Bookshop: Publishing Literary Blogs in Egypt', *Oriente Moderno*, Nuova Serie, Anno XCI, 1 (Between Everyday Life and Political Revolution: The Social Web in the Middle East), 75–89.

Pepe, Teresa (2015), 'Literature is on Trial in Egypt', *Mada Masr*, 13 November, https://www.madamasr.com/en/2015/11/13/opinion/culture/literature-is-on-trial-in-egypt (last accessed 3 September 2017).

Pepe, Teresa (2019), 'Critics, Moralists and Intellectuals: The Transformation of the (*udabāʿ*) in the Arab *nahḍah*: a Historical-Conceptual Approach', in 'Nahda Narratives', Special Issue of *Oriente Moderno*, 98 (3).

Peterson, Mark Allen (2011), *Connected in Cairo*, Cairo: AUC Press.

Pflitsch, Andreas (2010), 'Days of Amber, City of Saffron: Edwar al-Kharrat Remembers and Writes an Unintended Autobiography', in A. Pflitsch, A. Neuwirth and B. Winckler (eds), *Arabic Literature: Postmodern Perspectives*, London/Beirut: Saqi, 76–86.

Philipp, Thomas (1993), 'The Autobiography in Modern Arabic Literature and Culture', *Poetics Today*, 14 (3), 573–604.

Pickthall, Muhammad Marmaduke (1981), *The Meaning of the Glorious Qur'ān*, Cairo: Dar al-Kitab al-Misri.

Pitcher McDonough, Sarah (2011), *How to Read Autofiction*, Honors thesis, Wesleyan University, http://wesscholar.wesleyan.edu/etd_hon_theses/696 (last accessed 2 September 2017).

Poster, Mark (1995), *The Second Media Age*, Cambridge, MA: Polity Press.

Radsch, Courtney (2008), 'Core to Commonplace: the Evolution of Egypt's Blogosphere', *Arab Media and Society*, 6, http://www.arabmediasociety.com/countries/index.php?c_article=177 (last accessed 2 September 2017).

Radsch, Courtney (2012), 'Unveiling the Revolutionaries: Cyberactivism and the Role of Women in the Arab Uprisings', Rice University James A. Baker III *Institute for Public Policy Research Paper*, http://ssrn.com/abstract=2252556 (last accessed 2 September 2017).

Radsch, Courtney (2016), *Cyberactivism and Citizen Journalism in Egypt: Digital Dissidence and Political Change*, London: Palgrave Macmillan.

Rakha, Marwa (2009), 'Egypt: "Kleenex" Literature at the Cairo International Bookfair', *Global Voices*, 28 January, https://globalvoices.org/2009/01/28/kleenex-literature-at-the-cairo-international-bookfair (last accessed 2 September 2017).

Ramsay, Gail (2007), 'Speaking up with Yahoo: An Arabic e-mail novel', *Studia Semitica Upsaliensia*, 23, 179–90.

Ramsay, Gail (2017), *Blogs & Literature & Activism: Popular Egyptian Blogs and Literature in Touch*, Wiesbaden: Harrassowitz.

Reagle, Joseph M. Jr (2015), *Reading the Comments: Likers, Haters, and Manipulators at the Bottom of the Web*. Cambridge, MA: MIT Press.

Rettberg, Scott (2007), 'Notes on N. Katherine Hayles: Literature and the Literary: Why Electronic Literature is Key to Their Future', *ELMCIP (Electronic Literature as a Model of Creativity and Innovation in Practice)*, http://elmcip.net/critical-writing/notes-n-katherine-hayles-literature-and-literary-why-electronic-literature-key (last accessed 2 September 2017).

Reynolds, Dwight F. (ed.) (2001), *Interpreting the Self: Autobiography in the Arabic Literary Tradition*, Berkeley/Los Angeles/London: University of California Press.

Rifaat, Yasmine (2008), 'Blogging the Body: The Case of Egypt', *Surfacing*, 1 (1), 50–70, http://www.aucegypt.edu/GAPP/IGWS/GradCent/Documents/BloggingTheBody.pdf (last accessed 4 July 2018).

Rivlin, Paul (2009), *Arab Economies in the Twenty-First Century*, Cambridge: Cambridge University Press.

Rizk, Sherine (2007), 'The Language of Cairo's Young University Students', in C. Miller (ed.), *Arabic in the City: Issues in Dialect Contact and Language Variation*, London: Routledge, 291–308.

Robin, Regine (1997), *Le Golem de l'écriture: de l'autofiction au cybersoi*, Montréal: XYZ.

Robin, Regine (2000), 'Le text cyborg', *Études françaises*, 36 (2), 11–38, http://www.erudit.org/revue/etudfr/2000/v36/n2/index.html (last accessed 2 September 2017).

Rooke, Tetz (1997), *In My Childhood: A Study of Arabic Autobiography*, Stockholm: Stockholm University.

Rooke, Tetz (2011), 'The Emergence of the Arabic Bestseller: Arabic Fiction and World Literature', in S. Guth and G. Ramsay (eds), *From New Values to New Aesthetics: Turning Points in Modern Arabic Literature, vol. II: Postmodernism and Thereafter*, Wiesbaden: Harrassowitz, 201–14.

Rosenbaum, Gabriel M. (2000), '*Fuṣḥāᶜāmmiyya*. Alternating Style in Egyptian Prose', *Zeitschrift für Arabische Linguistik*, 38, 67–87.

Rosenbaum, Gabriel M. (2011), 'The Rise and Expansion of Colloquial Egyptian Arabic as a Literary Language', in R. Sela-Sheffy and G. Toury (eds), *Culture Contacts and the Making of Cultures* (Papers in Homage to Itamar Even Zohar), Tel Aviv: Tel Aviv University, 323–43.

Rustad, Hans K. (2009), 'A Four-Sided Model for Reading Hypertext Fiction', *Hyperrhiz: New Media Cultures*, 6, http://www.hyperrhiz.net/hyperrhiz06/19-essays/80-a-four-sided-model.

Schielke, Samuel (2012), 'Being a Nonbeliever in a Time of Islamic Revival: Trajectories of Doubt and Certainty in Contemporary Egypt', *International Journal of Middle East Studies*, 44 (2), 301–20.

Schmitt, Arnaud (2010), 'Making the Case for Self-narration Against Autofiction', *Auto/Biography Studies*, 25 (1), 122–37.

Selim, Samah (2004), *The Novel and the Rural Imaginary in Egypt, 1880–1985*, New York: RoutledgeCurzon.

Serfaty, Viviane (2004), *The Mirror and the Veil: An Overview of American Online Diaries and Blogs*, Amsterdam/New York: Rodopi.

Seykaly, Sherine (2013), 'The Body as a Site of Contest', *Jadaliyya*, 11 June, http://www.jadaliyya.com/pages/index/12162/the-body-as-a-site-of-contest_sherene-seikaly-on-t (last accessed 2 September 2017).

Shimon, Samuel (ed.) (2010), *Beirut 39: New Writing from the Arab World*, London: Bloomsbury.

Shoemaker, Pamela J., and Tim P. Vos (2009), *Gatekeeping Theory*, New York: Routledge.

Somekh, Sasson (1991), *Genre and Language in Modern Arabic Literature*, Wiesbaden: Harrassowitz.

Sorapure, Madeleine (2003), 'Screening Moments, Scrolling Lives: Diary Writing on the Web', *Biography*, 26 (1), 1–23.

Spear, Thomas (2010), 'Identité Virtuelle', in C. Burgelin, I. Grell and R. Yves-Roche (eds), *Autofiction(s)*, Lyon: PUL, 441–59.

Stagh, Marina (1993), *The Limits of Freedom of Speech: Prose Literature and Prose Writers in Egypt under Nasser and Sadat*, Stockholm: Almqvist & Wiksell International.

Stehli, Ulrike (2011), 'The Egyptian Magazine Galīrī 68: Truth, Innovation and Diversity', in S. Guth and G. Ramsay (eds), *From New Values to New Aesthetics: Turning Points in Modern Arabic Literature, vol. I: From Modernism to the 1980s*, Wiesbaden: Harrassowitz, 159–72.

Suleiman, Yasser (2003), *The Arabic Language and National Identity*, Edinburgh: Edinburgh University Press.

Suleiman, Yasser (2004), *A War of Words: Language and Conflict in the Middle East*, New York: Cambridge University Press.

Thorburn, David, and Henry Jenkins (eds) (2003), *Rethinking Media Change: The Aesthetics of Transition*, Cambridge, MA: MIT Press.

Tisseron, Serge (2003), 'Le désir "d'extimité" mis à nu', *Le Divan familial*, 2 (11), 53–62.

Tolino, Serena (2012), 'Identità omosessuale in tribunale tra l'Egitto e il Libano contemporanei', *Genesis, Rivista delle Storiche Italiane*, XI (1–2), 115–40.

Tonkin, Boyd (2008), 'Is the Arab World Ready for a Literary Revolution', *The Independent*, 15 April 2008, www.independent.co.uk (last accessed 20 August 2017).

Turkle, Sherry (1995), *Life on the Screen: Identity in the Age of the Internet*, New York: Simon & Schuster Trade.

Tyldesley, Joyce (1995), *Daughters of Isis: Women of Ancient Egypt*, New York: Penguin Books.

Unbrainwasher (2009), 'Didda Shuruq wa-Baqi al-Mutaffifin' ['Against Shuruq and the other defrauders']), *Unbrainwasher*, 16 February, http://unbrainwasher.blogspirit.com/archive/2009/02/16/anti-shorok.html (link no longer available).

Van Dijck, Jose (2004), 'Composing the Self: Of Diaries and Lifelogs', *Fibreculture*, 3, http://journal.fibreculture.org/issue3_vandijk.html (last accessed 2 September 2017).

Walker, Jill (2003), *Fiction and Interaction: how clicking a mouse can make you part of a fictional world*, Doctoral thesis, University of Bergen.

Walker, Jill (2004), 'Distributed Narrative: Telling Stories Across Networks', paper presented at *AoIR 5.0, Brighton, 21 September*, http://elmcip.net/critical-writing/distributed-narrative-telling-stories-across-networks (last accessed 2 September 2017).

Walker, Jill (2005), 'Blog', in D. Herman (ed.), *The Routledge Encyclopedia of Narrative Theory*, New York: Routledge, 45.

Walker, Jill (2008), *Blogging*, Cambridge: Polity.

Walker, Jill, and Torill Mortensen (2002), 'Blogging Thoughts: Personal Publication as an Online Research Tool', in A. Morrison (ed.), *Researching ICTs in Context: InterMedia Report*, 3, http://imweb.uio.no/konferanser/skikt-02/docs/Researching_ICTs_in_context-Ch11-Mortensen-Walker.pdf (last accessed 2 September 2017).

Wallace, Jo-Ann (1992), 'Subjects of Discipline: The Child's Body in the Mid-Victorian School Novel', in A. Purdy (ed.), *Literature and the Body*, Amsterdam: Rodopi.

Warschauer, Mark, Ghada R. El Said and Ayman Zohry (2007), 'Language Choice Online: Globalization and Identity Online', in B. Danet and S. C. Herring (eds), *The Multilingual Internet: Language, Internet, and Communication Online*, Oxford: Oxford University Press, 303–18.

Wasfi, Huda (ed.) (2011), 'Iftitahiyya' [Preface], *Fusul: Majallat al-Naqd al-Adabi* [*Fusul: The Journal of Literary Criticism*], 79, 72–234.

Weyman, George (2007), 'Speaking the Unspeakable: Personal Blogs in Egypt', *Arab Media and Society*, 3, http://www. arabmediasociety.com/countries/index.php?c_article=126 (last accessed 2 September 2017).

Wheeler, Deborah (2006). *The Internet in the Middle East: Global Expectations and Local Imaginations in Kuwait*, Albany: State University of New York Press.

Wirth, Louis (1945), 'The Problems of Minority Groups', in R. Linton (ed.), *The Science of Man in the World Crisis*, New York: Columbia University Press, 347–72.

Zack, Liesbeth (2001), 'The Use of Colloquial Arabic in Prose Literature: *Laban ilᶜasfūr* by Yusuf al-Qaᶜid', *Quaderni di Studi Arabi*, 19, 193–219.

Zakharia, Katia (2012), 'Guide de la littérature arabe médiévale et classique-sur-Web', *Maison de l'Orient et de la méditerranée Jean Pouilloux*, Lyon, février, http://www.mom.fr/guides/litterature.pdf (last accessed 2 September 2017).

Zargar, Cyrus Ali (2006), 'The Satiric Method of Ibn Daniyal: Morality and Anti-Morality in *Ṭayf al-Khayāl*', *Journal of Arabic Literature*, XXXVII, I, 68–108.

Zayani, Mohammed (2015), *Networked Publics and Digital Contention: the Politics of Everyday Life in Tunisia*, Oxford: Oxford University Press.

Zenith, Richard (1993), 'Fernando Pessoa and the Theatre of His Self', *Performing Arts Journal*, 15(2), 47–9, www.jstor.org/stable/3245710 (last accessed 18 July 2018).

Zipfel, Frank (2005), 'Autofiction', in D. Herman (ed.), *The Routledge Encyclopedia of Narrative Theory*, New York: Routledge, 36–7.

Primary Sources

Personal Blogs (all last accessed 20 April 2018)

A7lami al-Mob3athara, http://alienzero.blogspot.com
Africano, http://africano.manalaa.net
Akhir al-Hara, http://abdoubasha.blogspot.com
al-Banika, http://baneektshay.blogspot.com
Alexandria-Beirut, http://alexandriabeirut.blogspot.com
al-Haramlik, http://el7aramlek.blogspot.com
al-Kanabah al-Hamra, http://knbahmra.blogspot.com
al-Kuftah Tuday, http://onepenshow.blogspot.com
Allah, al-Watan, Amma Nshuf, http://allah-alwatan-amma-nshoof.blogspot.no
al-Tahir Sharqawi, http://alsharkawy.blogspot.com
ᶜArabiyyat Ful, http://al-karma.blogspot.com
ᶜAyzah Atgawwiz, http://wanna-b-a-bride.blogspot.com
Bint al-Qamar, http://bntalkamar.blogspot.com
Bint Misriyya, http://www.bentmasreya.net
EgypToz, http://egyptoz.blogspot.com
Ghawaya, Mujarrad Ghawaya, http://charkawy.blogspot.com
Hakadha Ana, http://hakazaana.blogspot.com
Hawadit, http://hadouta.blogspot.com
JarelKamar, http://jarelkamar.manalaa.net
Karakib Nuha Mahmud, http://nohaworld.blogspot.com
Kubri Imbaba, http://nournour.blogspot.com
Ma Bada Li, http://mabadali.blogspot.com
Maᶜa Nafsi, http://ma3nafsi.blogspot.com
Mulahazat Basita, http://simplenotesonlife.blogspot.com
Mustanqaᶜat al-Fahm, http://mostanqa3at.blogspot.com
Naʾil al-Tukhi, http://naelaltoukhy.blogspot.com

Nithar, http://azza-moghazy.blogspot.com
O7od!, http://o7od.blogspot.com
Shakhabiṭ, http://shkhabit.blogspot.com
SprinG, http://spring456.blogspot.com
Su᾽ al-Tafahum, http://karakeb.blogspot.com
Tanatīf Maᶜat, http://ma3t.blogspot.com
Taq Hanak, http://digressing.blogspot.com
Tayy al-Muttasal, http://zamakan.gharbeia.org
Tiyatro Sahib al-Saᶜada, http://zeryab.blogspot.com
Wa-ana Ma-li, http://wanamaly.blogspot.com
Wassiᶜ Khayalak, http://ahmednaje.net
Writing is a Green Dragon with a Purple Mustache, http://alaaeldin.blogspot.com
Yawmiyyat ᶜAnis, http://yawmiyat3aness.blogspot.com
Yawmiyyat Imra᾽a Mithliyya, http://emraamethlya.blogspot.com

Literary Websites (all last accessed 2 September 2017)

http://alketaba.com
http://arablit.wordpress.com
http://ofouq.com
http://www.alkalimah.net
http://www.alsakher.com/forum.php
http://www.alwaraq.net/Core/index.jsp?option=1
http://www.arab-ewriters.com
http://www.emilynasrallah.com
http://www.jehat.com/jehaat/ar
http://www.kikah.com
http://www.kotobarabia.com
http://www.mahmouddarwish.com
http://www.mernissi.net
http://www.nashiri.net
http://www.neelwafurat.com

Books Retrieved from Blogs

ᶜAbd al-ᶜAl, Ghada (2008), *ᶜAyza Atgawwiz* [*I Want to Get Married*], Cairo: Dar al-Shuruq.

Al-Buha, Ahmad, and Ahmad Mahna (eds) (2008), *Mudawwanat Misriyya lil-Jayb* [*Egyptian Pocket Blogs*], Vol. 1: *Mashruᶜ Watan* [*Project of a Nation*], Cairo: Dar

Uktub; Vol. 2: *Misr fi Qit*ᶜ*at Gato* [*Egypt in a Piece of Cake*], Cairo: Dar Uktub; Vol. 3: *Ana untha* [*I am female*], Cairo: Dar Uktub/Dar Dawwin.

Anwar, Salma (2009), *Allah, al-Watan, Amma Nshuf*, Cairo: Dar Dawwin.

Ashraf, Al-Baraa (2011), *al-Badin* [*The Fat Guy*], Cairo: Dar Dawwin.

Bassam, Rihab (2008), *Aruzz bil-Laban li-Shakhsayn* [*Rice Pudding For Two*], Cairo: Dar al-Shuruq.

Hasan, Muhammad Kamal, and Mustafa al-Husayni (2008), *Qahwat al-Misriyyin* [*The Egyptians' Coffeehouse*], Cairo: Dar al-Shuruq.

Hasan, Muhammad Kamal, and Mustafa al-Husayni, (2009), ᶜ*Indama Asma*ᶜ *Kalimat Mudawwana* [*When I Hear the Word Blog*], Cairo: Dār al-ᶜAyn.

Jirjis, Mina (2007), *Al-Nabi al-Ifriqi* [*The African Prophet*], Cairo: Dar Malamih.

Muhammad Mamud, Ghada (2008), *Amma Hadhihi fa-Raqsati Ana* [*This is my Own Dance*], Cairo: Dar al-Shuruq.

Nizar, Nirmin (2008), *Iskandariyya/Bayrut* [*Alexandria/Beirut*], Cairo: Dar al-Shuruq.

Thabit, Yasir (2009), *Yawmiyyat Sahir mutaqa*ᶜ*id* [*Memories of a Retired Magician*], Cairo: Dar al-Shuruq.

Literary Works

Naji, Ahmed, *Istikhdam al-Haya*, Cairo: Dar al-Tanwir, 2014.

Rakha, Youssef, *Bawlu*, Cairo: Dar al-Tanwir, 2016.

Interviews

Bloggers:

Abeer Soliman (ᶜAbir Sulayman), April 2011, Cairo.

Ahmad Abdalla, December 2011, Cairo.

Ahmad al-Fakharani ('Ziriyab'), February 2012, Cairo.

Ahmad Gharbiyya ('Alef'), March 2012, Cairo.

Ahmed Naji, (Ahmad Naji, 'Iblis'), May 2011, Cairo.

al-Baraa Ashraf, March 2012, Cairo.

Amani Khalil ('Bint al-Qamar'), February 2012, Alexandria.

Amr Ezzat (ᶜAmr ᶜIzzat), March 2011, Cairo.

ᶜAzza Mughazi, March 2012, Cairo.

Bilal Husni, February 2012, Alexandria.

Ghada Abdel Aal (Ghada ᶜAbd al-ᶜAl, 'Brayd'), June 2010, Cairo.

Haytham Shatir ('Sham3on'), February 2012, Alexandria.

Haytham Yahya ('JarelKamar'), February 2011, Cairo.

Imraᵓa Mithliyya ('Emraamethlya'), June 2010 and August 2012, email.
Jimmi Halim ("ᶜAlà Bāb Allāh'), December 2011, Cairo.
Mahmud Hassan, March 2012, Cairo.
Mahmūd ᶜIzzat ('NourNour'), March 2012, Cairo.
Michel Hanna, February 2012, Cairo.
Mohammad Rabie (Muhammad Rabiᶜ), March 2011, Cairo.
Mona Seif (Muna Sayf, 'Māᶜat'), February 2011, Cairo.
Muhammad Aladdin (Muhammad ᶜAlaᵓ al-Dīn), March 2012, Cairo.
Muhammad al-Hajj, March 2012, Cairo.
Muhammad Husayn, March 2012, Cairo.
Mustafa ᶜAbd al-Rahman, March 2012, Cairo.
Nael Eltoukhy (Naᵓil al-Tukhi), December 2012, Cairo.
Nirmin Nizar ('Alexandra'), February 2012, Cairo.
Radwa Usama, January 2012, Cairo.
Ramiz Sharqawi, February 2012, Cairo.
Rihab Bassam ('Hadduta'), June 2010, telephone interview.
Sharif Zuhayri ('Solo'), February 2012, Alexandria.

Others:
Ahmad al-Zayadi, director Dar al-Shuruq, June 2010, Cairo.
Ashraf Yusuf, editor Dar al-ᶜAyn, June 2010, Cairo.
Muhammad Hashim, owner Dar al-Mirit, March 2011, Cairo.
Muhammad Salah al-ᶜAzab, writer, June 2010, Cairo.
Muhammad al-Sharqawi, owner Dar al-Malamih, June 2010, Cairo.
Muntasir al-Qaffash, editor *al-Kalima*, February 2010, Cairo.
Sayf Salmawi, editor Dar al-Shuruq, June 2010, email interview.

Index

CPSIA information can be obtained
at www.ICGtesting.com
Printed in the USA
JSHW030347041120
9291JS00002B/22

9 781474 434003